Born and educated in Devon, Rachel Trethewey went on to read History at St Edmund Hall, Oxford University, where she won the Philip Geddes Prize for student journalism. During her subsequent journalistic career she wrote for the *Daily Express* and the *Daily Mail*, before switching to politics in 1995. In the 1997 General Election, she stood as the Liberal Democratic parliamentary candidate for East Devon, after which she became Education Correspondent on Westcountry Television. Now a full-time writer, she is married and lives in Devon.

'An elegant and deft first biography' *Sunday Times*

Mistress of the Arts

RACHEL TRETHEWEY

review

First published in 2002 by REVIEW
a division of Headline Book Publishing

First published in paperback in 2003 by REVIEW
a division of Headline Book Publishing

10 9 8 7 6 5 4 3 2 1

ISBN 0 7472 5503 2

Typeset in Garamond by Avon DataSet Ltd, Bidford-on-Avon, Warks

Printed and bound in Great Britain by
Mackays of Chatham plc, Chatham, Kent

HEADLINE BOOK PUBLISHING
A division of Hodder Headline
338 Euston Road
London NW1 3BH

www.reviewbooks.co.uk
www.hodderheadline.com

For John, Mum and Becky

Author's Note

I t seems the name the Duchess of Bedford chose to be called by was as changeable as her moods. Throughout her life she used the names Georgina and Georgiana interchangeably. She often signed her letters 'Georgy' or 'GB', but in a letter to her husband in 1806 she signs herself 'Georgiana' while in later letters to Mr MacKintosh in 1839 and Lord Brougham in 1849 she signs 'Georgina'. The people around her also showed a lack of consistency in which name they used. In a letter to the Duke of Gordon telling him of their engagement, the Duke of Bedford calls his future wife 'Georgiana'. Even contemporary newspapers are inconsistent; *The Times* in 1799, describing her coming-out party, calls her 'Georgina' but three years later, on 18 March 1802, the same newspaper calls her 'Georgiana'. When a poem was written in her honour in 1806, during her time in Ireland, she was called 'the fair Georgina'. In death, as in life, which name to use for the Duchess was not clear cut. Her death certificate from Nice at first had 'Georgina' written on it but then an extra 'a' was inserted! However, her will is in the name of 'Georgina, Duchess of Bedford' and the memorial plaque in her honour at Chenies church also has that version. Having closely examined the evidence, I would feel justified in calling her by either name, but for the purposes of consistency I have chosen one. Throughout this book the Duchess is called Georgina.

Contents

_____

Acknowledgements

A host of people have helped me, over the years, to turn Georgina's story into this book. First I have to thank the architectural historian and friend of our family John Wilson for introducing me to Georgina. It was due to him inviting me to lunch at the Duchess's Tavistock home, Endsleigh, and his telling the story of the house with such verve, that I was inspired to find out more about Georgina.

Since that time, researching the Duchess's life has been a challenging but fascinating experience. One of the highlights was visiting Barons Court in Northern Ireland, which was the home of Georgina's daughter Louisa, Duchess of Abercorn. The present Duke and Duchess of Abercorn showed such kindness to my husband and me during our visit, and their generosity has continued since that time as they are allowing me to reproduce in my book many of their wonderful Landseer pictures and sketches. The collection was photographed by the Courtauld Institute. I would also like to thank the Marquess and Marchioness of Tavistock and the staff at Woburn Abbey for all their support. The archivist, Ann Mitchell, and curator, Lavinia Wellicome, have given unstintingly both of their time and resources. Letters and pictures from Woburn are reproduced by kind permission of the Marquess of Tavistock and the Trustees of the Bedford Estate. While visiting the Doune, Georgina's home in Scotland, I met Philippa Grant, the present owner of the house. She provided me with information about the Rothiemurchus estate and put me in contact with Robert Lambert, who has co-edited an excellent book on the area.

Although a full-length biography of Georgina has never been written before, parts of her life story have appeared in other books. In particular, Campbell Lennie's biography of Edwin Landseer *The Victorian Paragon* and Georgiana Blakiston's books *Woburn and the Russells* and *Lord William Russell and his wife* gave me an excellent outline of Georgina's story and the characters involved in her life. I would like to thank Georgiana Blakiston's daughters Rachel Campbell and Caroline Blakiston for their kind permission to quote from private Russell papers used in the book on Lord William Russell and his wife Elizabeth.

Other invaluable primary sources have been Lord and Lady Holland's papers in the British Library and the Edwin Landseer papers in the Victoria and Albert Museum. Some of the Lord Auckland, Princess Lieven and Frederick Lewis papers in the British Library have also been of use.

Papers from the Gordon family are quoted in the book courtesy of the Trustees of the Goodwood Collections and with acknowledgements to the West Sussex Record Office and the County Archivist; their assistant county archivist, Mr McCann, was particularly helpful in providing me with the Gordon papers I needed. The letters between the Duke and Duchess and Lord Grey are reproduced by permission of Lord Howick of Glendale and Durham University Library. The letters between the Duke and Lady Bradford are quoted with the permission of Staffordshire Record Office. The Ellice, Lynedoch and Allen Thomson papers are used with the permission of the National Library of Scotland; their Principal Curator, Dr Iain Gordon Brown, was very generous with his time and expertise. The Public Record Office at Kew has kindly allowed me to use letters from Lord John Russell's papers. The Abercorn papers are quoted with the permission

Acknowledgements

of the Deputy Keeper of Records at the Public Record Office of Northern Ireland. Extracts from the letters between Landseer and Count D'Orsay are published by permission of the Houghton Library, Harvard University, while Falkirk Museums have generously allowed me to use the Forbes of Callendar papers.

Many other people have helped me in so many different ways during the writing of this book. Although it has been my enjoyable task to do the bulk of the research, I would like to thank Dr Roger Boulter for the invaluable research he did for me into Georgina's time in Dublin, and Beeta Duncan for researching contemporary newspapers for me.

Without my literary agent Dinah Wiener's support and faith in the story this book would never have been written. I am also very grateful to my publishers Headline and in particular their publishing director Heather Holden-Brown and my editors Lindsay Symons and Jo Roberts-Miller, who shared my enthusiasm for Georgina.

Finally, I want to thank my family for all their help during the writing of the book – my husband John for sharing the excitement of the research trips and taking photographs of Georgina's special places; my mother Bridget for being a patient first listener and my sister Rebecca for being a skilled first reader of the manuscript.

FAMILY

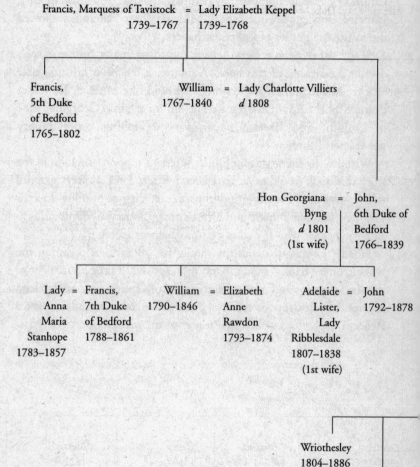

Francis, Marquess of Tavistock = Lady Elizabeth Keppel
1739–1767 | 1739–1768

Francis,
5th Duke
of Bedford
1765–1802

William = Lady Charlotte Villiers
1767–1840 | *d* 1808

Hon Georgiana = John,
Byng | 6th Duke of
d 1801 | Bedford
(1st wife) | 1766–1839

Lady = Francis,
Anna | 7th Duke
Maria | of Bedford
Stanhope | 1788–1861
1783–1857

William = Elizabeth
1790–1846 | Anne
| Rawdon
| 1793–1874

Adelaide = John
Lister, | 1792–1878
Lady
Ribblesdale
1807–1838
(1st wife)

Wriothesley
1804–1886

Edward
1805–1874

TREE

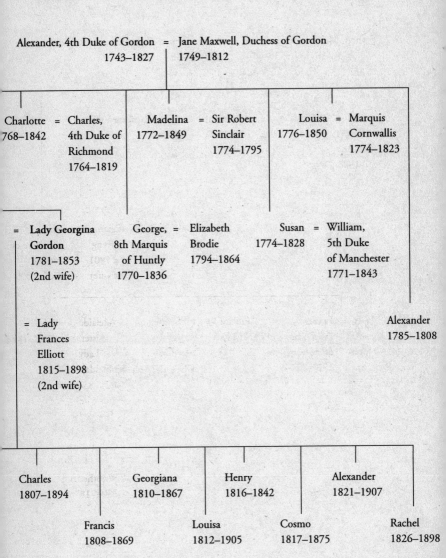

Alexander, 4th Duke of Gordon = Jane Maxwell, Duchess of Gordon
1743–1827   1749–1812

Charlotte = Charles,   Madelina = Sir Robert   Louisa = Marquis
768–1842   4th Duke of   1772–1849   Sinclair   1776–1850   Cornwallis
      Richmond   1774–1795   1774–1823
      1764–1819

= **Lady Georgina**   George, = Elizabeth   Susan = William,
   Gordon   8th Marquis   Brodie   1774–1828   5th Duke
   1781–1853   of Huntly   1794–1864   of Manchester
   (2nd wife)   1770–1836   1771–1843

   = Lady   Alexander
     Frances   1785–1808
     Elliott
     1815–1898
     (2nd wife)

Charles   Georgiana   Henry   Alexander
1807–1894   1810–1867   1816–1842   1821–1907

    Francis   Louisa   Cosmo   Rachel
    1808–1869   1812–1905   1817–1875   1826–1898

Introduction

$\mathcal{V}$isiting Endsleigh for the first time, I found myself caught in a seamless web of past and present. As we drove past the ornate gatehouse down the long, heavily wooded drive to the grey stone shooting and fishing lodge, it was as if the years had fallen away and I had travelled back almost two hundred years. Once inside the house, the impression became even stronger. This was no pseudo reproduction of the Regency era; this was the genuine thing. I could touch the original rosebud chintz cushions in the bedroom, walk on the sheep's knuckles cobbles on the terrace and look through the rustic tree-trunk colonnades at an unchanging view of the River Tamar.

Wandering around the picturesque gardens, discovering surprises around every corner, from the Marie Antoinette-style miniature dairy to the scenic Swiss cottage, I realised this was a very special, secret place. I had never experienced anything like it before, where the past was so palpable; I was enchanted and I wanted to know more about

Georgina, sixth Duchess of Bedford, the inspiration behind this magical house and gardens. Surely only a remarkable character could have left such a lasting impression of her impeccable taste and style. Almost two centuries since she first came to Endsleigh, her personality still pervaded the place; her feminine imprint was on everything from her name carved on the foundation stone in the stableyard to the scenic walks, the Upper and Lower Georgies, named after her. She had left Endsleigh for the last time well over a hundred years before my visit, but the rooms, although faded and slightly dusty, seemed to be so unaltered she could have walked back into them and immediately felt at home. It was as if, although she was no longer there in person, her spirit and scent, Esprit de Rose, still lingered in the air.

When it was time to tear myself away from Endsleigh, my step back into the past had been so convincing that it seemed incongruous to be driving away in a car instead of a carriage. Once away from the house, Georgina's spell remained unbroken. I felt that a woman with such a powerful, creative spirit must have lived an extraordinary life, and I wanted to know more about her.

Over the years, while working as a journalist, thoughts of Georgina never left me for long. Whenever the opportunity arose I would piece together information about her. The more I found out, the more tantalising her story became – there were rumours of an affair with the leading artist of the day, Edwin Landseer, who was twenty years younger than her, and hints that they had a love child together. I had always wanted to write a book but I now knew the subject I wanted to write about was Georgina. Five years after my first visit to Endsleigh, the time was right to concentrate on bringing my idea to fruition. My father had just died and journalism no longer seemed fulfilling; the only project that aroused more than a flicker of enthusiasm in me was the thought of writing Georgina's story.

When I began researching her life I did not know exactly what I would find or how much information would be available but to my relief, as the research progressed, Georgina never let me down. As I read her letters and discovered what other people had said about her, I found she was an even more fascinating character than I had hoped. In an era when many women were victims, unable to fulfil their potential, often caught in loveless marriages but unable to divorce easily, Georgina was different. She was a woman who in modern parlance was able to 'have it all' and on her own terms – she kept a doting husband and an adoring younger lover enthralled; she had a family of ten children but also created an active and stimulating life of her own.

Although born in the eighteenth century, she had so much in common with many modern women. She was the child of separated parents, a second wife and a stepmother who in her forties took a much younger lover. But in other ways she was the epitome of her time: as the wife of one of the wealthiest men in England, her lifestyle vividly reveals what it was like to live at the centre of society during the decadent Regency era. Her world was full of powerful characters, from her mother, the controversial political hostess Jane, Duchess of Gordon, to her stepson, the Prime Minister Lord John Russell; their stories intertwine with Georgina's. Her biography explores the complex relationships and strong passions surrounding this magnetic and manipulative woman.

In many ways Georgina lived a charmed life, but her letters reveal there were sometimes fissures behind the façade. She was a woman who inspired intense emotions and people either loved or hated her. Her stepsons loathed the dominant woman who exerted such a great influence over their father the Duke, but her greatest enemy was her stepdaughter-in-law, Elizabeth Rawdon, an intellectual beauty whose hatred of the Duchess led to a family feud.

Few situations depressed Georgina for long because she was naturally good humoured and knew just how to get her own way. Even when her beauty faded her sex appeal remained and throughout her life she attracted men. Her enduring allure kept both her husband and lover besotted even beyond the grave. After Georgina died, Edwin Landseer's fragile emotional balance collapsed and he gradually went mad.

During two years of extensive research I read everything I could about Georgina and visited the places where she had lived, hoping to capture the essence of this complex woman. The Duchess came alive in my imagination at Endsleigh and I wanted that frisson again. I experienced that same sensation of past reaching out to present when I visited Barons Court in Northern Ireland, the home of Georgina's daughter Louisa, Duchess of Abercorn (now the home of the present Duke and Duchess); at this house they still have the sketches Landseer did of Georgina that were such an important part of their love story. Laid out on the polished table in the splendid rotunda at Barons Court were four large boxes of pictures by the artist. As I opened each box my excitement increased. These were no ordinary sketches. They were so tender and intimate that they confirmed in the most evocative way all my research into their affair. The sensuality of their relationship came alive as I looked at Landseer's simple sketch of the Duchess from behind, showing her elegant neck and curvaceous figure. Again, as at Endsleigh, the distance between past and present evaporated, and the sketches looked so fresh they could have been drawn the day before; even the lead from Landseer's pencil strokes still glinted silver in the sunlight.

It is this freshness that has made Georgina's story such a pleasure to uncover. Although over the years the Duchess has been mentioned in many books, no one has ever written a full-length biography, nor have many of the pictures and sketches of her and her family ever been published before. In death, as in life, she was no dull and dusty Duchess; she was always scintillating and humorous. It is those qualities which cut across the centuries and make her story as relevant to us today as it was in her own era. For readers who want to go back to the Regency period, Georgina is an excellent and entertaining guide, while for others who want to read about a true mistress of the feminine arts, the Duchess will not disappoint.

CHAPTER ONE

The Early Years

Born on 18 July 1781 at Gordon Castle, Fochabers, Banffshire, Georgina was the flamboyant daughter of unconventional parents. Although her birthplace was in the north of Scotland, far away geographically from the seats of power, as part of the Gordon clan she grew up at the centre of late eighteenth-century political, cultural and social life. Her up-bringing set the pattern for much of her later life; many of her attitudes and tastes can be traced back to her intellectually cosmopolitan yet physically remote childhood. Her love of nature, interest in the arts and view of marriage stem from her early experiences.

At the centre of Georgina's early life was her mother, Jane, Duchess of Gordon. Few girls could have had a more overpowering parent. Jane moulded her daughter in her own image and in adulthood Georgina's strengths and weaknesses echoed her charismatic mother's personality.

Jane was an exceptional woman by the standards of any era, but particularly by the criteria of the eighteenth-century world in which she lived. She behaved as if women were equal to men long before feminism became an ideology, and she taught her daughters to have the same advanced attitude. Born into genteel poverty in Edinburgh, the young Jane Maxwell had the indomitable nature and endless energy to rise to the top. As the second daughter of a baronet, Sir William Maxwell, and his wife Magdalen Blair, she was a member of the minor aristocracy. Home for the family was a large second-floor flat in Hyndford's Close, Edinburgh. Many Scottish aristocrats lived in flats at this time, but some of the closes and streets were so narrow that people could shake hands with their opposite neighbour through the window and Hyndford's Close was not the most salubrious address. The Maxwells' flat was far from luxurious. The rooms were linked by a dark passage where, due to lack of space, the family's washing was hung up to dry. Not having a large staff, the Maxwell children were brought up to be practical. Jane's sister Eglantine used to be sent across the road to fetch water from the fountain for cooking and cleaning.

Pretty though Jane undoubtedly was, there was always an element of coarseness about her. Contemporaries described her as 'a boisterous young hoyden' and they had many anecdotes to illustrate her tomboyish behaviour. One describes how, as a young girl, she rode up the High Street on a sow belonging to Peter Ramsay, the stabler in St Mary's Wynd, with her sister following behind thumping the pig with a stick.

Exuberant and ambitious, Jane blossomed into a high-spirited beauty known as 'The Flower of Galloway'. So great were her powers of attraction that the song 'Jenny of Monreith' was composed for her. One contemporary described her appearance in detail: 'The shape of her face was a very beautiful oval, but her chin rather too long. Her hair, eyes and eyebrows were dark, her upper lip short and her mouth, notwithstanding a certain expression of determination, was sweet and well defined.' However, it was her personality as much as her physical appearance that made her unforgettable. The description continued: '[She was] above middle size, very finely shaped, she had dark expressive eyes, very regular features, fine complexion, and a most engaging expression. She was eminent for agility and grace in the performance of those exercises which display beauty and symmetry, and for the gaiety, spirit and brilliancy of humour and with which so agreeably set off her acute and vigorous understanding.'

When she was a teenager, she met and fell in love with a young officer. They were devoted to each other but were forced to part when he was sent abroad with his regiment. Shortly afterwards, news reached her that he had been killed. Jane was devastated by his death and she suffered what would now be called a nervous breakdown. She was still grieving for her lost love when she met Alexander, fourth Duke of Gordon, at a ball in the Old Assembly Rooms in Edinburgh.

In many ways, Alexander seemed to be the perfect match. Not only was he extremely rich with a large estate in the Highlands, he was very attractive, reputedly the handsomest man in Scotland. He was also charming. When he met the beautiful 'Flower of Galloway' he fell in love at first sight but it seems that Jane was less immediately infatuated. However, it would be an upward move socially for her and the rumour spread around Edinburgh that an engagement was imminent. Needing to economise, Jane was walking to a ball in Edinburgh when she discovered a hole in her cotton stocking. She went into the nearest silk draper's shop, pulled off her stocking and asked for a needle to repair it. The owner of the shop came forward with a pair of fine silk stockings, asking in return only the honour of her patronage when she became a duchess. The Duke proposed to her that night at the ball and her patronage was ever afterwards bestowed on the helpful draper's shop.

When Jane accepted Alexander's hand, her head was ruling her heart. She was still in love with her dead soldier but her friends and family told her that the Duke's offer was too good to miss. Through him, Jane was offered the chance to become a member of one of the most important families in Scotland.

Gordons, French in origin, were to be found taking key roles in Scottish history throughout the centuries. Early records show that in the eleventh century Adam Gordon was granted land in Berwickshire by Malcolm III. His descendants proved to be fearless fighters, willing to take on the strongest in the land. In 1199, Bertram de Gordoun killed Richard Coeur de Lion at Chalus; then, in the reign of Henry III, Adam Gordon won fame during the wars against England by fighting in single combat against Prince Edward (later Edward I, Hammer of the Scots) which ended in a draw. Skilled in diplomacy as well as combat, Gordons helped to shape the future of Scotland. In 1320, Adam's grandson, another Adam Gordon, was one of the Scots ambassadors who laid the Declaration of Arbroath before the Pope.

Over the years, the Gordons extended their lands and power until they virtually ruled the north-east of Scotland. Alexander Gordon, Earl of Huntly, commanded one wing of the Scots army at Flodden. When his grandson George succeeded him, he was made Lieutenant of the North and Chancellor in 1547. While visiting George at Huntly Castle, the Queen Regent, Mary of Guise, called him 'Cock o' the North' and this became the term by which all Gordon chiefs were known from then on.

During the Jacobite Rising of 1715, Alexander, Marquis of Huntly, was an ardent Jacobite. He brought 2,300 men to fight with him at the battle of Sherriffmuir. He was taken prisoner by the government but received a pardon and became the second Duke of Gordon in 1716. The rest of the Gordons remained staunch Jacobites, although Georgina's grandfather, Cosmo George Gordon, the third Duke, became a Protestant and took no part in the Second Jacobite Rising in 1745.

Cosmo George died in 1752, making his son Alexander a duke and chief of the clan at only nine years old. Despite this early elevation and the duties it entailed, Alexander's life continued in much the same way as it would have if his father had lived. Like many aristocratic boys in the eighteenth century he was educated at Eton, then undertook the obligatory Grand Tour of Europe. His education and travelling gave him an air of international sophistication so that by the time he met Jane he was a polished twenty-four-year-old looking for a wife.

The young couple married on 28 October 1767 at the house of Jane's brother-in-law, Mr Fordyce, at Number Two Argyle Street,

Edinburgh. After the ceremony, the Duke and his new Duchess went to Mr Fordyce's estate at Ayton in Berwickshire. Legend has it that during the honeymoon, Jane received a letter addressed to her in her maiden name and written in the well-known hand of her first love. He was writing to tell her that he was on his way home to marry her and complete their happiness. On reading the letter Jane fled distractedly from the house, her emotions in turmoil. According to local tradition, after a long search she was found 'in a swoon' by her husband, who read the letter and realised where his new wife's true affections lay. The honeymoon fiasco was to cast a long shadow over the rest of their married life and it seems the Duke never forgave his wife for making him feel second best.

Despite the disastrous start to their marriage, the Duke and Duchess lived up to their dynastic obligations and soon started a family. They were to have seven children, two sons and five daughters; Charlotte, born a year after their marriage, then George, Marquis of Huntly, Madelina, Susan and Louisa at two-yearly intervals. There was a five-year gap before Georgina was born, then four years later in 1785 they had another son, Alexander.

Jane's children were not Alexander's only offspring. He was a serial womaniser who was to father nine illegitimate children by at least four different women. Nor was fathering children outside marriage a new experience for the Duke – his first 'natural' child, George, was born a year before Alexander married Jane. It seems he had more energy and enthusiasm for creating children than for naming them; by the time he fathered his eighth and ninth illegitimate daughters he had run out of inspiration and named them after two of his legitimate daughters, Charlotte and Susan. Alexander's natural children grew up in contact with their father and half-brothers and sisters, and as adults were provided with a house and land. Jane showed an almost saintly tolerance in her treatment of these children. In fact, such genuine mutual affection developed between them that one of the Duke's illegitimate sons named his daughter after the Duchess.

In the early years of her marriage, Jane made the most of all the trappings of being an eighteenth-century duchess, throwing herself into public life to compensate for her unhappy private life. Her success was immediate and she was soon known as the Queen of Edinburgh society, becoming 'the sole arbitress' of fashion in the city. No praise seemed too exaggerated; one contemporary claimed she had 'a brilliancy and radiance about her like the rays round the head of an apostle', while another observer recalled that in her heyday she was 'unquestionably the most beautiful and fascinating woman in Great Britain'.

She gave lavish parties and knew just how to upstage every other woman in the room, as the writer Pryse Gordon's description of her appearance at a masked ball reveals: 'The Duchess was just a flower girl, and changed her costume before supper for a superb court dress. She was unmasked and glittering with diamonds. I had read the Arabian Tales and was transported to the regions of that fanciful work.'

As an acknowledged beauty she was painted by the greatest artists of the day. In 1772, Angelica Kauffman portrayed her as the goddess Diana; three years later Sir Joshua Reynolds captured her on canvas dressed in white and gold. Deified and adored, the only person who seemed immune to Jane's beauty was her husband.

By the time Georgina was born, her parents' marriage was on the wane. They were incompatible on many levels and wanted to lead very different lives; the Duke was home-loving while Jane knew there was an exciting world to dominate. As their marriage gradually disintegrated, the Duchess spent a great deal of time in Edinburgh while the Duke stayed in the Highlands. He was an easy-going man of mediocre talents who, unlike his wife, did not wish to take centre stage at a national level. Although he supported William Pitt the younger, politics was low on his list of priorities, coming far below his main preoccupations of rural pursuits and field sports. As a major land-owner, he applied his innovative skills to improving his estate. He introduced semaphores to give notice of the movements of the deer, kept hawks and bred deerhounds. Although Alexander was not a good husband, he was a good father and a likeable man, as a family friend explained:

The Duke, though more inclined to a retired life, is in no respect inferior [to his wife]. I have never known a man of a sounder judgement, of more acute parts or of a more candid and benevolent temper; and in the company of people whom he knows, there cannot be a more facetious, a more cheerful, or a more agreeable associate. His passion for astronomy and other parts of science, his abhorrence of drinking and gaming, and his attachment to his children, keep him at a distance from the dissipations of high life.

With Jane often away, how much Georgina saw of her mother in her early childhood is open to question. When she was with her, the Duchess certainly doted on her adorable youngest daughter, but that did not mean she was willing to sacrifice her own independent life to provide Georgina's day-to-day care. As a baby, Georgina was wet-nursed by a young Scottish woman called Helen Taylor. Jane's desire to avoid the most intimate elements of child-care was not unusual among aristocratic women and wet-nursing was common at the time. Fashionable women believed breast-feeding would ruin their figures and make them prematurely old. In some cases, the boned corsets that eighteenth-century fashion demanded were so tight that they damaged breast tissue and nipples and made breast-feeding physically impossible. In any case, a wet nurse was a status symbol, particularly in France where during the time of Louis XVI and Napoleon, breast-feeding was regarded as bourgeois and simply not done.

Earth mother was certainly not the image Jane intended to create. Having conquered Edinburgh society, she moved on to London, where she carved a niche for herself as the leading Tory hostess, in rivalry with the Duchess of Devonshire, her Whig equivalent. The competition between the two women became the talk of society and was even captured in a satirical novel, *A Winter in London* by T.S. Surr. Apparently, 'the Duchess of Belgrave' (a thinly disguised version of the Duchess of Devonshire) was not amused when 'the Duchess of Drinkwater' (alias the Duchess of Gordon) appeared on the London scene. Surr described the rivalry in terms of an epic battle:

The Duchess of Drinkwater appeared upon the field of fashion, and threw down the gauntlet of defiance to Belgrave: an event which produced upon the fashionable world an effect precisely similar to that which the natural world sustains from the convulsion of an earthquake; or which the moral world experienced from the French revolution.

Before this challenge was given, to have doubted that the will of Belgrave was the law of fashion would have been deemed an abrogation of loyalty itself . . . What then must have been the surprise, the horror of a people cherishing such sentiments when they beheld the Duchess of Drinkwater erecting her standard of revolt against the object of their allegiance and their worship, and promulgating with undaunted zeal a code and creed diametrically opposite to the principles of their former obedience and faith.

At her house in Pall Mall, which belonged to the Marquis of Buckingham, Jane held large soirees for supporters of the Tory administration. In the relaxed atmosphere she created, they could plot the tactics of the party and discuss intrigues. In politics, as in all other aspects of her life, Jane would stop at nothing to achieve her goals. She had a ruthless streak that was plain for all to see. Nathaniel Wraxall wrote of her that while she was 'far inferior to the Duchess of Devonshire in grace and accomplishment she possessed indomitable pertinacity, importunity and unconventionality'. She used her considerable presence to cajole, or if necessary intimidate, weaker mortals. In Surr's satire she was portrayed as bellowing her commands 'with the lungs of a boatswain'. It was said that during one General Election she even kidnapped a supporter of a rival candidate and kept him locked in a cellar to ensure her friend Captain Elphinstone was elected. She became known as 'the whipper in' of the Tory party. Wraxall wrote: 'Confiding in her rank, her sex, and personal attractions, she ventured to send for members of Parliament, to question, to remonstrate, and to use every means for confirming their adherence to the government.'

Gradually she gained a degree of political influence rare for a woman of her era. Few women since, unless they reached the rank of cabinet minister or Prime Minister, have wielded such parliamentary power or patronage. Wraxall observed:

> The Scottish Duchess reserved all the energies of her character for Ministerial purposes. Desirous of participating in the blessings which the Treasury alone can dispense, and of enrolling the name of Gordon with those of Pitt and of Dundas if not in the rolls of fame, at least in the substantial list of court favour and benefaction, the Administration did not possess a more active or determined partisan.

Rather than concealing her sexuality, she blatantly used it to get her own way. To the disgust of some, she cleverly employed her considerable charm and wit to become the confidante of the party's leader William Pitt, and critics were soon describing him as 'the dupe' of a designing woman. However, Jane genuinely admired her leader and her admiration was not just for his political skills. She wrote:

> There is an elegance in his taste, and a wise kind of folly in his social hours of conversation that raises him more in my estimation than even his political talents . . . there is a rectitude of mind, a steady firm principle of honour in every word.

Perhaps her appeal to Pitt was that she treated him informally, as a friend not a statesman, and they exchanged banter. On one occasion, after a long absence, the Duchess said to him, 'Pray Sir, have you talked as much nonsense as ever since we parted?' to which he replied, 'I do not know, Madam, but I certainly have not heard so much!'

Like the Duchess of Devonshire, her role was to make politics sexy and glamorous. Party politics took on a whole new meaning as she held dinners and balls for Pitt, aimed at creating a sense of Tory party unity against the Whigs. There was no excuse for mistaking Jane's parties for her rival's events because they were clearly marked with her distinctive style. She introduced Scottish reels to London for her balls, which sometimes went on until five in the morning, and she made wearing tartan a fashion statement. Balls were used as battles in the long 'war' between the two duchesses, as Surr explained:

> The Duchesses never met without betraying some signs of approaching hostilities. The patroness of reels cracked the shoulder straps of sixteen dresses by exercising herself in shrugs at the Duchess of Belgrave . . . At length the war was openly declared by both parties, and the first blow was struck by the Duchess of Drinkwater, who gave a grand gala the same night on which her rival had previously announced one.

As time went on, Jane's parties became more fashionable than the Duchess of Devonshire's, partly because she had novelty value but also because they were so much fun. One of her most opulent events was a ball held by members of White's at the Pantheon on 30 March 1789, given to celebrate the recovery of George III after the Regency crisis earlier that year.

The crisis had begun in November 1788 when the King became seriously ill, suffering from the mental illness that plagued him. Remedies such as blistering, bleeding and purging, or taking quinine and laudanum, failed to improve his condition and his doctors could not agree on a treatment. In this difficult situation it seemed likely that a Regency under Prince George would be established and William Pitt would be dismissed from office, allowing Charles James Fox, who was a friend of the Prince, to form an administration.

While William Pitt played for time to keep himself in power, Fox, eager for office, asserted the Prince's right to assume control. He even demanded in the House of Commons that the Prince's royal powers should be unfettered rather than restricted. This was a volte-face for the Whig leader as he was now defending the royal prerogative he had spent his political life attacking. Understandably, Pittite MPs mocked the former 'people's champion' for his hypocrisy.

With Fox standing up for monarchical privilege, William Pitt was left to defend parliamentary power. He insisted that the Prince could only become Regent with the consent of Parliament and subject to conditions set out by Parliament. There was self-interest in Pitt's move; Parliament would have control over the Prince, who would then be unable to dismiss Pitt and put Fox in power.

The carefully drafted Regency Bill was passed by the Commons and was ready to go to the Lords, but in the event Pitt's delaying tactics worked; the King recovered before it got there. For William Pitt and the Duchess of Gordon it was time to celebrate the good news. More than two thousand guests danced the night away, drank champagne and sang 'God Save the King'. To add to the stylish atmosphere, Jane and the Duchess of Richmond, who were the patrons of the event, decided that all the guests should wear white and gold. It was a moment of triumph for Jane as she walked into the ball arm-in-arm with Pitt to the sound of loud applause.

Such showmanship did not appeal to everyone and some contemporaries complained that Jane's behaviour was brash. Wraxall wrote:

> Her conversation bore a very strong analogy to her intellectual formation. Exempted by her sex, rank and beauty from those restraints imposed on women by the generally recognised usages of society the Duchess of Gordon frequently dispensed with their observance.

Jane was not willing to abide by society's rules when she thought they were wrong, or worse still dull. She always said exactly what she thought – even to the Prince of Wales. At a ball in 1789, many of the ladies were wearing the Prince of Wales' feathers in their caps as a sign of support for the Prince and the Whig party. The Prince asked the Duchess to put on a similar cap but as a supporter of the Tory party and the King she said she would 'sooner be hang'd'. Although sometimes there was a serious motive behind Jane's outrageous behaviour, often it was just her way of puncturing pomposity and expressing her tremendous sense of humour. She once caused 'a great riot at the Opera' by kissing a member of the French royal family. A young aristocrat had told her it was a sign of respect to kiss royalty when introduced when in fact it was a breach of etiquette.

As a small child, Georgina's time was divided between Gordon Castle, her mother's house in Pall Mall and her parents' unpretentious cottage in the Highlands. The Duchess's London life left little time for her daughter as she filled every moment to the full, often leaving the house at dawn one day only to return at dawn the next. Horace Walpole described Jane's hyperactive lifestyle:

> The Duchess of Gordon uses fifteen or sixteen hours of her four and twenty. I heard her journal of last Monday. She first went to Handel's music in the Abbey; she then clambered over the benches, and went to [Warren] Hastings' trial in the Hall; after dinner, to the play; then to Lady Lucan's assembly; after that to Ranelagh, and returned to Mrs Hobart's faro-table; gave a ball herself in the evening of that morning, into which she must have got a good way; and set out for Scotland the next day. Hercules could not have achieved a quarter of her labours in the same space of time.

Her mother's absences do not seem to have done Georgina any harm. She was a very intelligent child and with typical Gordon loquacity she began to talk at an early age. When she was two years old, her mother wrote: 'From morning to night Georgina's cheerful note is to be heard, talk of mama, and all her new friends, the goats, the kids, the deer, and sisters, Papa, Doctor Beattie is even to be heard in her interesting rhapsodies.'

As the youngest girl in the family she became the pampered pet of her parents and older siblings. Her elder brother George, Lord Huntly, doted on her and when he returned home from boarding school for the holidays, she was 'his delight'. But as a spoilt four-year-old she did not reciprocate his affection and took some time to be 'reconciled to the intrusion of this little stranger' who threatened to steal her limelight.

Surrounded by affection and all the advantages of wealth, Georgina grew up in a privileged environment. Her family home was like a fairytale castle, complete with a fifteenth-century turreted tower fit for Rapunzel, where Georgina and her sisters could let their imaginations run wild as they lived out their childhood fantasies. This tower was one of the few remaining parts of the original house. The Duke had had Gordon Castle rebuilt by the architect John Baxter of Edinburgh. No expense was spared to create an elegant Georgian house surrounded by exquisite formal gardens. The effect was impressive. The Reverend James Gordon described it as 'one of the noblest palaces in Britain, and [it] attracts the notice of all travellers, who never fail to be highly gratified'. Beneath the immaculate façade, extensive work had been required to create the Duke's dream castle; costly drains had been needed to turn bog land into an enchanting landscape. Away from the manicured lawns there were plenty of places for children to explore; the fine plantations of trees and shrubs surrounding the castle and the distinctive large clusters of holly bushes in the grounds provided ideal hiding places.

The estate reflected the Duke's love of field sports. There was a large deer park near the house and all types of wildlife were attracted to the area, including woodcock in the autumn and green plover in the spring. Built in the far north of Scotland on the banks of the River Spey, Gordon Castle could be a difficult place to reach at certain times of the year when floods and winds made the river hard to cross. Until 1804 when the Fochabers Old Bridge was opened, a ferry was the only means of crossing the Spey. Communication with the outside world could become a problem for Georgina and her family as visitors were sometimes deterred from travelling to this remote part of Britain. Living in such splendid isolation meant that Georgina and her sisters often had to rely on their neighbours from all classes for company; this experience helped to shape adults who could relate to people from all sections of society.

The nearest town to the castle was Fochabers, and its position in relation to the castle was very like Blenheim Palace's relationship with Woodstock. Reflecting the lengths to which aristocrats were willing to go in order to create an aesthetically pleasing view, during the eighteenth century the town was moved south, a mile away from the castle. The same architect who built the castle, John Baxter, was commissioned to build the new town and he created a rectangular street plan around an extensive square. Although Fochabers was by no means a sophisticated shopping centre, it had everything the local community needed. When Georgina was a child, weekly markets for butter, cheese, eggs and poultry were held in the town and several shops and two inns were open throughout the week. The major manufacturing business was weaving – cotton stockings, and thread and worsted material for waistcoats and breeches. A local merchant dealt in lint, thread and tobacco.

Much of the wealth that sustained the Gordons' expensive lifestyle came from the area. The Duke owned a salmon fishery on the Spey run by Messrs Gordon and Richardson which gave him a rent of £1,500 a year, a considerable sum. The average wage for common labourers in the area was 6d a day in winter and 8d a day in summer, and a manservant could be employed for about £6 a year. Thousands of salmon were sent to London early in the season covered with ice, and any fish left over were salted and sent abroad.

The Duchess, rather than the Duke, managed the family finances and she proved to be a determined businesswoman. During her time, the Gordon fortunes grew. Her main aim was family aggrandisement, both socially and financially, but the spin-off helped her tenants. Perhaps because of her origins, she had a well-developed social conscience and a great empathy with the poor. She never forgot seeing people starve during the famine years of 1772 and 1773, their suffering helping to put her marital problems into perspective. Showing a reflective side to her extrovert character, she wrote:

When I look at the thatch roof and think how many more deserving beings there are than me, pine under the same rustic covering without even the necessaries of life and that I should repine, because the person I wish to be perfect, has one fault when perhaps myself and others have many more – at those moments I think nothing would distress me, but alas we are weak mortals, the same scene would cause the same feelings.

Jane's sympathy for the less fortunate went further than just fine words; she also made sure practical help was provided. Part of the Duchess's financial plan was to encourage local industries. By introducing the wearing of tartan into fashionable society she was not just making a fashion statement, she was also trying to boost Highland manufacturing. In the early years of her marriage, she took over the farm of Cuttlebrae near Gordon Castle and was soon producing the best flax in Scotland. Typically practical, she made sure that she understood all the different methods of dressing flax, coming to the conclusion that flax should not be dressed by the cottagers in their homes because they often put the flax too near their hearth which caused dangerous fires. Instead, she set up a mill at Fochabers where her tenants could work during the day. Spurred on by the success of this first mill, she worked with her friend Lord Kaimes, who was one of the Trustees for Manufacturers, to set up a lint mill at Kingussie in Badenoch.

Although her support of local industries improved the Highland economy, as an astute political woman she realised that more long-term solutions were needed to help the poor improve their lives. She wrote to a political friend:

For years I have given premiums for all kinds of domestic industry – spinning, dyeing etc . . . But there is an evil I cannot remedy without a sum of money. The children are totally neglected in body and mind: cold, hunger and dirt carries off hundreds. The cowpox [vaccination against small pox] would save many; no doctors for thirty miles, make many orphan families. They say they may be better in a foreign land; they cannot be more wretched . . . I wish to add to the comforts of the aged, and take the children – teach them to think right, raise food for themselves and prepare them to succeed to their fathers' farms with knowledge of all the branches of farming.

Georgina was to continue her mother's tradition of *noblesse oblige* when she became mistress of her own staff and tenants. Throughout her life there are many examples of small, thoughtful gestures to her employees. From her mother she had learned that with great privilege came responsibilities to those who were less fortunate.

At Gordon Castle, Georgina grew up in a cultured and happy environment where music, dance and poetry flourished. The Duke composed verses and wrote a famous comic song, 'There is Cauld Kail in Aberdeen'. The Duke and Duchess became well known for generously supporting other people's talents. Their butler, Marshall, was encouraged to compose strathspeys that were danced with gusto by the Gordons. They also became patrons of Neil Gow, the celebrated Scottish fiddler who composed more than two hundred Scottish airs.

The Duchess enjoyed her role as patron of the arts and found the company of writers stimulating. The poet and philosopher Dr Beattie, who wrote *The Minstrel* and *The Essay on Truth*, became a great friend and she was soon calling him her 'guardian angel' and expressing 'sentiments of love and gratitude' to him. Determined to better herself not just socially but intellectually, she thoroughly enjoyed Dr Beattie's entertaining company. As her literary guru, he directed her reading and was often astonished at the rapidity with which she grasped the salient points of a book. If he gave her a book one day, he often heard her discussing it the next evening at dinner with her guests. The Duchess was hungry for knowledge and she read with a voracious appetite. As a perfectionist, she became frustrated when she could not express her thoughts as lucidly as her exacting standards demanded. She explained to Dr Beattie:

> I think I write more to you than any other body, the reason
> is plain, I wish to excel – and forget it is folly and amusement
> you wish to find in your female friends – not serious
> reflections – I am sure in society I have as much of those
> former qualifications as any body – but the moment I take
> up a pen – all bright ideas leave me.

Her attempts to become a literary hostess were watched with cynicism
by some contemporaries who believed it was just a passing fad. Mrs
Grant of Laggan wrote:

> Her Grace's present ruling passion is literature – to be the
> arbitress of literary taste and the patroness of genius – a
> distinction for which her want of early culture and the flutter
> of a life devoted to very different pursuits has rather
> disqualified her. Yet she has strong flashes of intellect,
> immediately lost in the formless confusion of a mind ever
> hurried on by contending passions and contradictory objects.

As a member of the Scottish literati, the Duchess mixed with many
of the Edinburgh writers and intellectuals of the time. The greatest
star in the Gordon circle was the poet Robert Burns. Writing to John
Ballantine in December 1786, Burns listed the Duchess as one of his
'avowed Patrons and Patronesses'. To help his career she invited him to
her drawing-room parties in Edinburgh and introduced him to her
friends. Mrs Alison Cockburn wrote:

> The town is all agog with the ploughman poet who receives
> adulation with native dignity and is the very figure of his
> profession, strong and coarse, but has a most enthusiastick
> [sic] heart of love. He has seen the Duchess of Gordon and
> all the gay world.

Burns commemorated his visit to his patrons' Highland home in his
song 'Gordon Castle', which describes the atmosphere:

Wildly here, without control
Nature reigns and rules the whole;
In that sober pensive mood,
Dearest to the feeling soul,
She plants the forest, pours the flood,
Life's poor day I'll musing rave
And find at night a sheltering cave,
Where waters flow and wild woods wave,
By bonie [sic] Castle Gordon.

Burns also recorded in his *Journal* his impressions of the castle's inhabitants: 'The duke makes me happier than ever great man did – noble, princely; yet mild, condescending and affable, gay and kind – the Duchess charming, witty and sensible – God bless them.' The Duchess was equally impressed by the poet, as she told Sir Walter Scott: 'He was the only man I ever met who carried me off my feet.'

Although many contemporaries were cruel and critical of the Duchess, Burns never forgot her early support. In 1789 he wrote angry letters to two newspapers that had published a sneering stanza about Jane, allegedly by Burns. He wrote in extreme terms to the editor of the *Star*:

I never composed a line on the Duchess of Gordon in my life. I have such a sense of what I personally owe to her Grace's benevolent patronage, and such a respect for her exalted character, that I have never yet dared to mention her name in any composition of mine, from a despair of doing justice to my own feelings.

I have been recollecting over the sins and trespasses, peccadilloes and backslidings of myself and my forefathers, to see if I can guess why I am visited and punished with this vile calamity. To be at one time, falsely accused of the two most damning crimes, of which, as a man and as a poet, I could have been guilty – INGRATITUDE and STUPIDITY.

Despite the grandeur of her surroundings and the importance of the guests, Georgina grew up in an informal atmosphere. No matter how elevated the company, life with the Gordons was never stuffy and contemporaries witnessed Georgina jumping over backs of chairs and taking part in rowdy games. Through her parents she met the most talented men from the worlds of politics and art, but as a precocious child she took it for granted that these great men were her 'friends'. Her mother wrote proudly to Dr Beattie:

> She [Georgina] always insists upon calling Mr Dundas Doctor Beattie and no care can prevent it – great minds must give a resemblance to the countenance for she still says: 'Well Mr Dundas – you are so like my friend Doctor Beattie.' She astonishes Edinburgh with her cleverness.

Georgina was brought up by her mother to be able to talk to anyone, rich or poor. The Duchess used to say, 'I have been acquainted with David Hume and William Pitt, and therefore I am not afraid to converse with any body.' Jane always spoke with a Scottish accent and although she was a social climber she was not a snob. She reserved her acerbic comments for the powerful not the vulnerable, as was shown one evening when a poor tenant came to visit her during dinner. He had never before met a duchess and overawed he replied to all her questions, 'Deed no, my Lady Duchess', or 'My Lady Duchess, deed yes.' She looked at him throughout as though she had never been addressed differently and she avoided exchanging glances with the amused circle of guests around her, in case she wounded the man's feelings.

Although life at Gordon Castle, with its wide range of different characters visiting, was never dull, some of the happiest times in Georgina's childhood were spent at her parents' cottage at Glenfiddich, Banffshire. It gave her a taste for the simple, rural life she was to recreate in later years. The Duchess of Gordon called Glenfiddich 'this dear romantic Glen' and wrote of its 'rural delights' – 'You cannot think how delightful it is, the stillness, the fragrance, after the tiresomeness of a London life . . . it is in the most beautiful part of the mountains, woods, lakes and rivers.' While the Duke enjoyed excellent shooting, the Duchess created a farm where her children could play with animals and develop a love of nature. She encouraged her daughters to be unashamed sensualists and to revel in the sounds, sights and smells of their native country. The Duchess described the pleasure she experienced during a visit:

> I came there from Edinburgh and never experienced such delightful sensations as when I first saw the dear hills and met each gale loaded with perfume, the children were skipping about amidst the heather like fauns of which there were millions. Before night I was upon the top of every hill and went to every favourite spot as if I had expected to find a beloved friend there. Indeed this summer has yielded me nothing but delight and when I regret sensuality I call it a fatal gift from heaven.

At Glenfiddich the Gordons could enjoy family life in privacy, away from the large staff and frequent visitors who filled the castle. Jane watched with delight as her children developed their own favourite pastimes. Louisa became 'the first botanist in the world', climbing across rocks looking for plants, while Georgina was put in charge of the goats. Her mother wrote: 'a pretty little dairy maid she is – in short it is perfect rural felicity surrounded with every beauty of nature.' Georgina's role was not just for picturesque effect; the goats' whey was needed because her mother was a great believer in its ability to cure all types of illness. She insisted her daughters drank this elixir, and recommended it to her friends as well as her family.

Many years later, Georgina's sister Susan recalled their Highland holidays with affection. She described to Arthur Young 'running up and down the hills bare-footed, driving down the goats and milking them; and being delighted with the place and the life, though no human being within many miles except the family and an old woman of the solitary house. This was the case of all the girls; she never went to school and laid in a fine stock of health.'

Although Georgina's life was superficially idyllic, beneath the surface tensions between her parents threatened her security. Despite her positive personality, Jane could not always keep depression at bay and it seems that most of her misery stemmed from her marriage. Her letters to James Beattie, when his wife was suffering from a mental illness, show she knew all too well the depths of unhappiness and had developed her own ways of coping with it:

> I am afraid you rather indulge the luxury of woe, as try to alleviate it by some society, or at least the conversation of a friend. Under any depression of spirits, one shudders at the idea of interruption – and the first struggle is the most painful. But after a little time we see their kind sympathy, and make an exertion to amuse them, which insensibly banishes, or at least soothes our griefs for a time.

By the time Georgina was twelve her parents were leading virtually separate lives. In 1793 the Duke formally recognised the situation by giving the Duchess an allowance of £4,000 a year for the first year, to be reduced to £3,500 annually thereafter. The Duchess was not happy with the settlement, believing she needed more money to sustain her high-powered lifestyle, but she had little choice in the matter. The couple still put on a united front for family occasions and the Duchess, at this stage, still used Gordon Castle, but for the majority of the year they lived apart.

As Georgina was growing up she witnessed both her parents openly having extra-marital affairs. No doubt this influenced her attitude to infidelity in her own marriage, and showed that as long as a certain amount of discretion was shown, affairs could be conducted openly. The Duke had several mistresses in the 1790s, but the most permanent and important was Jean Christie, the daughter of a tenant farmer. Plain and homely, Jean was not at all like the Duchess, but this seems to have been a large part of her appeal for Alexander – her meekness was evidently more appealing than his wife's pushiness. With the Duchess away in London for much of the year, the Duke did nothing to conceal his affair from his wife or children. In 1791 Jean gave birth to Catherine, the first of her children by Alexander. They had four more children together, and eventually, after the Duchess's death, Jean became the Duke's wife. The Duchess was also unfaithful and it is widely believed she had a long-term affair with Henry Dundas, the leading Tory politician and Pitt's right-hand man.

As the Duchess became increasingly estranged from the Duke, a farmhouse at Kinrara, near Aviemore, became her rural retreat instead of the family cottage at Glenfiddich. During her teenage years, Georgina often joined her mother at her Highland home in the Cairngorms. The vibrant world they created is vividly portrayed by Elizabeth Grant in her *Memoirs of a Highland Lady*. The Grants were neighbours of the Gordons, living at a house called the Doune on the Rothiemurchus estate. As this remote area was sparsely populated, Elizabeth and her family often socialised with the Duchess and her daughters and a real sense of community grew up between them. Elizabeth described the enchanting atmosphere the Duchess created at Kinrara:

> It was a sort of backwoods life, charming to young people amid such scenery, a dramatic emancipation from the forms of society that for a little while every season was delightful, particularly as there was no real roughing it ... [people] flocked to this encampment in the wilderness during the fine autumns to enjoy the free life, the pure air, and the wit and fun the Duchess brought with her to the mountains.

At Kinrara, the house was almost always full to overflowing with guests, so Georgina and her mother shared a bedroom, simply decorated with white calico, whitewash and plenty of flowers. Away from the formality of stately home life, the Duchess and her daughters enjoyed getting back to nature. They got up at five every morning and washed in the burn in preparation for a long day.

The Duchess took running her farm seriously, employing twenty or thirty workers every day and taking an interest in every aspect of their work. But Kinrara, as well as being a working farm, was also run like a hotel, with a constant flow of visitors coming to see the Gordons. Once all the bedrooms were filled, a barn was turned into a dormitory for ladies and a stable was set aside for men. The kitchen was in the out-buildings and here the French cook created delicious meals with limited equipment. He had one large black pot that he divided into four using two pieces of tin sheet. The only disadvantage was that the chef had to cook all white sauces one day and all brown the next.

An eclectic mix of people found themselves thrown together under the Duchess's roof. On one occasion the literary hostess Mrs Thrale, who was a friend of Fanny Burney and Dr Johnson, came to stay; at another time the formidable lady traveller, the Honourable Mrs Murray Aust of Kensington, visited. London politicians and writers mixed with members of the Gordon and Maxwell families in a relaxed atmosphere. The Duchess's attitude was 'the more the merrier' and so once every space in her drawing room and dining room was filled, not to mention the barn and stable, and the butler had resorted to sleeping on top of the kitchen dresser, she would requisition her neighbours' spare rooms.

Parties were impromptu but frequent, with music provided by Long James, a handsome, violin-playing footman. He was always the core of the band but anyone else who could play an instrument was urged to join in the entertainment when the Duchess held a dance in the drawing room or the servants' hall. Georgina had joined the servants and neighbours to learn Scottish dancing from a dancing master, and there was plenty of competition to see which of the young people could dance the strathspeys the most elegantly. The Duchess's dances were energetic events that often went on until midnight, the visiting glitterati from London dancing reels with neighbours from all classes. Elizabeth Grant recalled: 'A few candles lighted up bare walls at short warning, fiddles and whisky punch were always at hand, and the gentles and simples reeled away in company until the ladies thought the scene becoming more boisterous than they liked remaining in.' The Duchess's skill at party planning developed into what became known as 'The Northern Meeting'. Once a year, in October, she persuaded friends and acquaintances from all the northern counties to come to Inverness for a week of parties. Dinners and balls were held in the evenings while days were spent visiting friends and enjoying the scenery.

Through her mother's influence, Georgina became adept in social skills, but her formal education seems to have been more limited. As a young eighteenth-century aristocratic woman, the aim was to become a feminine creature pleasing to men, not a blue-stocking who might intimidate a potential husband. However, although the Duchess of Gordon did not want her daughters to be intellectuals, she did want their minds to be 'enlightened' and to have 'principles founded about divine matters'. She believed that religion was the only consolation in distress and trusted in 'a kind providence who ever protects and watches over innocence and virtue'. To instil the same beliefs in her daughters she took them to hear sermons from the great preachers of the day.

She also turned to her friend the old judge Lord Kaimes for advice on their education. He impressed upon her the great responsibility of her position and he encouraged her to make sure her children learned practical skills. He was delighted to find his 'dear pupil' had followed his advice, 'training the young creatures about her to habits of industry, the knitting of stockings among the young folk of both sexes and other useful occupations'. Evidently the Duchess was ahead of her time, expecting her sons to be as adept at handling a pair of knitting needles as her daughters. Lord Kaimes told the Duchess that he had started writing a book on education in the hope of improving the Gordon girls and that he was going to dedicate it to her. The Duchess was slightly annoyed when at the last minute he decided to change the dedication to Queen Charlotte instead; Jane did not like coming second to anyone, even the Queen.

It seems that like most eighteenth-century aristocratic girls Georgina was given lessons in French, drawing and dancing. She showed an early aptitude for art, as Pryse Gordon confirmed when he described a visit to the Duchess. While she was writing letters in her morning room, 'two of her daughters, the ladies Louise [sic] and Georgiana, were employed in drawing beautiful and interesting sylphs; lovely subjects themselves for the pencil.'

Whatever her other potential may have been, Georgina was brought up with one aim in life – to marry well. Like an aristocratic Mrs Bennet, the Duchess of Gordon made it her life's mission to secure the maximum status for her five daughters. From an early age, Georgina learned how a woman could use her femininity to get her own way on a large or small scale. In 1794, for example, the Duchess of Gordon took her daughters with her on her famous Gordon Highlanders recruiting mission.

When the Napoleonic wars started in 1796, the King turned to Scotland for soldiers, although there was still much bitterness between the Highlanders and the English after the Jacobite rebellion. In 1745 Charles Stuart, known as Bonnie Prince Charlie, the grandson of the exiled Catholic monarch, James II, had attempted to regain the throne, supported by the Catholic Scottish Highlanders. Although Georgina's grandfather, Cosmo George, did not join the rising, his brother Lord Lewis Gordon did, leading a strong contingent of clansmen in the campaign which ended at Culloden.

The Gordons suffered relatively mild reprisals after the uprising's failure. Lord Lewis fled to France where he died in 1754. However, Bonnie Prince Charlie's crushing defeat was to have terrible consequences for many Highlanders. Supporters of the Stuarts were dispossessed of their lands, homes and often their lives. The English government disbanded the Clans and banned the wearing of kilts and playing of bagpipes as these were seen as signs of Scottish nationalism.

The clan system had worked well for generations as each clan was ruled by a chief who treated his 'subjects' as family members. However, during the eighteenth century many of the chiefs became more interested in a sophisticated London life than their Highland estates. To finance these expensive lifestyles they needed more money so at the end of the century many tried to improve their income by introducing large-scale sheep farming. Although Jane was intoxicated with London life her husband was always happiest in the Highlands and he remained in Scotland. The Duke and Duchess tried to establish new industries on their estates to help their tenants adapt to the changing world.

Many of their fellow landlords showed no concern for their tenants. They cruelly evicted families who had lived on their land for centuries, burning their houses and possessions. Dispossessed and deprived of their homes, many Highlanders moved into pitiful crofts along the shore or emigrated to America or Australia. The glens fell silent and in the place of thousands of people were just a few shepherds and many sheep. The brutal experiences during these years did nothing to endear the English or the wealthy Scottish lairds to the Highlanders and recruiting Scots into the English army was difficult.

On 10 February 1794, the King authorised the Duke of Gordon to raise a regiment but as he had recently recruited a regiment of 'fencibles' (temporary recruits for home service), Alexander found it difficult to sign up enough men. Ingenious as ever, the Duchess stepped in and developed a strategy that filled the regiment in just three months. Dressed in regimental-style outfits and escorted by six pipers, Jane and her daughters travelled around local markets and fairs offering the incentive of a kiss and a guinea to each man who joined up. There is an anecdote that the recruiting sergeants wanted to enlist one particularly fit young man, but nothing they offered attracted him – until the Duchess arrived. Lured by her kiss, the young man accepted his first day's pay and the kiss, then tossed the money to the crowd to show what had finally persuaded him to sign up.

By 24 June, more than a thousand men and officers had enlisted. The next day the Duchess's recruits marched through Aberdeen, starting the impressive tradition of the Gordon Highlanders. Always aware of the importance of image, Jane decided that the regiment should wear the Black Watch tartan, but with a yellow stripe added for the 'Gey Gordons' (as 'gey' meant overwhelming or self-important, perhaps this term suited the recruiter better than her recruits). The Duchess and her daughters could not resist wearing the material themselves; when they joined members of the royal family at a review of the Gordon Fencibles, all the Gordon women wore Highland bonnets and their new tartan.

Jane was very proud of her role as a recruiting officer and afterwards frequently recounted the story. In the salon of a Whig grandee, a young man said to her, 'I wish I had been present, I would have taken the kiss and the shilling myself.' Jane replied, 'But you would not have understood what I said in broad Scotch.' 'Oh yes I would; I understand Scotch however broad,' the young man claimed. 'Well, I will try you,' said the Duchess, 'and if you tell me what I mean, I'll give you a kiss.' With great rapidity she said, 'My canty carle, come pree mi mou.' The young man exclaimed, 'Oh! That's French not Scotch!' To which the Duchess replied, 'You have lost your kiss my lord, what I said was Scotch and means "My handsome fellow, come taste my mouth." '

Georgina was brought up in a racy atmosphere full of flirtation, as Pryse Gordon's description of a visit to the Duchess and her daughters illustrates. Staying with Jane was a 'facetious and lively friend Mrs G – – whom I soon discovered, young as I was, to be a considerable coquette,' he wrote. 'I was placed by her side at dinner, when she played off all her airs, on which she was rallied by the Duchess who complimented me on the readiness of my repartees.' After dinner, Pryse played whist in the drawing room with the ladies and won a couple of guineas. Although he intended to leave the next morning, the Duchess used her charm to persuade him to stay on. He ended up staying a week, 'living on the fat of the land, filling my purse with half crowns and flirting with the gay widow'.

Jane knew just how to charm men and Georgina learned through imitation. The secret of the Duchess's success was that she gave every man an opportunity of speaking on the subject on which he supposed he could speak well. She would then flatter him in the most fulsome terms, unscrupulously pandering to the susceptible male ego. As the youngest daughter, Georgina watched her mother, through a mixture of determination and sheer cheek, marry her daughters to the most eligible bachelors in the land. Her tenacious methods became the talk of society and the butt of many jokes. Wraxall wrote:

Her conjugal duties pressed on her heart with less force than did her maternal solicitudes. In her daughters centred principally her ambitious cares. For their elevation no sacrifices appeared to her to be too great, no exertions too laborious, no renunciations too severe.

Jane's eldest daughter Charlotte was at first destined for her friend William Pitt. He had shown some 'partiality' to her and many attentions, so Jane, accompanied by Charlotte, began to drive in her carriage to Wimbledon, where Pitt lived, when she knew that he was there. The Duchess's plan seemed to be going well but Dundas did not want his friend to marry his lover's daughter because it would have given Jane more power over Pitt than he had. As cunning as the Duchess, Dundas decided to counteract her design by pretending he was now interested in the daughter, not the mother.

One night the Duchess and her daughters were spending an evening with Pitt and his friends, making up verses, when Dundas remarked to his leader what a fine woman Charlotte was and what small feet she had for her size. At the time Jane did not appear to have heard, but when she left to go home she said, 'Though you have not done your game, gentlemen, I must bid you good night, and the next time you are capping verses let me beg of you to take care that you don't put in more feet than belong to them!'

Pitt, who had never shown more than a slight interest in Charlotte, withdrew his attentions, so Dundas, having achieved his aim, stopped courting the daughter and returned to her mother. No doubt Jane was annoyed at being outwitted, but she soon turned her match-making attentions elsewhere and her sights were now set on Colonel Lennox, the future Duke of Richmond.

Captain Lennox (as he then was) had been sent to Edinburgh because he had the audacity to challenge the Duke of York to a duel after the King's son had made an offensive remark to the young Captain. The duel took place on Wimbledon Common. No one was seriously hurt but Lennox's bullet grazed the Duke's face. The officers of the Coldstream Guards passed a resolution that Lennox had 'behaved with courage but from the peculiarity of the circumstances not with judgement'. Having developed a taste for duelling, he then fought a second duel with Theophilus Swift, who had written a critical pamphlet about him. Shortly afterwards, Lennox was sent to Edinburgh as Colonel of a regiment. The courage he had shown in his duels had made him popular and on his arrival he was given the freedom of the city, and the castle was illuminated in his honour. It is probable that it was at this time he met Charlotte. Although she was by no means a beauty, they fell in love and were married at Gordon Castle on 9 September 1789.

Jane was delighted with the match and, with more mercenary than maternal instincts, she could not wait to relinquish her own parental role in her eldest daughter's life because it was to another duke and duchess. She wrote to a relative, Charles Gordon:

> It will give you pleasure to hear how the Duke and Duchess of Richmond received my beloved Charlotte. The house everything they could wish, silver plate with their crest and the Duke and Duchess like the kindest parents. She is constantly with them, indeed I wished her to go up when we were in Scotland and to know them well and dedicate herself to his family for life.

Having caught one future duke for her daughters, the Duchess was after her next one. She wanted Susan to marry William, fifth Duke of Manchester, because as well as having the vital title, he was rich and handsome. Elizabeth Grant described him as 'the most beautiful statue like person that ever was seen in flesh and blood'. In fact, he was so good-looking he had been painted as Cupid by Sir Joshua Reynolds. He was also a keen sportsman and a great oarsman who, in his youth, impressed his friends with his exceptional strength.

At first, he was decidedly unenthusiastic about taking a Gordon bride, but it was no easy task to escape the Duchess's clutches. Jane took Susan to Newmarket Races in the hope of seeing William but she was disappointed to discover he was not there but at Valenciennes, which had recently surrendered to the allied army and the Duke of York. Not to be thwarted, the night before she left Newmarket the Duchess sent a message to William's home, Kimbolton, ordering supper and beds to be prepared for the next night. She arrived with Susan the next morning and went all over the house and park to make sure Manchester met her demanding material requirements for a son-in-law.

When a friend asked William if he was to marry Susan, he claimed he had not the smallest intention of doing so. 'Then why are you constantly with the Duchess of Gordon?' the friend asked. William replied, 'Because I cannot help it. She will not let me rest, but comes and sends for me constantly: but I am soon going to Scotland to the Duke of Montrose's.' His friend replied, 'Then she will certainly carry you to Gordon Castle and as certainly marry you to her daughter.' He was right. There was to be no escape and Susan married the Duke of Manchester on 7 October 1793 at Eaton near Edinburgh. Lady Stafford observed an immediate change in William as his life was taken over by domineering Gordon women. She wrote: 'His Grace of Manchester before marriage disliked hunting; his "fair" partner now makes him skip over hedges and ditches and rules him, they say, as her Mother has done her father.'

This double ducal success was very encouraging 'to so enterprising a genius' and like an addicted gambler playing cards, Jane would not rest till she had a full set of dukes in her hand. Never a woman to waste time, she immediately started on her next project which was to marry her fourth daughter, Louisa, to the Duke of Bedford that winter. This time romance did not flourish, but Jane found an alternative eligible prey in Lord Brome, the future Marquis Cornwallis. The couple fell in love and were engaged to be married, but Lord Brome's father called off the engagement, expressing concern that madness ran in the Gordon family. Determined not to let a future marquis slip through her net, Jane arranged a meeting with his father to clarify the situation. Apparently, sacrificing her own reputation was not too high a price to pay, and she told him, 'I know your reason for disapproving of your son's marriage with my daughter, now, I will tell you one thing plainly

– there is not a drop of the Gordon blood in Louisa's body.' The Marquis believed her and by the time the young couple married in April 1797 he was able to write with genuine enthusiasm to the Duke of Gordon:

> From what I have had the pleasure of seeing of Lady Louisa, I feel most perfectly happy at the prospect of the union which is to take place this day. I am much flattered by the connexion with your Grace's family and hope that the most cordial intercourse and friendship will exist between us.

While Jane pursued partners for her daughters, she tried to protect her eligible sons from any similarly predatory women. Her youngest son Alexander was only a teenager at this time and little is known about his romantic history as he died unmarried at the age of twenty three. But her eldest son, George, Marquis of Huntly, was already seen as a catch by many aspiring mothers and daughters. He was known as the Prince of Wales of the North and gained a reputation as a brave soldier after he became Colonel of the Gordon Highlanders.

Elizabeth Grant described him as 'young, gay and handsome'. He was the life and soul of the parties at Kinrara and 'so general a favourite that all people seemed to wake up as it were when he came amongst them'. But there was one large obstacle that stood in the way of prospective brides; his mother. Jane was very close to George and they spent a lot of time together. It seems no one was good enough for her dashing son and she interfered in his love life at least as much as she did in his sisters'. According to Elizabeth Grant the Duchess prevented him from marrying the love of his life, a beautiful but unsuitable young girl. Apparently Jane carried the girl off to Paris and married her to an old merchant while George was away with his regiment. The ploy worked and Jane remained the most important woman in her son's life. In fact, George only married after his mother's death.

Perhaps Jane's only match-making disappointment was with her second daughter, Madelina. Although Elizabeth Grant considered her 'the best bred amongst them, she showed to less effect among the list of great names', marrying her cousin, Sir Robert Sinclair of Murtle, who was only a baronet.

With all her other daughters married off and her sons safely single, Jane was left with Georgina, who many people thought was the most eligible of them all, as much due to her vivacious personality as to her appearance. Elizabeth Grant described Lady Georgina at this time as 'much liked; kind hearted . . . then in her early youth, she was quiet and pleasing as well as lively. Unchangeable in amiability of manner, she was very variable in her looks; one day almost beautiful, the next day, almost plain.' Jane intended to capitalise on her youngest daughter's beautiful days to make sure Georgina became at least a duchess.

CHAPTER TWO

Courtship

The Georgian marriage market was a competitive arena where nubile young girls were paraded before a selection of prospective husbands. Every year ambitious mothers prepared for their daughters' presentation at court and coming-out balls with great precision. It was important that a girl made a success of her season and costly balls and dinners were seen as a worthwhile investment if it led to a good marriage. With her reputation as the most accomplished match-maker of the day to maintain, the Duchess of Gordon spared no expense when she launched Georgina into fashionable society in February 1799. The day after she was presented to Queen Charlotte at court, her mother gave a grand coming-out ball for her, inviting three hundred of the most fashionable society guests to the Marquis of Buckingham's Pall Mall house. It was one of the most eagerly awaited debutante events of that season, and *The Times* wrote a flowery account describing Georgina and the party in detail:

Fair and lovely as the rest of the Duchess's female offspring
are undoubtedly, Lady Georgina, like

'A Flower just opening to the view,'

seems to out-rival them all. Her eyes with magic power
endued, fired many a youthful heart, and produced many a
wistful glance; but on all she

'Smil'd like a knot of Cowslips on a cliff,
Not to be come at by the willing hand.'

Georgina opened the ball by dancing with Lord Petty (the youngest
son of the Marquis of Landsdowne) to a lively tune played by the
violinist, Gow, who had been brought down to London to give a
Scottish flavour to the party. It was a cold winter's night outside, but
in the ballroom the Gordons created a warm and enticing atmosphere.
Apparently, Georgina's 'fascinating form, grace of gesture, and pleasing-
ness of manner . . . quickly inspired the whole company, and made
them totally forgetful of the severity of the season or the cares of the
world'.

The Scottish dances continued until three in the morning, when a
sumptuous supper was served. *The Times* continued:

Mirth and plenty reigned around. The Noble Hostess
herself, who was all attention, pleasantry and conviviality,
looked not for these ten years past more engaging or more
youthful. The Marquis (of Buckingham) officiated as
Landlord; and where he presides hilarity and good humour
are diffused on every countenance.

The Ladies eager to resume the mazey dance, soon
summoned the Gentlemen from the supper table. After two
or three country dances, Scotch reels commenced, which did
not finish till six in the morning, when each with seeming
regret separated from a society in which all were delighted.

Georgina's coming-out ball was a triumph. Among the guests was the
Prince of Wales, and although he went home early because he had a

cold, his brother Prince Edward stayed. It was a stylish occasion with the girls dressed in the latest fashions of coloured muslin or silk empire-line dresses trimmed with silver, and feathers or jewels in their hair. To the Duchess of Gordon's delight, Georgina outshone all the other debutantes and was soon described as 'the incomparable Lady Georgina'.

However, a successful season was measured by weddings not balls, and the Duchess of Gordon would not rest until Georgina had walked down the aisle with a duke. Georgina's main rival was Georgiana Cavendish, known as Little G, the daughter of her mother's arch enemy, the Duchess of Devonshire. Little G was slightly younger than Georgina so she was not presented at court until May 1800, but the girls soon found themselves competing for the same man.

The most eligible bachelor on the scene was the Duke of Bedford. Georgina Gordon had the advantage of being the more beautiful; Georgiana Cavendish was plain and gauche in comparison. As one contemporary wrote, she was 'a tall, gawky, fair girl, with her head poked out and her mouth open'. However, political allegiances favoured Little G as the Bedfords, like the Cavendishes, were Whigs while the Gordons were staunch Tories. As the leading Whig duke, the Duke of Bedford was expected to marry the daughter of the top Whig hostess, the Duchess of Devonshire. He was an important member of the Devonshire House set and an old friend of the family, so the marriage was seen as part of his dynastic duty. In 1800, Lady Holland wrote of the Duke in her *Journal*: 'The probability is that . . . he will not marry, unless indeed he should fix upon Lady Georgiana Cavendish, an alliance long arranged for him by the world.'

For the two rival Duchesses, the battle for the Duke of Bedford's hand was like the culminating battle in a long war. This clash of the maternal Titans became the talk of society. In his satirical novel, Surr gives the Duchess of Belgrave a speech which perfectly captures the way in which the two women were, like generals, planning their strategies. The Duchess of Belgrave tells an ally:

The town must be carried by storm. While such cold calculators as the Duchess of Drinkwater [Gordon], with all the frigid economy of her native north, are collecting a little money and a few forces to meet us, reckoning upon our weakness, we must by a display of unbounded magnificence, taste and expense . . . at once overwhelm their puny preparations and strike a blow that shall palsy every effort of our rivals for the remainder of the season . . . I am decidedly for a grand masked gala.

Such tactics were necessary because the stakes were so high for both women. Francis, fifth Duke of Bedford, was one of the wealthiest men in Britain, owning estates in Bedfordshire, Buckinghamshire, Devon, Cambridgeshire and London. His family was also politically powerful. For many generations they had been one of the most important Whig dynasties. The Russell family began its rise to fame and fortune when in 1506 John Russell, a wine importer from Weymouth, helped the Habsburg Archduke Philip to London after he was shipwrecked. Once he reached court, John Russell never left, becoming a polished courtier. He was made a baron and an earl and was rewarded with land. The link with Whig history began in 1683 when William, Lord Russell, heir to the fifth Earl, was executed for his part in the Rye House plot to assassinate Chares II and his brother, James, Duke of York (later James II). After the Revolution of 1688, William became a Whig martyr for his stand against the monarchy's abuse of power. His suspicions of James were proved right when he became King and tried to govern as absolute monarch and restore Catholicism. Once James was forced into exile and William and Mary were on the throne, the Protestant faith and the liberties of Parliament were secure. The Russells flourished and his father was made a duke.

Like Georgina's father, Francis inherited the title at an early age. Born in 1765, he was orphaned when he was three years old. His father Francis, Marquess of Tavistock, was killed by a fall from his horse in 1767 and a year later his mother Elizabeth died from consumption or, as many people believed, a broken heart at the loss of her husband. On the death of his grandfather when he was only six, Francis became the fifth Duke. The tragic loss of his parents made the Duke particularly close to his two brothers John and William Russell. A lifelong solidarity developed between the three boys, who were brought up by their domineering grandmother, Gertrude.

As an adult, Francis continued his family's Whig tradition by taking an active part in the House of Lords. Despite the fact that at the age of twenty-four he had hardly opened a book and he at first feared he might speak incorrect English, he became a heavy-weight debater. His friend Lord Holland wrote in his *Memoirs of the Whig Party*:

> Deficient in wit and imagination, though wonderful in fluency, it was by perspicuity of statement and solidity of argument alone that he could arrest the attention of his audience . . . He had, too, another great defect, he always seemed to treat the understandings of his adversaries with contempt, and the decision and even the good will of the audience which he addressed with utter indifference.

The Duke became an important supporter of Lord Lauderdale and Charles James Fox. He opposed the war against France in 1793, protested against the suspension of habeas corpus in 1794 and denounced the suppression of the rebellion in Ireland in 1798. Fox wrote:

> I look upon him to be one of the main pillars of the party. You know I am one who think both property and rank of great importance in this country in a party view and in addition to these, the Duke of Bedford has a very good understanding; I wish I could add popular manners.

As well as politicians, Francis was close to royalty. He was a great friend of the Prince Regent, becoming known as his 'boon companion'. They shared a love of horse racing, often attending Newmarket and

Epsom together. Francis was such a close friend that he was chosen as one of the two bachelors who literally supported the drunken, weeping Prince at his wedding to Princess Caroline on 8 April 1795.

The royal marriage was ill-fated from the start, not least because the Prince already had a string of mistresses. A decade before, he had committed himself to one of his lovers, Mrs Maria Fitzherbert, in a secret and illegal 'marriage'. The Fitzherbert union was illegal because, under the 1701 Act of Settlement, no one married to a Catholic could become monarch of Great Britain. It was also against the terms of the Royal Marriage Act of 1772 which stated that if a member of the royal family under the age of twenty-six got married without the sovereign's consent, the marriage was void.

The Prince's promiscuous past was not the only problem when George was forced to make a legal marriage; unfortunately, the groom found his Brunswick bride completely unattractive. As the union was arranged and not a love match, George did not meet Caroline until shortly before their marriage. Apparently when he first saw the large, coarse woman who was to be his wife, he turned to his aide and said, 'Harris, I am not well. Pray get me a glass of brandy.' Evidently he did not feel any better by his wedding day.

The only potential threat to the Prince and Duke's friendship was that George feared his friend might outshine him. This fear was well founded, as Horace Walpole's description of Francis's arrival at court for the King's birthday reveals: 'The Duke of Bedford eclipsed the whole birthday by his clothes, equipage and servants: six of the latter walked on the side of the coach to keep off the crowd – or to tempt it; for their liveries were worth an argosie.' In fact, many people thought this dashing dandy was the Prince of Wales and even the guard stood to arms when he arrived.

The Duke was a leader of fashion with a strong, rebellious streak. Although it led to him being barred from Brooks's Club, he abandoned powdered hair and wigs in favour of simple, cropped hair. It started as a political gesture, showing he opposed Pitt's decision, following a bad harvest, to tax powder which was made from flour. However, his mark of sympathy for the poor who needed the flour for bread worked to his advantage. Unpowdered hair looked so good on him that soon many of his friends copied him and it became the fashion.

Handsome, in a slightly overweight and debauched way, Francis had reached his mid-thirties without marrying. Until the two Georgies came on the marriage market, the Duke had shown no inclination to follow the Prince of Wales's unappealing example. It would take quite something to persuade this experienced man of the world to give up his unconventional love life.

From an early age he had enjoyed women's company, but he realised many predatory mothers were trying to track him down to marry him off to their daughters. His eligibility attracted the mothers while his good looks appealed to the daughters. Even the King's daughter, Princess Charlotte, asked her brother to arrange an alliance between her and his friend. Francis was determined to avoid being trapped and he soon learned how to enjoy love affairs without marriage. He had no intention of limiting himself to virginal aristocrats; instead, he had affairs with experienced women of all classes and ages. Perhaps his unhappy childhood made him seek mother figures, but whatever the reason may have been a succession of practised mistresses filled his life.

For many years he lived in a *ménage à trois* with an older woman, Lady Maynard, and her husband. They met in France when the nineteen-year-old Duke was sent abroad with a tutor on the Grand Tour. Lady Maynard was a woman with a notorious past; as Nancy Parsons or Mrs Horton (or Haughton) she had been the mistress of several wealthy men. While she was the Duke of Grafton's mistress, she had scandalised society by appearing with him at the opera when Queen Charlotte was present. However, when Grafton eventually divorced his wife he married Elizabeth Wrottesley, not Nancy. Undaunted, she soon found a new lover, the Duke of Dorset. Again she was treated as mistress not wife material; although Dorset took her abroad with him, he refused to marry her. When that affair ended, she finally found a man who wanted to marry her in Lord Maynard, who at twenty-five was at least fifteen years younger than her.

Although some contemporaries considered her to be common, she was highly intelligent and knew just how to flatter men. She listened to each man with rapt attention and treated him as though he was the most interesting person in the world. Her charm evidently worked on the young Duke of Bedford because he dismissed his tutor and set up home with the Maynards in France. Lord Maynard seemed to be quite happy with the situation, often leaving Nancy alone with the Duke and returning to her when Francis visited England. Lady Maynard's appeal was not purely physical; she gave Francis lessons in literature, reading him love poems and teaching him to recite Ovid by heart.

When the young Duke reached his majority in July 1786, he returned to England, bringing Lord and Lady Maynard with him. He was quite open about the *ménage à trois* and was often seen with his mistress and her husband at events in London.

Lady Maynard was not his only mistress. He soon installed Mrs Hill, another older woman, at Woburn Abbey. Described as 'an old Madame' by some contemporaries, the Duke was not seen with Mrs Hill at society parties, but she was a good horsewoman and Francis enjoyed riding with her around the park at Woburn.

Francis was very good at compartmentalising his life. It seems no single woman could satisfy all his needs so he had different women to fulfil different roles in his life. Another mistress, Mrs Marianna Palmer, entertained him in London and had two children by him – a boy, Francis, and a girl, Georgiana. For intellectual stimulation and gossip he turned to Lady Melbourne, who was described by contemporaries as like Madame de Merteuil in *Les Liaisons Dangereuses*. No doubt her manipulative mind attracted Francis and provided him with the sophisticated company he enjoyed.

However, at thirty-five the Duke realised it was time he selected a wife who could be the official mistress of Woburn and a mother to legitimate heirs. At last the long-awaited time had come and the Duchesses of Gordon and Devonshire were ready to meet the challenge, each believing her daughter to be the perfect candidate for Bedford's hand. At first, the Duchess of Devonshire seemed to be ahead. At Little G's coming-out ball he was one of her most frequent dancing partners and in the autumn he was invited to Chatsworth to socialise with the Cavendishes in a more relaxed atmosphere. During his stay, Francis seemed to be giving out contradictory signals. At times he was attentive, but at others he seemed determined to rebel against the expected match. James Hare commented that 'a certain person's behaviour is unaccountable', but perhaps it becomes more understandable when the Gordons' manoeuvres are put into the equation.

The Duchess of Gordon was determined to beat the Duchess of Devonshire at the match-making game, using every weapon in her armoury. So ardent was her pursuit that it was satirised in a cartoon by Gillray showing a fat, florid Duchess of Gordon accompanied by Georgina, chasing after 'the Bedford bull'. Enlisting additional troops in the battle, she persuaded her son-in-law the Duke of Manchester to help catch the Duke of Bedford for Georgina. Jane was very skilful at using one alliance as a base to launch another, making dynasty-building a project that involved the whole family. The Duchess of Devonshire wrote: 'The Duke of Manchester and the other Brother-in-law follow up the Duchess' game whenever she starts it.'

As part of the scheme, the Duke of Bedford was invited to the Manchester estate at Kimbolton to meet 'the young one' as Georgina was called. At twenty, Georgina's dark-haired, fresh-faced beauty – captured by Hoppner in a portrait of her wearing a simple white muslin dress – must have provided a stark contrast to the Duke's faded and jaded mistresses. As a contemporary engraving of Georgina shows, she had a knowing look about her, even in her youth, that added to her attractions. Her sensuous, full mouth and curvaceous figure gave her a sexual allure to rival the experienced women Francis usually chose.

Perhaps the Gordons' candid if sometimes coarse approach to life also appealed to the Duke as he, too, was noted for his frankness that often verged on rudeness. Lord Holland wrote in his *Memoirs*:

> His heart was affectionate, and he joined to all these qualifications great firmness of mind and the purest simplicity of manners that I ever knew. No man's

conversation was so sure an indication of his feelings and thoughts; he was truth itself, sometimes too naked, and possibly sometimes disagreeable, but always plain, undisguised truth and real benevolence.

No doubt the family's uninhibited parties, described by contemporaries as 'frolic and fun' aimed solely at making people 'laugh and be merry', also attracted Francis.

Within a short time, Georgina's youthful beauty and *joie de vivre*, combined with her family's liveliness, worked and the Duke abandoned the Cavendishes for the Gordons. The Duchess of Devonshire was devastated and wrote outraged letters to her friend Lady Melbourne. While the Duchess had lost a prospective son-in-law, Lady Melbourne had lost her lover to a woman thirty years her junior but as a great intriguer and gossip, this was one affair that surprised even her. Both women were horrified, not just at the personal but also at the political loss; the thought of losing the most eligible Whig bachelor to a Tory family, and worse still to the Duchess of Gordon, was too much to bear. The Duchess of Devonshire wrote to her friend:

> I suppose it must be so and we are all undone. Loo's [their nickname for the Duke] first error, when he resolved against the connection was allowing himself to be surrounded by the tribe – he exposed himself at Kimbolton to the temptation of all others he was most likely to yield to – and tho' his good taste will I suppose disgust him with the different society he is about to mix with – yet as they will be all prepared to flatter him and as he is sometimes entertained with observing original character – of which God knows he will have enough . . . I believe he must be very unhappy – and indeed cannot conceive his being happy unless he becomes different from what he is. I think her very pretty, very bewitching and clever certainly, and I have liked some of the things I have seen in her. But certainly there have been stories enough to make one tremble . . . What a futurity

for Loo to be surrounded with plotting, shabby Scotts [*sic*] men. The very amiabilite that some times arises from the grotesque originality of Scotch people is in a line very different from what one should have thought would be Loo's election for the Mistress of Woburn. However if he can like the kind of specimen of broad jokes (covering however artful designs) which he has seen with the Manchesters – one has nothing to say . . . No possible event could have so thoroughly overthrown the habits of our society as this.

Despite the uproar it caused in high society, Georgina's relationship with the Duke was flourishing when tragedy struck. In February 1802, Francis was playing a strenuous game of tennis when he suffered a strangulated hernia. The problem stemmed from a childhood strain suffered while he was at school; the old injury was aggravated during the game of tennis when a fit of coughing caused the rupture.

His doctor, Halifax, was called to Woburn and told the Duke that an operation was required. A surgeon, Dr Kerr, who had come from Northampton, wanted to operate immediately before the other surgeons arrived but Francis asked for a respite of two hours in order to arrange his affairs. He used this time to write detailed instructions to his brothers about what he wished them to do if he died.

As news spread that his life was in danger, his brother John and his friends, including Lord Holland, rushed to Woburn Abbey. But Francis chose to avoid the pain of taking leave of his friends and refused to see anyone except his two brothers. Although in great pain, he talked to John, his heir, at length about running the family estates and 'entered with his usual calmness and sagacity into the details of many arrangements which he thought might be conducive to the credit or happiness of those who survived him'. It was a disturbing, emotional experience for John and he wrote in his diary: 'I but ill bore this cruel scene; I kissed the hand of this kind and amiable brother and bathed it with my tears. When I tore myself from his bedside I went into my own room and gave full vent to my bursting heart.'

Once Francis had settled his affairs he asked for the surgeon, Sir James Earle, to be called in. By this time, the part of his intestine that had ruptured had become gangrenous. The operation began at about half past six and as *The Times* recorded:

> . . . although it is impossible for the mind to conceive of any thing more dreadful than the operation, the Duke evinced a fortitude and resignation well worthy of his high spirit and character. After the first incision he never suffered a word to escape him. He was convinced from the moment Dr Halifax had pronounced his opinion that he was a dead man.

After the operation the Duke asked his doctor how long he thought he was likely to survive. When he was told not more than half an hour, he asked that he might be moved to a couch and for a pen and paper to be brought to him, but he was in so much pain he never wrote another word. In fact, he survived longer than expected, but the next day he suffered from nausea and by Monday morning the symptoms were very bad.

Dr Kerr was amazed at the extraordinary courage the Duke showed during those final hours. The doctor commented, 'in the agonies of pain and death, he could have governed the world'. At half past eleven on 2 March, Francis died. His brother John was with him and described the scene in his diary:

> The tide of life was ebbing apace and in a few minutes, without a struggle this amiable and excellent man, this kind and affectionate brother expired in my arms – God's will be done! But this dreadful blow . . . is more than I shall be able to sustain.

One of Francis's last requests was for a lock of his hair to be taken to Georgina Gordon. In those final hours he had also requested that his funeral should be conducted without ostentation. He did not want his friends and relations to attend, perhaps because he feared a grave-side clash between his many mistresses and prospective brides. Instead, mourners were hired and his solicitor, Mr Gotobed, took the role of chief mourner. His brother John obeyed his brother's wishes about not attending the funeral and, in any case, was so distraught that he was advised by friends to stay away. He wrote: 'My head has been sadly confused, and is so still – Pray God, my friend to give me strength to get through this Trial – I have a world of cares upon me – too much for my weak nature to bear.'

The funeral turned into a bizarre event, moving from tragedy to black farce. At eleven o'clock the night before, the hearse left Woburn in order to reach the family church at Chenies by noon the next day. Perhaps the most poignant sight was the late Duke's empty carriage following the hearse. The journey was about thirty-six miles and along the route the procession passed through streets lined with Francis's tenants, staff and local people who wished to pay their last respects.

By the time the cortège arrived at the church, there were at least five thousand people gathered in the village. But the dignified atmosphere was soon shattered: just as the coffin was going into the church, the crowd tried to force their way in by breaking the windows; someone stole the escutcheons from the hearse; and a notorious gang of pick-pockets from London robbed some of the mourners of considerable sums of money.

Despite the unfortunate events at his funeral, Francis was genuinely mourned by his family and friends. His death, in his prime, seemed a particularly cruel blow. The Prince of Wales was so upset about the loss of his friend that he cancelled his engagements and stayed at Carlton House for several days. Politicians were also deeply distressed as the Whigs believed they had lost one of their leading statesmen. *The Times* obituary observed:

> There seemed every reason to believe that his Grace would become one day a leading man in the political history of his country. As a private character we have never heard his Grace's name mentioned but with marks of the greatest

respect and love. He was a generous and kind relation, hospitable to his friends, a munificent encourager of the Arts, and a liberal landlord.

However, not everyone eulogised the Duke. Some contemporaries criticised his lack of morality. Arthur Young wrote:

> This Duke ... set an example of an utter neglect, if not contempt of religion: all was worldly in his views; all his motives tending that way and his example mischevious to religion and the souls of men ... He set so very bad an example in morals and want of piety.

Whatever the public assessment of Francis, the two people most affected by his death were Georgina and his brother John, although at first they were divided, not united, in their grief. After Francis's death, the Duchess of Gordon claimed Georgina was privately engaged to him. Always a great believer in dressing the part, the Duchess immediately put her daughter in mourning and sent her to grieve in private with one of her sisters, while she launched a propaganda offensive on London. First she visited Francis's great friend Lord Lauderdale, but evidently he did not support her engagement theory as they had a violent quarrel. In the following weeks she invited to her house only people she called 'orthodox', which meant those who accepted that Georgina had been engaged to the Duke.

Determined to win over as many people as possible, the Duchess went to other people's parties and briefed anyone who would listen on just what had happened, according to her. She even told her story to the Prince of Wales. Apparently, there had not only been a private engagement, the Duke of Bedford had also told the Duke of Manchester of his intentions. A few days before he became ill he had sent a message to Georgina's brother-in-law explaining that the obstacle which had previously prevented his marriage had been removed, that is, his relationship with Mrs Palmer was over. He was just waiting for Georgina's return from Scotland to declare their engagement publicly.

John, the new Duke, refused to confirm there had been any formal commitment, while his friends over-zealously launched a counter-offensive to contradict the Duchess's story. Sir Robert Adair said he had the new Duke's authority to contradict the story and Lord Lauderdale said it was all a fabrication of the Duchess of Gordon's. The disagreement between the two factions became the talk of London society although many people considered it was bad taste on both sides to argue over Francis's intentions so soon after his death.

By the summer, the Duchess of Gordon realised the dispute was damaging Georgina's reputation. She was not willing to stand by and let a scandal ruin her most attractive daughter's future marriage prospects, so she took direct action. Jane contacted John's sister-in-law Lady Bath, and asked her to arrange a meeting between Georgina and John. The Duchess later explained to the Duke her reason for taking this step. It was 'the most respectful way of claiming your pity – for an amiable being possessed of every virtue to beg your protection to silence the malignity of the world', she wrote, 'and to tell you your conduct added pangs to one already doomed to eternal regret'.

Eventually, the sensitive meeting between John and Georgina took place at Barnes. Their discussion went well; the Duke explained his motives for not supporting the engagement story and she appeared to understand his reasons. It seems the harmonious meeting sowed a seed in the Duchess of Gordon's scheming mind; at the end of July she decided to consolidate Georgina's position by writing the Duke a 'vindication of my daughter's fame'. Her earlier aggressive campaign was replaced with a subtle charm offensive. Practised in under-standing male psychology, she knew just how to manipulate John's emotions, claiming that she had delayed writing before out of respect for his grief but felt that after his successful visit it was time to explain her motives:

> I thought the moment would come when you would see the matter as I do – of course restore her [Georgina] to that high place in society she held – Clouded by your silence which the world judge as a denial of what they are pleased

to call my assertions. The malignity of some envious wretches when they first discovered her engagement to your brother made it necessary to show this engagement did exist – had it been derogatory to the character of the first of men I might have felt doubtful of making it public. His conduct did him honour . . . I never doubted in your loudly agreeing to every word I advanced.

However, the Duchess's letter revealed her proof of an engagement was based on circumstantial evidence rather than hard facts. It seems all she could suggest was that the late Duke was about to propose, not that he had actually been engaged:

> She [Georgina] had every consolation a woman in her situation could have – being remembered with affection in his last moments and desired to wear his hair – it raised her above all others in my opinion and proved it was not the fond partiality of a mother that made me love and value her as I do. I need not tell you of his opinion of her – you know it – but I fear you don't know the motive that made him express his sentiments to you – had it been only a message of consolation he would have sent for Manchester.

Cunning as ever, it seems Jane was already pursuing the next Duke of Bedford for her daughter. Using a mixture of flattery and emotional bribery, she attempted to establish a link by claiming that asking John to give Georgina a lock of his hair was a sign that Francis wanted his brother to take care of her:

> . . . it was to gain her a friend and protector from the malice of the World. He had often talked to her of you as the friend of his heart and pride of his family – did he think you would permit her name to be the sport of a newspaper, me the object of abuse because I was her mother.

In case her letter had the wrong effect, Jane was careful to distance Georgina from it and to portray her as a self-effacing martyr:

> She is so afraid of disturbing your peace that she would prevent my writing tho she knows her fame and all that is valuable in life depends on your interference ... let me express my grateful thanks for your kind visit to her – your goodness gave her much comfort and the resolution has cheated time of many a miserable hour.

When John replied to the Duchess's letter he admitted he found himself 'at a loss' in knowing how to answer it and his letter was equivocal. He admitted:

> [The subject] has been a painful one to me, and has cost me many moments of regret and disappointment ... that the part I had taken in it should not have met with your Grace's approbation – you may rest assured that it was dictated only by the respect I owed to the memory of a much loved and lamented brother.

In his letter he did not confirm or deny an engagement, nor would he tell the Duchess what Francis had said about Georgina on his deathbed:

> What he communicated to me in his last moments was in strict and sacred confidence and as such will find a faithful sanctuary in my heart to my dying hour – No one has heard anything from me on this subject except that when he named your daughter to me it was in terms of the most unfeigned and unbounded respect ... Lady Georgiana Gordon's character is dear to me because I know it was so to him; but surely your Grace would not call upon me to publish to the world the confidential death-bed communications of a friend and brother on account of the supposed censure of a few misjudging individuals ... no one who

had the slightest knowledge of my brother could for a single instant doubt that his object his views and his intentions were most pure and honourable.

Although Georgina and her mother left England for France in August, the communication between the two sides continued. Before leaving, Georgina wrote a warm letter to the Duke, apologising for departing without seeing him again to be given Francis's lock of hair, but asking him to keep it for her return. She thanked him for his 'flattering and very satisfactory letter' which had made her mother 'perfectly happy', and she shared with him her feelings on leaving England. She wrote: 'They may carry me to new scenes and different climes but nothing will ever obliterate the awful events of this year – pray let me have a place in your remembrance.'

By travelling to Paris, Georgina and her mother were following many members of London's fashionable society who had decamped to the city since the Treaty of Amiens was signed in the spring, temporarily ending the war against the French Republic. The Duchess and her daughter joined Charles Fox and his wife, formerly Mrs Armistead, Lady Holland, Lady Oxford, Lady Elizabeth Foster, Lady Bessborough and the Duchess of Cumberland. Despite the fact that England had for so many years been at war with Napoleon, the Whig aristocracy had continued their love affair with all things French. Once in Paris, they happily mixed with the leading soldiers of their erstwhile enemy. General Massena, General Menou, General Moreau and General Andreossi were welcome guests, while to be presented to the First Consul Napoleon and Josephine at the Tuileries was the height of chic.

France provided just the distraction Georgina needed from the arguments about her abortive engagement. It was a vibrant society with good restaurants, theatres and parties. More egalitarian than Britain, it provided an eye-opener for some of the English aristocrats. Lady Bessborough wrote:

Nothing can be more extraordinary than the look of the Theatres, as in the boxes next to you you see women who appear to be the lowest kind of tradespeople – the Men worse still – and in coming out of the Opera, you are surrounded by men whom you would only see at the Hustings.

Fashions, too, shocked some of the English; the French women were dressing more informally than they were used to, in flimsy empire-line dresses that allowed a 'gross display of bosom'. Male styles were also simplified; Parisian men dressed in black or dark blue coats and immaculate white linen. Like the Duke of Bedford, instead of powdered hair or wigs, their hair was cut short into styles modelled on Roman statues.

Luxury industries were flourishing, boosted by the influx of English tourists. During the winter of 1802–03, more than one million yards of satin and tulle were sold to make up the dresses worn at an estimated five thousand dinner parties and eight thousand balls.

Georgina and her mother moved into the apartments Charles Fox and his wife had stayed in and soon the Duchess of Gordon was putting on regular balls and dinners. Evidently, Georgina had recovered sufficiently from her grief to attend parties and the opera. Among the more exotic events were Madame Récamier's 'Thursdays'. Juliette Récamier was a *nouveau riche* society hostess whose house was decorated like a stage set. Mixed with reproduction antiques were fashionable Egyptian decorations, lions' paws and muzzles, and sphinxes. Guests were a cosmopolitan élite that included politicians, foreign visitors and the Bonaparte family. At her balls the new waltz was danced, but each evening ended with Juliette dancing for her guests, or rather posing in a series of 'attitudes' taken from ancient Greek vases; no doubt for English visitors it was like another visit to the theatre.

The English in Paris formed a competitive, gossipy society with many pushy mothers and eligible young girls vying for attention. But with the engagement fiasco fresh in their memories, all eyes were on Georgina to see how she was behaving and what she would do next. On 14 October, Lady Bessborough wrote to Lord Leveson Gower:

Lady G Gordon is consoling herself with Lord Hinchinbroke and danced at the Salon in her weeds (this is the disadvantage of proclaiming too much sorrow; real deep grief does not want publicity), but les grands eclats undertake more than they can keep up to.

A few weeks later Lady Bessborough observed:

Lady Georgiana Gordon appeared out of mourning last night; the Duchess is at home almost every evening and I suppose she may be glad herself to let things be forgotten. She has chose to take up a tone of great civility to me; I shall go to her in an evening sometimes for Caro's sake [her daughter Caroline, the future infamous Caroline Lamb] . . . [Caro] is exposed to the worst set of English women here. However, luckily there are some samples of English manners and looks – and Lady Conyngham, Lady Louisa Gordon [*sic*] and Lady Georgiana Gordon redeem a little.

It seems that the Duchess of Gordon was in a prickly mood, irritated by the uncertainty of Georgina's marriage prospects. During her stay in Paris she fell out with many of her compatriots including Lady Bessborough and Lady Conyngham, but her most sustained attack was saved for Sir Robert Adair. She still had not forgiven him for undermining her engagement story. On 2 October, Sir Robert wrote to Lady Melbourne: 'You will hardly believe that the Duchess of Gordon persecutes me even here.'

The Duchess's rudeness was not restricted to the English. At first she was scathing about Napoleon and did everything possible to offend him. One evening she was invited to a prestigious dinner at the Tuileries where all the flashy formality of Napoleon's court was evident. Guests would walk up the Tuileries stairs between a line of grenadiers, then pass through several antechambers where military music was playing. In the yellow salon they would meet Josephine, dazzling in diamonds.

The conspicuous display continued during dinner as Napoleon and his wife sat on a dais while their guests were seated at long tables decorated with fragrant roses and orange blossom.

Such pomp certainly did not overawe the Duchess and, as usual, she happily broke all the rules by arriving with the English ambassador Lord Whitworth half an hour too late for dinner. The Russian ambassador Markoff admiringly observed: 'Jamais je n'ai vue de ma vie plus d'assurance. Oui d'assurance pour ne rien dire de plus. Elle s'est placé de la manière la plus extraordinaire. Certainement sans le moindre embarrass, auprès du premier Consul.' (Never in my life have I seen such confidence. Yes, confidence, there is no better way to describe it. She positioned herself in the most extraordinary way. Certainly, without the slightest awkwardness, next to the First Consul.)

Then, almost overnight, the Duchess's attitude to Napoleon totally changed. Contemporaries recorded that she could be seen paying 'obsequious court' to the Bonapartes; acting like a lady-in-waiting, she passed her shawl to her and held up the train of Napoleon's step-daughter Hortense. She started inviting Napoleon and his family to her balls and instead of sending just a card, borrowed the ambassador's carriage and servants to send with the message, as this was the etiquette the consular family expected. She was even willing to sacrifice her country in her attempt to ingratiate herself with the Bonapartes – apparently, she said she hoped to see Napoleon 'breakfast in Ireland, dine in London and sup at Gordon Castle'. Lady Stafford wrote in disgust:

> I have thought that though her Grace of Gordon continually acted absurdly yet, it was occasion'd by her zeal to bring about a marriage, to have interest with ministers, or in short with a view of advantage or profit to herself and her relations, and that she was not a fool, but what can she mean by this conduct on the continent? What advantage can she or her family desire from the sort of language she holds at Paris.

In fact, there was maternal method in her apparent madness, and it seems likely that her *volte face* was because she had suddenly had the idea of engineering a match between Georgina and the First Consul's handsome young stepson, Eugene Beauharnais.

Eugene was Napoleon's golden boy. Born in the same year as Georgina, in September 1781, he was the son of Napoleon's wife Josephine and the General Alexandre, Viscount de Beauharnais. Eugene's father, although born an aristocrat, embraced the revolution and renounced his titles. He became a member of the Estates General and president of the Constituent Assembly. In 1793 he was made Commander of the Army of the Rhine, but when he failed to relieve Mainz that August, the Jacobins relieved him of his command and had him imprisoned. He was guillotined on 22 July 1794 at the height of the Terror.

Legend has it that Eugene was instrumental in bringing the future Emperor and Empress together. When he was fourteen years old, Eugene was sent by Josephine to ask Napoleon if she might keep her dead husband's sword (the citizens of Paris had been ordered to give up their arms to the authorities). Napoleon, who was a general at the time, was impressed by Eugene's charm and granted his request. It seems Josephine was so grateful she invited Napoleon to visit her.

After marrying Josephine in 1796, Napoleon treated Eugene like a son, even making him his aide-de-camp during the Egyptian campaign. He was evidently grooming his stepson for high office in the future. In 1804 he received the title of Prince; a year later he was made Viceroy of Italy; then, in 1806, Napoleon formally adopted him.

If Eugene's status proved irresistible to the Duchess of Gordon, it is likely his physical charms exerted an equal hold on Georgina. Unlike the Duke of Bedford, he was the same age as her and with his elegant figure and masculine Roman haircut, his appearance embodied what was considered good-looking at the time. The Duchesse D'Abrantes wrote:

> His personality displayed an elegance much more attractive from the fact that it carried with it one thing rarely found in

combination – an unassuming frankness and gaiety. His laugh was that of a child's, but his hilarity was never called forth by an ill-timed jest. He was amiable, gracious, polished without being obsequious, a joker without being impertinent . . . He was a good actor, a delightful singer, danced as his father had danced before him, who had earned the nickname of 'Beauharnais the beautiful dancer'.

He had also proved his bravery on the battlefield. In 1798 he had been present at the Battle of the Pyramids, and was badly wounded in the head at the Siege of Acre. Two years later he fought against the Austrians at Marengo and in 1802 he became colonel of a regiment. After Marengo, Napoleon wrote to Josephine: 'Your son is marching with rapid steps towards immortality. He has covered himself with glory in all his battles. He will eventually become one of the greatest captains in Europe.'

With his impeccable pedigree, Eugene was soon on the Duchess of Gordon's guest list and began to attend her balls. Frederick Foster, the son of Lady Elizabeth Foster, wrote:

He seems gentlemanlike and unassuming. By the bye the Duchess of Gordon in her happy manner and choice French took the opportunity of observing to Mr Seger whilst Beauharnais was standing close by him, that Bonaparte only wanted to equip his fleets to declare war against England.

No doubt he was more interested in the daughter than the mother's opinions; Georgina knew just how to appear to her best advantage and it seems she was learning new arts from the sophisticated Parisiennes. Lady Bessborough described one of the Duchess's balls to Lord Leveson Gower in a letter of 23 December: 'My Caroline made her debut in public at the Duchess of Gordon's where there was some beautiful dancing but quite like the stage. The best by far were Mademoiselle de Coigny, Lady G Gordon and Bessy Monck, who look'd beautiful.' At this time Georgina became close friends with Eugene's sister Hortense.

Many years later Hortense claimed that Eugene and Georgina had been very much in love, but there were so many difficulties in the way of their marriage that the relationship faltered. It seems that in Napoleon the Duchess of Gordon had met her match in ruthless dynastic match-making. He had already overruled his stepdaughter Hortense's feelings, making her marry for position not love. The pretty blonde darling of his court was married off to his brother Louis Bonaparte, a man suffering from a persecution complex and from an 'undiagnosed' physical disease, believed to be gonorrhea. Hortense was to become Queen of Holland, but it was an unhappy marriage.

For Eugene, Napoleon had equally grand plans and he wanted to link his family to European royalty, not a Scottish Duke's daughter. Obedient as ever to his stepfather, Eugene gave Georgina up, although they remained friends. Three years later, Napoleon married him to a princess he had never met, Augusta Amalie of Bavaria, eldest daughter of the Elector of Bavaria, Maximilian Joseph. Fortunately, Eugene fell in love with Augusta at first sight; perhaps it was because the Princess, with her dark good looks, bore more than a passing resemblance to Georgina.

For Georgina, the failure of her relationship with Eugene was yet another romantic disappointment. Worn out by constant emotional strain, she became seriously ill. Although there is no record of exactly what the illness was, the Duchess insisted Georgina was treated by the surgeon from Eugene's regiment and he 'bled and blistered her without mercy'.

So far, despite her many attractions, Georgina had been unlucky in love but her fortune was about to change. It was at this moment that John, sixth Duke of Bedford, arrived in Paris to deliver Francis's lock of hair. His attitude to Georgina had begun to soften when he visited her at Barnes, but when he saw her in the Gordons' Paris home, compassion turned into love. During dinner Georgina burst into tears when she saw that waiting behind John's chair was the same servant who had attended his dead brother. Her reaction made the Duke feel he had found a kindred spirit to share his grief. Perhaps John also found Georgina's vulnerability attractive. Instead of her usual Gordon exuberance she was subdued, her confidence knocked by the failure of her relationships with Francis and Eugene. John noted that during his visit she looked very ill and this brought out the protective streak in his character.

Even the Duchess of Gordon handled the situation more sensitively than usual. The Duke wrote to his sister-in-law Lady Bradford about the visit: 'I have seen the Duchess of Gordon who has received me most graciously and has not even given a hint upon any subject which could be unpleasant to me.' He later described his impressions of Georgina: 'I have more reasons than one to believe her to be most perfectly amiable – I have seen her in the most trying situations acting with the utmost propriety, and with a feeling and dignity of conduct which I must ever admire.'

The rapport between Georgina and John was built on mutual suffering; they had both loved and lost the same man and they were both still grieving for him. John had also recently lost his first wife, Georgiana Byng, who had died from consumption on 10 October 1801.

His first marriage had started as an impetuous romance. Lord John Russell, as he then was, had married Georgiana, the daughter of Viscount Torrington, in March 1786 when he was nineteen. Their love for each other had at first been intense; Georgiana wrote a letter to him repeating over and over again, 'I love you.' When she became pregnant she spoke with awe about giving birth to his child. The couple had three sons, Francis, William and John, but although the boys were a delight to their mother, childbirth was to sap her limited energy.

In the early years of their marriage, Lord John pursued a career in politics. He became the MP for Tavistock in 1788 and was a keen parliamentary reformer. Although his career meant they spent less time together, Georgiana worshipped him and admired his work. Unfortunately, this adoration was no longer mutual and as the years went by John became bored with his wife. Although she was very pretty, sweet-natured and a devout Christian, she did not offer the intellectual stimulation and challenge John needed.

Following the difficult birth of their third son, John, in 1792, she was often ill and suffered from depression. John spent more time away from his wife and at times she felt he no longer loved her. In 1800 she wrote an emotional letter to him explaining her feelings of rejection:

> Your letters are ever precious to me and I feel doubly gratified by that appearance of kindness which your manner has for some time convinced me I must no longer expect; Believe me I do not mean those sentiments of tenderness to which my Youth had been accustomed but the esteem and confidence which Years of Dutiful and faithful services might make me look for is so entirely wanting that I feel myself a useless person in your family . . . I experience each day some new instance of your Neglect . . . If you have ceased to value my friendship . . . if you are grown to despise my very small stock of sense and to dislike ever to consult me . . . Believe me it would be happier for us both to live separate.

Needy as she was for affection from her husband, a few kind words from John appeased her. She knew that her mental and physical illnesses put a strain on their marriage and that not all the fault lay with her husband. In a letter she wrote to John to be delivered immediately on her death she admitted:

> Your goodness to me has been much more than I deserved. My faults were so many and my total want of merit so apparent that I had no right to that goodness which I always experienced from You but for which I am very grateful – Most bitterly have I lately regretted the having been deprived by ill Health of the means of rendering myself useful to You . . . You must not My Friend suppose that it was from neglect or from any change, three Years incessant Ill Health and a lowness of Spirits which it was at times impossible to conquer may have given to my manners an appearance

Courtship

which was unpleasant to You but it was unintentional and
there is no species of suffering which I would not prefer to
giving You pain.

After his first wife's death, John experienced tremendous guilt about
the way he had treated her. He wrote to her sister Lady Bradford on
Georgiana's birthday, 23 November 1802:

Alas! my dear friend, I have much need of consolation – the
'accusing spirit' will not rest within me – every moment's
pain or sorrow or uneasiness or vexation which I have caused
to that blameless and incomparable woman, come upon me
with increased force and I humble myself with shame and
compunction . . . today I retire within myself, a solitary and
almost unconnected being.

As part of coming to terms with his grief, John reinvented his wife as
a perfect 'angel of truth and virtue'. He wrote to her sister that despite
his inconsiderate treatment:

. . . not a reproach or even a complaint ever escaped her
lips, and I know they never entered her heart; all was
kindness, Patience, submission and resignation, and I may
add to all was kindness, forgiveness and benevelonce . . . I
have lost my dearest friend, my companion and my
comforter.

After Francis's death, he found living without both his wife and
brother a torment. In other letters to Lady Bradford he wrote of his
overwhelming depression and his broken spirit. At first he was reluctant
even to sign himself as the Duke of Bedford, and he told his friend
Lord Holland that all the business his new position involved exhausted
his mind and body. He also found it difficult bringing up his sons as a
single parent. He told Lady Bradford: 'I am constantly apprehensive
of failing in doing what may be most essential to their future

happiness.' For advice and support in taking care of his sons, he turned to his sister-in-law and Lady Holland.

When the Duke met Georgina in Paris, she attuned herself to his melancholy mood and by sympathising with his suffering won a place in his heart. After their meeting she wrote him a subtly manipulative letter that echoed his feelings and sometimes even his phrases. Although she had only met Georgiana socially, she struck just the right tone by expressing her admiration for his 'lost angel':

> The mention of her too, whose virtues form the emulation of my soul, whose moments of pain are always soothed by the recollection of that affectionate kindness she possessed and in a manner so peculiar to herself, gratifies my whole heart . . . The return of the season, does indeed diffuse much melancholy into the minds of those who were blessed in belonging to her, but these feelings are mixed with great pleasure from witnessing the goodness of the Almighty in being bestowed on you, one, whose every thought and feeling is rendered subservient to softening by a continued chain of affection and devotion, the affliction with which it pleased him to visit you.

Georgina emphasised the good she saw in the Duke and how much she valued his 'friendship'. Her view of him helped to bolster his shattered self-esteem. She wrote to him:

> I feel for your virtues and kindness, every sentiment that it is possible should exist in the warmest breast . . . much as I value the love of many persons, there are none, whose good opinion and affections contribute so very much as yours does towards the joy, comfort and pride of my life.

Recognising the complexity of the emotions John felt about his first wife, she did not try to replace her. Perhaps after the turbulent times she had been through, she was willing to accept a relationship built on friendship not passion. Shortly after their meeting, John confided to Lady Bradford:

> I trust . . . That you will not consider it a want of respect or affection for the memory of our lost, ever loved and ever lamented angel, no my Dear Lady Bradford, my sorrows and regrets for her have taken a deep and lasting root, and are never to be removed, but I feel a reasonable and well grounded belief that she to whom I have determined to unite my lot will feel for and sympathise in my afflictions. I have formed no wild or visionary schemes of happiness – I look not again to that it was once my blessed lot to enjoy. I seek only for ease and tranquility of mind, for relief from care and oppression, and these I trust I shall obtain.

John was different from Georgina's other suitors; while they had been glamorous and flamboyant, he was a plain, shy man. His easy-going nature and love of the country were reminiscent of Georgina's father, the Duke of Gordon, and his quietness seemed to complement her vivacity. The fact that he was fifteen years older than her seemed to add rather than subtract from his suitability, giving him an attractive air of maturity.

By the end of May 1803 the couple were engaged. The Duke's first duty was to write to his future father-in-law, the Duke of Gordon, telling him the news:

> I take the earliest opportunity of acquainting your Grace that I have been fortunate enough to obtain Lady Georgiana Gordon's consent to unite her lot to mine, and as my object will ever be to promote and secure her happiness, I am inclined to flatter myself that it may meet with your Grace's approbation.

Georgina's father was delighted:

> I feel highly flattered that my daughter Georgina had been
> so fortunate as to be the object of your Grace's choice. I can
> only add that nothing in this world could have given me
> greater satisfaction.

Not everyone was so supportive. Lady Bradford refused to write and congratulate her brother-in-law, while the Duchess of Devonshire claimed John was only doing it to save Georgina from her dreadful mother. Even the Bishop of Oxford wrote to the Duke: 'I hear a strange report that you are going to marry a daughter of the Duchess of Gordon. It cannot be true. God forbid.' The Duke was well aware of what people thought of him becoming the son-in-law of the dreaded Duchess of Gordon. He wrote: 'I feel that the world will be busy in conversation and conjecture, the arts and intrigues of the Duchess of Gordon will give rise to many, and I shall in all probability be pronounced to be dupe to them.' But he begged his friends 'to distinguish between the daughter and the mother and know how to respect a pure and generous conduct in a person truly amiable'.

Despite all the negative comments, Georgina knew that once John had made up his mind in her favour she was secure. She wrote to him:

> You know me, and in this, as well as in the steadiness you
> ever evince to those opinions you have once been able to
> fix, I place an implicit reliance that all my actions however
> faulty they may appear will ever be understood and this
> conviction makes me inexpressibly happy.

Predictably, the Duchess of Gordon was ecstatic that Georgina had finally caught her duke. Although she was an ardent Tory it seems she had no qualms about her daughter marrying into a leading Whig family. In her hierarchy of aims there was one thing that came before political allegiances and that was family advancement. The fact that Bedford was a duke was far more important than his political beliefs, and no doubt she enjoyed a frisson of excitement at snatching the most eligible Whig widower from under the noses of any Whig hostesses who had designs on him to marry their daughters. She wrote to an old family friend, Lord Buchan: 'In the midst of my joy I remember your friendship for Georgiana and am happy to tell you she is to be married to the Duke of Bedford. He is the most amiable of men.'

As the peace concluded at Amiens came to an end and war was declared on France in May 1803, the Duchess returned to England triumphant. Once back in London, her extraordinary match-making powers were given full recognition – when she walked into the opera house, the whole audience turned to her and burst into applause as she took her seat.

CHAPTER THREE

Early Married Life

*Y*ears of planning and hard work by the Duchess of Gordon and her daughter finally reaped their reward when Georgina at last married her duke on 23 June 1803 at Fife House in Whitehall. The actual ceremony was surprisingly restrained, with the rector of Chenies performing the service in front of just the Duke and Duchess of Gordon and close members of the Gordon and Russell families. Perhaps the wedding ceremony was on a small scale because of the controversy surrounding the alliance and also to show respect for John's dead brother and his first wife.

Although the wedding service was understated, Georgina was radiant. No doubt relief was one of the emotions she experienced as she had at last lived up to her mother's expectations and fulfilled her destiny. The *Morning Post* recorded: 'Lady Georgiana Gordon looked most beautifully and was in high spirits.' She was 'most splendidly dressed' although she chose a simple rather than flashy style, not even wearing the stunning jewels the Duke had given her as a wedding present the night before.

Having exchanged their vows, at half-past five in the afternoon the Duke of Bedford and his new Duchess set off in a chariot and four for the family seat, Woburn Abbey in Bedfordshire. Once the bride and groom had left, the Duchess of Gordon, no longer having to show the dignified moderation expected by her new son-in-law, was able to express her pride and joy in the alliance in her own inimitable way. It would have been unnatural for her to leave the moment of her greatest triumph unmarked and she gave 'a most splendid dinner' for five hundred members of the 'haut ton'. The party started at ten o'clock at night, and an hour later the country dancing began. *The Times* described the scene: 'The ball-room was most beautifully fitted up and decorated with artificial flowers and the Ladies seemed to vie with each other in the splendour and elegance of their dress, which rendered it altogether a scene of the most delightful kind.' At two in the morning a lavish supper was provided in three supper rooms 'fitted out in the most magnificent and expensive style'. Vast tables, forty feet long and three feet wide were laden with an ostentatious display of plate – of course ordinary china would not suffice as the Duchess of Gordon reached the zenith of her match-making career. After supper, exuberant dancing continued until seven in the morning. The happy atmosphere was contagious and 'the excessive delight and rejoicing' spread to the servants and the whole neighbourhood, who shared in the celebrations by receiving white favours, wine and cake.

The couple's honeymoon initiated Georgina into what being the Duchess of Bedford entailed, as she was taken on a tour of the Bedford estates in Cambridgeshire and Northamptonshire. When they returned to Woburn she was welcomed to her new home with a series of celebrations. One of the first events Georgina hosted was a ball given in honour of her twenty-second birthday. No doubt eager to see how the young Duchess was settling into her role, a large group of 'the Gay World' came to Woburn for the party, and in the evening a ball was given for the servants.

The early months of the couple's marriage were taken up with a round of visits from their respective families. During the school holidays in August, Georgina was introduced to her stepsons, then her predecessor Georgiana Byng's family, the Torringtons and Bradfords also visited. Once the marriage was a *fait accompli*, they had little choice but to accept the new Duchess who had replaced their demure sister. Georgina's own sister Susan, the Duchess of Manchester, and her husband were frequent guests. Their estate at Kimbolton was not far from Woburn so Susan and Georgina were able to spend a great deal of time together.

Georgina took to being the wife of one of the premier dukes with extravagant enthusiasm. As there had not been a young Duchess of Bedford for more than three decades, Georgina was able to make a great impression, immediately bringing to the role a glamour the Russells had previously lacked. A neighbour, Charlotte Orlebar, described the Duchess's first appearance at Bedford Races in September 1803:

> The moving scene of the carriages had a pretty effect. Duke of Bedford who is pleasing tho' far from handsome like his late noble Brother drove his handsome Dutchess in an elegant Phaeton; she array'd all in pink with an immense Lace Veil thrown loosely all over her person; in a Barouche (which being an open Carriage shew'd to advantage) the Dutchess of Manchester, with three nice children but her and the Duke having been married as many years as the other have months, he rode on horse back amongst the Gentlemen.

Between three and four o'clock in the afternoon the company left the racecourse. At about nine o'clock that evening they went to the Race Ball, which was 'a most brilliant one in every respect, both as to company, jewels etc.'. Charlotte Orlebar noticed that Georgina was beautifully dressed, wearing 'a sort of Muslin Gause [*sic*] with silver sprigs, a profusion of jewels her necklace remarkably fine; her Hair dress'd in a pretty style ornamented with a diamond crescent'.

On her marriage, Georgina became mistress of Woburn. The stately grandeur of the house was on a far larger scale than the enchanting elegance of Gordon Castle. Woburn had originally been a Cistercian monastery but in 1538 Henry VIII confiscated the land and in 1547 it was granted to John, first Earl of Bedford, for services to the crown. The tree from which the last abbot was hanged was still there when Georgina arrived, a grisly reminder of the house's past. In 1619 Woburn became the Russells' family seat. Most of the buildings at the Abbey today were built by the Palladian architect Henry Flitcroft in 1747 but more work was done in 1786 under the direction of Henry Holland.

As a woman who cared about the aesthetic qualities of her surroundings, Georgina wanted to put her mark on the house so the couple spent lavishly on improving Woburn. They had several apartments refurbished with clocks, candelabra, bronze and porcelain that the Duke had bought in Paris during the Peace of Amiens in 1803. The landscape gardener Humphry Repton was employed to improve the gardens after he had done some work for the Duke at Russell Square on the Bedfords' London estate. When he was commissioned to prepare some designs for Woburn, he created one of his famous 'Red Books' for the estate. Within a slim volume, bound in red leather, was set out, in his son's immaculate copperplate handwriting, his proposals for changes. Maps, plans and 'before' and 'after' drawings were included to illustrate his ideas. The Red Book for Woburn was one of the largest he ever produced; it was eighty-nine pages long and included forty-eight drawings, maps and diagrams. Although Repton admired some of Henry Holland's work, particularly the 'ever-green drive', he had many ideas of how the landscape could be improved to capitalise on the 'greatness' which he saw as the essence of Woburn. He suggested creating a terrace near the house, American and Chinese gardens, a private garden for the family, a rosary or dressed flower garden in front of the greenhouse, a botanic garden and 'an animated garden' or menagerie. Georgina took a keen interest in his work and even helped him to design her own flower garden. Repton was obviously pleased with the result of his designs because he later wrote: '. . . the improvements I have had the honour to suggest have nowhere been so fully realised as at Woburn.'

Such extravagance encouraged criticism of the Duke and Duchess. The agriculturalist Arthur Young was particularly disapproving of this 'profusion of expense'. He wrote:

> This poor Duke of Bedford, whose nominal income is so enormous will, I fear, involve himself with the same imprudence [as his brother] . . . An extravagant duchess, Paris toys, a great farm, little economy and immense debts, will prove a canker in all the rosebuds of his garden of life.

Georgina was censored not just for her spending habits. Although she brought fun and laughter into the stately formality of Woburn, some people complained about the uninhibited freedom of speech and frankness of the new Duchess and her guests. After staying at Woburn, Arthur Young complained:

> I am tired of the whole, and long for the retirement of Bradfield [his home] and this finishing of hurry and bustle. I would not have another week of it for a hundred pounds . . . They are never cool, and have no time for reading or thought . . . What a spectacle at Woburn was that miserably swearing profligate Major B of Sussex, at the age of eighty one sticking to the last moment to worldly dissipation, and utterly regardless of what is to become of him hereafter . . . It is a sin and ought to be repented to go into such company.

Whatever pious critics thought, Georgina's high spirits were just what the Bedfords needed. Her *joie de vivre* was a marked contrast to the depression of John's first wife, and Georgina was the one person who could always dispel the Duke's black moods. Just a few months after their marriage John wrote to Lady Bradford about the transformation Georgina had brought about in his life:

I cannot forget my sorrows, but I have now an amiable and kind hearted friend near me who by every pleasing and gentle attention soothes and lightens their burden and by the most constant and unvarying endeavours to promote my happiness, dispels the dark clouds which so lately blackened the horizon before me and made every hour of my existence painful and gloomy – she asks me not to forget former days and former scenes, but with uncommon goodness shares the feelings which the recollection of them gives birth to, and with endearing kindness consoles and softens my affliction.

Georgina's method of dealing with the Duke's depression was to deliver gentle lectures to remind him of his many 'blessings'. Although she was fifteen years younger than him, she was the dominant partner in the marriage and she readily gave him advice. She wrote to him:

Why my own Johnny will you give way to unpleasant thoughts when you have so many charming reflections, that you ought to make and so many bright prospects before you. Can a human being stand higher in everyone's estimation than you do, is there a father in the world more beloved by his children or a husband more adored by his wife than you are, has heaven ever formed a human creature more perfection . . . then why heart of mine allow too much humility to prevent your 'shining in all your glory'? Rouse yourself and shake off your false notions and rely on my word, that the more you are known the more you must be loved, respected and admired.

When she married the Duke, Georgina was not just becoming his wife, she was also becoming stepmother to his three sons, Francis, William and John. She tried to be a good stepmother to them, but inevitably, as she was only a few years older than them, her role had to be more as a friend than a mother. It seems the boys were not quite sure what to make of their father's new wife. Her boisterous behaviour was the opposite of their mother's refined sobriety.

As time passed, each of Georgina's stepsons related to her in a different way, partly due to age, but also due to their temperaments. The eldest son, Francis, was already almost grown up and had least to do with his stepmother. The Duke's second son, William, was hot-tempered but straight talking and he became particularly close to Georgina, treating her as a trusted confidante. The youngest son, John, was most in need of maternal love as he was still a young child and had been his mother's favourite. The year before her death she wrote to her husband:

> It is not in my power to express the merits of that Child, his sense, his cleverness, his quietness and sweetness of temper and disposition surpass all I ever witnessed, his attentions to me are those of a grown person of superior sense, he reads to me, he talks to me on those things only by which he thinks to amuse and interest me – he hates to be absent from me.

John recalled many years later: 'I was very fond of her. I used to call her in the morning, and from that hour during the whole of the day she showed me the utmost affection.' Her death when he was nine years old was a devastating loss.

When Georgina first met John he was a frail eleven-year-old who was just four feet two inches tall and weighed only three stone twelve pounds. He was often ill, suffering from colds, coughs and fainting fits. Although young, Georgina already had a maternal streak, and she tried to take her youngest stepson under her wing. Knowing he was an intellectual child, the first present she gave him for his birthday was the works of Shakespeare.

The three boys went to Westminster school, but John was too delicate to stand the harsh life of the public school. Georgina saw it was not right for him and intervened with the Duke. John was taken away and taught at home. At first Dr Cartwright, the domestic chaplain, taught him, but after a few months John was sent to Mr Smith, the vicar of Woodnesborough near Sandwich, where he lodged with six other boys.

Both Georgina and John shared a love of the theatre. During the winter months they went to plays with the Duke, sometimes several times a week. Perhaps the highlight of the season was seeing the leading actors Kemble and Mrs Siddons in *Macbeth*. Evidently, John also enjoyed acting as he happily took part in the amateur theatricals Georgina staged at Woburn. *The Mayor of Garratt*, *The Village Lawyer* and *The Rivals* were performed first to guests and servants and then to the neighbours.

Talented in all forms of communication, John wrote playful poems and he even dedicated a particularly facetious one to his stepmother. His dedication gives an insight into the impression Georgina made on her new family:

> I shall here attempt not after the usual manner of dedications
> to describe your good qualities to those who know you it
> would be superfluous, and to those who do not it would
> seem either a fabulous invention of my brain or a copy from
> the character of the heroine in a modern novel.

The Duchess's time for her stepsons became more limited when she started a family of her own. In May 1804 her first son, Wriothesley, was born; it was an event which delighted the whole family, and naturally Georgina wanted to involve her parents as much as possible. Shortly after the birth, the Duke wrote to his father-in-law:

> I have great pleasure in being able to inform you that I left
> Georgiana in town this morning continuing as well as
> possible and I have now to request that you will have the
> goodness to be Godfather to our little boy . . . Georgiana
> charged me to give her kindest love to you and the Duchess
> and to say that she hopes the Duchess has not forgot her

promise of being also responsible for the sins of her new born grandson.

A year later, Georgina gave birth to a second son, Edward. Over the next twenty years, the Duchess was to be almost constantly pregnant; she gave birth to twelve children, nine boys and three girls (two of her sons dying shortly after birth). She was a very involved parent, and unlike her own mother, nursed most of her babies herself. By the time Georgina was a mother, the merits of wet-nursing were being challenged. Towards the end of the eighteenth century Dr William Cadogan wrote an essay on nursing and the management of children from birth to age three. He observed that peasant women who nursed their own babies had healthier children and that early breast-feeding prevented mastitis and engorgement. He therefore recommended breast-feeding as of benefit to both the mother and the child.

With a young family and an active social life, the first years of John and Georgina's marriage were very happy. Their relationship developed from a good friendship into a mutually supportive commitment that was central to both their lives. He doted on his 'darling little girl' and she adored her 'darling old man'. A few years after their marriage, Georgina wrote:

> Remember my own Johnny that you are dearer to me, than children, relations and all the world, that your love, esteem and confidence are the blessings that I would sacrifice all those tender ties to preserve, and what I told you three years ago, I repeat now, 'la vie n'est rien sans toi.'

Although the Duke never doubted he had married the right woman, at times he must have wondered about the wisdom of linking himself to her family. Shortly after their marriage, the Gordons caused embarrassment when Georgina's sister Susan left her husband, the Duke of Manchester, and ran off with a gamekeeper. Elizabeth Grant in her *Memoirs of a Highland Lady* wrote: 'The Duchess of Manchester (a crude, coarse talking woman) was driven from the house of the husband she disgraced.' But not everyone thought Susan was at fault; some people blamed her husband. When Arthur Young visited the couple at Kimbolton he was enchanted by this unpretentious young Duchess who preferred country life to London society and was very critical of the Duke of Manchester for openly flaunting a mistress. After his visit he wrote:

> [Susan has] a sweetness of temper and simplicity of character which, joined with an excellent understanding, contributed so much to form her as she is at present, calculated to be a blessing to her husband. She loves him and behaves with a most exemplary and unexampled patience and mildness under his connection with Mrs – . . . The spectacle in this age of seeing a very plain table, a plain unaffected way of living and everything about them modest and moderate in scale, very little company and never at London, yet all cheerfulness and content, even under the above circumstances speaks a good heart and an amiable temper.

Although Susan was playing her husband at his own game when she committed adultery, like many women of her era she paid a much higher price for her indiscretion. By taking a lover from a lower class, Susan had broken the social rules and so became an outcast from society. Most cruel was the fact that when she left her husband she was forced to leave her two sons and six daughters behind. The boys were sent to Eton while five of the girls were put under the care of a governess, overseen by the Duke's mother the Dowager Duchess of Manchester. The eldest daughter, Jane, chose to live with her maternal grandmother, the Duchess of Gordon, instead.

At this time, the Duchess of Gordon was causing almost as much controversy as her errant daughter. After her successful visit to France, Jane remained a staunch supporter of Napoleon. Such behaviour was seen as unpatriotic by many contemporaries and her position in society was in jeopardy. Lady Malmesbury wrote: 'The Duchess of Gordon is returned from Paris raving about Bonaparte and talked such real treason that if it would not give her too much consequence, she ought to be sent to the Tower.'

Her relationship with her husband had also deteriorated. When the Duke tried to make their informal separation permanent, Jane fought an acrimonious matrimonial battle with him. A series of letters from Jane to Francis Farquharson, an Edinburgh accountant who acted as mediator between the couple, reveals how bitter the fight was. Although they were separated, the Duchess of Gordon demanded the Duke should keep her in the style befitting the mother of so many duchesses. In 1804 she wrote:

> Now my family are settled as my fondest ambition or tenderness could desire – so that where I live is of little consequence to me – but I must live as mother of such daughters. However my Duke may encroach upon my privileges as a Wife and Mistress of his family I never shall forget what I owe to myself.

She added in a later letter: 'I am Duchess of Gordon – He is Duke – and I feel I have done as much credit to the name as any Duke ever did.' However, the Duke was unwilling to increase the amount of money he gave her and he apparently told her: 'By God Ma'am you are a swindler. Your extravagance has ruined me.'

Georgina and John were sympathetic to the Duchess, but all her son-in-laws begged her to settle the matter as soon as possible to avoid further embarrassment. It seems Georgina had the most influence over her mother as the Duchess of Gordon wrote:

> These scenes upon nerves a good deal shattered by former unmerited sufferings made me very ill. Georgiana begged I would leave town and let the rage excited by my superior situation in point of character and public esteem be a little evaporated before any more discussion.

Once her anger had abated, the Duchess accepted her family's advice and she settled with the Duke. On 31 October and 4 November 1805 the warring couple signed a Decree Arbitral. The Duke of Gordon was quite happy for the terms to be generally known as he thought the allowance he had made was 'very handsome and in every respect suitable to the ranks of the parties'. He agreed to pay Jane an annuity of £4,000 (about £120,000 in today's money) per annum and an additional sum of £2,000 (approximately £60,000) to provide furniture, plate, linen and other items she might need for her separate establishment. The Duchess was not happy with the situation but explained her reasons for accepting the terms:

> Wishing to avoid throwing disgrace on a family I have raised
> to the highest dignities – and upon those now connected
> with them – I bid Mr Adam do every thing he could to bring
> on an amicable separation – but one that would take me out
> of the power of a man void of every generous principle . . . A
> giddy head and broken heart is all I am left with.

After the final separation from her husband, Jane became 'a wanderer', moving from hotel to hotel or staying with her children. Her reputation was damaged further when her lover Henry Dundas, now Lord Melville, was disgraced. He had been First Lord of the Admiralty, but the commission appointed to enquire into frauds and abuses in the Royal Navy contained serious charges against him, and he was accused in the House of Commons of misappropriating funds during his time as Treasurer of the Navy. Due to the allegations, Melville resigned and his name was immediately erased from the list of Privy Councillors. He was then impeached before the House of Lords but was finally acquitted in June 1806. Loyal to her lover, the Duchess of Gordon supported him throughout, writing: 'Poor Lord Melville has been tortured by all that malice or malignity could invent – the papers tell all – so adieu to the painful subject – nobody has felt more for him than I have done.'

The Melville scandal undermined William Pitt as Dundas had been his right-hand man. In January 1806 Pitt died and the King turned to the Whigs. Lord Grenville formed a coalition cabinet known as 'the ministry of all the talents', which included Charles Fox as Foreign Secretary. Lord Holland, who was very close to Fox, pushed for the Duke of Bedford, as a leading Whig supporter, to be made Lord Lieutenant of Ireland in the administration.

It was a controversial appointment because the Prince of Wales and some politicians were already questioning whether such a responsible post should be filled by a peer. The number of potential candidates was limited as the expenditure it involved required the Lord Lieutenant to have a substantial private income. In 1783 the viceroy's salary was set at £20,000 per annum but the actual vice-regal expenses were at least double this amount. This led to the choice being made with more regard to a person's private means than their capacity for public service. There were calls for the Lord Lieutenancy to be replaced by a council headed by the Prince of Wales. The Duke was aware of the criticism and was anxious about taking on this potentially poisoned chalice. He later told Lord Howick (soon to become Earl Grey):

> I came to this country [Ireland] at the earnest solicitation of Fox – the partiality of his friendship and that indulgence so natural to his nature gave me a fitness for the office I undertook, which I felt an unaffected conviction did not belong to me ... was I now to follow solely my own inclinations I should desire to be permitted to retire to that private station and turn of habits of life which I reluctantly quitted.

Georgina and her mother felt no such reluctance. They were both delighted with the Duke's appointment; in fact the Duchess of Gordon was so excited that when she caught sight of her son-in-law at a party, she ran towards him in such haste she tripped over her shoes and fell flat on her face. Showing an ambitious streak worthy of her mother, Georgina told her husband he would be a worthy successor to Charles Fox (who died that year). She wrote to him:

How it warms my heart . . . to hear that they look up to the first man certainly now in the world, yes darling, it is the truth, you are the person that ought to replace Mr Fox to his party and you are the only man fitted for the arduous task, you possess abilities much greater than you are yet sensible of, they only require to be called forth to show how superior they are to those looked up to upon many occasions. Your principles are not to be shaken, your manners are most pleasing and your temper gentle, this is not half what I think, but all I dare tell you for fear of appearing what I abhor, a flatterer.

Although Georgina had been brought up in a strong Tory family it seems she found no conflict of interests in becoming the wife of a leading Whig politician. Throughout her life she cared more about people than party politics. In her letters she rarely discussed politics but she did, like her husband, have a strong sense of justice and she often supported the under-dog in a situation. Her mother had trained all her daughters in the art of flattery as a way of pleasing their husbands so it came naturally to Georgina to be a political chameleon. Now she was the Duchess of Bedford, she supported Whig men and measures whole-heartedly.

In 1806 the Duke, Georgina and their two young sons moved to Dublin. On 25 March they sailed from Holyhead to Ireland on board the King's yacht, *Dorset*, and three days later, early in the morning, they arrived in Dublin. Georgina was extremely tired by the journey but was soon energised by the euphoric welcome they received. After meeting the Lord Mayor, Alderman, sheriffs and commons of Dublin, the Duke and Duchess, attended by a squadron of dragoons, set off for Dublin Castle. The streets were packed with people eager to see the new Lord Lieutenant and his wife. *Walker's Hibernian Magazine* described the scene:

The acclamations of the people were unbounded. At Macartney's bridge they endeavoured to take the horses from

the new viceroy's carriage, but their views were frustrated by
the activity of postillions, and the procession from that
moment proceeded with most rapidity to the castle, through
the line formed by the military.

At eight o'clock in the morning the Duke and Duchess arrived at
Dublin Castle where a reception was held to welcome them by the
out-going Lord Lieutenant, the Earl of Hardwicke. At three o'clock
that afternoon a privy council assembled and the Duke was sworn in
as Lord Lieutenant, invested with the collar of the Order of St Patrick
and given the sword of state. To mark the occasion, a royal salute was
fired by the great guns in Phoenix Park and this was answered with a
volley of musketry by the soldiers drawn up on College Green. At four
o'clock a levee was held at the castle to introduce the new Viceroy and
his wife to the leading people in Dublin and, as a finale, in the evening
'an illumination' was put on.

The following morning the Duke rode through the streets of
Dublin to meet the people he was to govern. Many years later he
recalled: 'The old women assembled round me and received me most
cordially. I remember one of them called out to me – "Long life to
your Excellency! Let me give you only one small bit of advice, don't
drink too much of the Whiskey Punch!" '

As the wife of the Lord Lieutenant, Georgina's life in Ireland revolved
around hosting parties for important visitors and the leading members
of Dublin society. In 1806 Dublin's population was just under 200,000
people. Since the Act of Union in 1801, the ancien regime of aristocrats
living in the city had been replaced by a new order. As the aristocracy
retired to their country seats or moved to London, prosperous
merchants, doctors and lawyers filled the vacuum they left. The middle
classes became Dublin's new élite and for the first time they were
invited to the castle.

Georgina's Gordon flamboyance made her the perfect icon for this
upwardly mobile society. The beautiful young Duchess's enthusiasm
for her role captured their imagination. The people of Dublin immediately responded to her warmth and her first drawing room was more

'A Flower just opening to the view.' Georgina as a young woman, wearing a simple white empire-line dress. Portrait by Hoppner.

'The Flower of Galloway, Jane Maxwell, Duchess of Gordon.' This portrait by Angelica Kauffman in 1772 shows Georgina's mother at the height of her powers, portrayed as the goddess Diana.

Reputed to be one of the handsomest men in Scotland, Alexander, fourth Duke of Gordon, was painted by Angelica Kauffman during the early years of his marriage to Jane.

Cartoon by Gillray of the Duchess of Gordon with 'Georgie' chasing 'the Bedford Bull'. Just one of the many satirical attacks on the Duchess's manipulative match-making tactics.

An eligible bachelor worth fighting for, the Duchesses of Gordon and Devonshire were soon in competition to marry off their daughters to Francis, fifth Duke of Bedford. Portrait by Hoppner.

Lord John Russell, later sixth Duke of Bedford, as he looked at the time of his first marriage to Georgiana Byng. Portrait by Sir William Beechey.

Pious and pretty Georgiana Byng, painted during the first years of her marriage when she was happy, before ill health and depression marred her life. Portrait by Samuel Cotes.

The Duke and Duchess's picturesque cottage *orné*, Endsleigh, in Devon soon became known as 'the Garden paradise of the West'. Pictures from Humphry Repton's Red Book show the view across the Tamar (*above*) and the children's pond (*below*). The house was specially designed so that Georgina could watch her children playing while she worked in her study.

Above left Elizabeth Rawdon, an intellectual beauty. After her marriage to Lord George William Russell, Elizabeth became Georgina's arch enemy. This portrait by Vogelstein captures Elizabeth's haughty good looks.

Above right Georgina's step-son Lord George William Russell in Hussar costume by an unknown artist. As a dashing soldier in Wellington's army he attracted many women and broke several hearts, earning himself the description of 'a gay deceiver'.

Right Georgina's youngest step-son, Lord John Russell was more sympathetic than his brothers were to their stepmother. John was to become a future Whig Prime Minister, and a leading advocate for parliamentary reform. In this portrait by Sir Francis Grant, Lord John is pictured holding the Reform Bill in his hand.

Edwin Landseer in his prime. As an artistic genius and a handsome young man, the aristocracy courted him to be their artist and guest. Portrait by Sir Francis Grant.

Above left A naughty child. This picture, one of Landseer's most famous child portraits, is thought by some critics to be modelled on Lady Rachel Russell.

Above right Ladies Louisa and Georgiana Russell at the time of their coming out. Lady Louisa was the beauty of the family while Georgiana was described as a 'dull dowdy'. Picture by A. R. Chalon.

Below left James, first Duke of Abercorn, married Georgina's daughter Louisa in October 1832. He was very handsome and extremely eligible as this portrait of him by Landseer reveals.

Below right Georgina's daughter, Louisa, Duchess of Abercorn at about the time of her wedding. Contemporaries described Louisa as looking just like Georgina had as a young woman; certainly this picture has echoes of her mother also painted by Landseer at about this time (*see over*).

Above Time for contemplation. As Georgina grew older she became increasingly religious, turning to her faith in times of trouble. This portrait by Landseer shows Georgina deep in thought.

Left A mellow man. John, sixth Duke of Bedford, gave Georgina steadfast love and security. Portrait by Landseer.

'numerously and splendidly attended than we have witnessed these many years'. When she first went to the theatre, she was treated like a modern film star. As she entered the vice-regal box, the entire audience rose and the band started to play 'God Save the King'. The Duchess was clearly delighted at the flattering reception and made 'the most polite acknowledgement'.

The lively informality of Dublin society perfectly matched Georgina's style. Edward Wakefield wrote:

> In all public places the company mix freely, without restraint or formality, and the consequence is, a general knowledge of each other, a circumstance which gives more animation to crowded circles in Dublin than is to be met with either in London or Paris, where people may frequently meet, and yet acquire very little acquaintance with each other. A social disposition and love of amusement seems to provide all ranks and the dance is often kept up with as much spirit in the back room of a shop-keeper, as in the splendid mansion of a peer . . . The gaiety of Dublin, during the fashionable season, exceeds all descriptions, there are many who never pass an evening out of visiting parties, either at home or abroad.

The Viceroy had to be as aware of public relations as politics at this time because, after the Act of Union, the Irish were very sensitive to any suggestion that they were inferior to the British. Part of the Viceroy's responsibility was to hide the loss of Dublin's political status by increasing the trappings of power. Therefore as real power ebbed away from Dublin, the pomp and pageantry increased. The Bedfords were just the right couple to implement this calculated policy; living lavishly came naturally to them.

During their rule in Dublin, the Duke and Duchess divided their time between the vice-regal lodge in Phoenix Park and Dublin Castle. The Lord Lieutenant's Lodge had been built in 1751 and was occupied by Lords Lieutenant from 1782. It stood in seventeen acres of grounds in Phoenix Park and was used as the Viceroy's summer home when the Dublin social season ended in May.

Dublin Castle was more formal and during the season the Bedfords lived like royalty. The castle had ornate state apartments including a throne room (originally known as Battleaxe Hall) and St Patrick's Hall, which was used for important occasions. The hall was decorated in gold and white, with gold Corinthian columns. Its ceiling, painted by Vincenzo Valdre, depicted George III between Britannia and Hibernia, St Patrick converting the Druids, and Henry II receiving the surrender of the Irish chieftains. In this ostentatious room, Georgina and the Duke hosted magnificent balls. The Lord Lieutenant and his wife sat on 'thrones' on a dais at one end of the hall and no lady was allowed to dance before the vice-regal couple had taken to the floor.

The Duke and Duchess were expected to provide all the events offered by a royal household so there were regular levees, drawing rooms and audiences. They attended concerts and benefit performances in support of an eclectic range of charities, including ones for the benefit of 'Decayed Musicians', 'The Lying-in Hospital' and for 'Sick and Indigent Room-Keepers'. The Duchess also made 'royal visits' to the National Museum and the Lying-in Hospital. She established an immediate rapport with the people she met, as the description of her visit to the hospital reveals. She 'went through the different wards, and with celestial feelings opened the curtains of the beds, looked at the children, and enquired most minutely about them'.

One of the most important dates of the vice-regal year was the King's birthday. There was a court in the morning and a ball at night, while during the trooping of the colour, crowds filled the castle yard to watch military exercises to the sound of martial music. As the Duke reviewed the troops, the Duchess passed along the line in her superb state landau, drawn by six blood horses, richly decorated.

Family life was fitted in around the formality and during the school holidays Georgina's stepsons came to stay. They spent their time playing cricket, riding and shooting, but the highlight of their visit was a fancy-dress ball hosted by Georgina in honour of the Prince Regent's birthday. For the party, three hundred 'gay and fashionable' people were invited to the vice-regal lodge where Georgina put on a display her guests would never forget. The *Dublin Evening Post* described the evening:

> All the avenues to the Lodge were illuminated and the whole suit [*sic*] of apartments were decorated in a style that reflects the highest credit on our Vice-Queen. In the varied ornaments of each room, some striking allusion to the day was most happily blended – the idea of the Prince seemed to pervade every spot. In the Ball-room, beneath the Coronet and ostrich plumes, and encircled with laurel wreaths were the initials of the Prince's name, and his motto composed of the most vivid mixture of roses, lilies, anemones and jasmine, harmonising most admirably with the festoons that hung all around with the gay fancy dresses of the company.

The Duchess looked extremely beautiful in an Elizabethan costume. Her guests had entered into the spirit of the occasion and were dressed as Swiss peasants, Arcadian shepherdesses, Turkish sultans and Grecians. Entertainment was provided by Dublin's leading actors and singers. The party dined at two o'clock in the morning then returned to the ballroom to dance until five.

During the boys' visit, the family went to the theatre and young John was impressed when, as they entered their box, his father and stepmother were received with 'great applause'. The audience was anxious to see what the Duchess was wearing because in just a few months she had become a leader of fashion, admired for her style and beauty. Every detail of her clothes was described in the Dublin papers although it was not only her dresses that were noted. During this time she used her extensive jewellery collection to great effect and gave the people the glamour and glitter they wanted from their vice-queen.

She attended one ball looking 'uncommonly elegant' in white and silver with a profusion of diamonds. When she went to the theatre she wore a turban with a plume of white ostrich feathers to match her white muslin dress trimmed with roses. In her hair was a wreath of diamonds to match a 'brilliant necklace and splendid ear-rings'. On another visit to the theatre she appeared in a blue muslin dress with a matching blue cap trimmed with a feather and a wreath of diamonds. Her style was not subdued even when the court went into mourning for the Duke of Brunswick. Her black muslin dress was trimmed with white lace and gathered in at the waist with diamonds while a flamboyant touch was added by a Spanish hat made of black velvet and trimmed with a plume of white ostrich feathers and a black rose. A swansdown tippet and white gloves completed the outfit.

Georgina thoroughly enjoyed being the centre of attention and she revelled in the flattering admiration she received. At the Chief Secretary Mr Elliot's summer fete at his villa in Phoenix Park, the *Dublin Evening Post* recorded:

> It must be confessed the charming Duchess stood unrivalled, 'the first in beauty as in place' – her form is symmetry itself and she dances with the airy lightness and grace of a nymph: she was simply attired in a morning dress of tamboured muslin, lined with pale rose colour, a cap to match, a splendid white scarf and veil.

Commentators noted that the Duchess's elegant example led to an improvement in the way Dublin women dressed. The same paper recorded: 'We were happy to observe a visible change in the costume of several of our fair country women, who of late years, so obstinately indulged in a propensity to appear in the most careless and least expensive dresses possible to be procured.'

The Duke and Duchess became the most sought-after guests for Dublin hostesses. Georgina's attendance at events was said to give 'a new zest to the enjoyment of the evening'. Waltzes and poems were soon being composed in her honour, including a particularly fulsome ode that was performed at a concert at the Rotunda:

The Caledonian muse with kindred charms,
With many a lay of love and gen'rous arms,
Of Scotia's fair-one, and her martial youth,
For beauty form'd, for courage and for truth
Delighted let her plume her raptur'd wing
But high o'er all the fair Georgina sing
Her sister muse, and not less form'd for song
The full responsive note shall pour along
And glad proclaim where beauty's throng resort
Gordon the brightest gem of Britain's court.

Fortunately, Georgina was not blinded by such flattery and she remained self-aware enough to recognise her weaknesses as well as her strengths. Like her mother before her, she showed a desire for self-improvement. During this time she privately expressed a concern that her education had been deficient. When she was not required to take part in official duties, she decided it was time to improve her knowledge of literature. Mornings were spent reading Sir Walter Scott's latest tragedy and *Gulliver's Travels*. Aware of her poor spelling, letters were written carefully with a dictionary by her side.

Despite all the splendour and sycophancy, she did not lose touch with normal life. In the afternoons, Georgina visited friends or went shopping, finding yet more extravagant objects to fill Woburn, including a pair of alabaster vases for fifty guineas. Although she was cut off from her friends and family, Georgina was kept up-to-date with the gossip by letters from home. Predictably, her mother kept her well informed about the latest marriages and extra-marital affairs.

While Georgina was flourishing in her high-profile role, the Duke was experiencing more testing times. Governing Ireland was never easy, but with rebellion fresh in people's memories and the Act of Union so recent, the Irish problem had become one of the most explosive issues of the day.

Since the French Revolution in 1789 the political atmosphere in

Ireland had been unsettled. The Irish saw that in France religious inequality had been abolished and a democratic government set up. Irish Catholics wanted equality, while Irish Protestants wanted parliamentary reform; both groups wanted economic reform.

Moderate Irish politicians believed that Ireland should support Britain in its time of crisis but more extreme politicians such as Lord Edward Fitzgerald and Wolfe Tone wanted an independent Ireland that would break the connection with England. To achieve their end they set up the United Irishmen in 1791 to unite Catholics and Dissenters against Anglican rule.

As a canny politician Pitt knew action had to be taken. In 1793 the Irish Parliament was persuaded to pass the Catholic Relief Act. This gave Catholics the right to vote but, although they could stand as candidates, they were still not allowed to take a seat in Parliament. The Irish were hopeful that there would be further reform when Earl Fitzwilliam was made Lord Lieutenant of Ireland in 1795. He was a Whig who believed Catholics should have complete political equality. But his reign was short-lived; within three months George III recalled him in disgrace.

The situation in Ireland became more dangerous in the following years, with outbreaks of sectarian violence. The United Irishmen encouraged the French to help them gain Irish independence. In reaction to this foreign threat the Irish Protestants formed the Orange Order to protect Protestantism in Ireland.

In 1796 the United Irishmen put their plans into action and 15,000 French troops arrived off Bantry Bay; but bad weather prevented them from landing and a major opportunity was missed. After this incident the British carried out a campaign of terror against the United Irishmen and dozens of the group were executed.

By 1798 many of their leaders had been arrested and the remaining men felt forced to call for an immediate rising. Across Ireland people supported the rebels for a variety of reasons. Peasants, who were often treated like animals, forced to live in terrible conditions by their landlords, resented the fact that everyone, regardless of their religion, had to pay a tithe to the local Anglican clergy. They hoped rebellion would lead to the tithes being abolished. Roman Catholics wanted an end to discrimination, while nationalists wanted independence from Britain.

By the autumn the rebellion was defeated, tens of thousands of rebels were dead and the British Government was determined to stamp out the potential for any future uprisings.

Pitt believed that Ireland could not be allowed an independent parliament because it might then become an independent nation and support France. To prevent this happening, and despite much opposition, Pitt pushed through the Act of Union which tied Ireland firmly to Britain. The King and peers holding Irish estates opposed any concessions to the Catholics so the terms were tough. The Act led to the Dublin Parliament, which had existed for more than four hundred years, being abolished. Instead, Ireland was to be represented at Westminster by one hundred MPs, four Lords Spiritual and twenty-eight Lords Temporal. The Anglican Church was recognised as the official Church of Ireland and no Catholics were to be allowed to hold public office.

The Act of Union just aggravated the problems between Ireland and Britain. As Lord Lieutenant of Ireland, the Duke of Bedford had to try to govern a deeply divided country, and at times this quiet, fair-minded man felt out of his depth. John based his political philosophy on the principle that all governments should be made for the happiness of the many and not for the benefit of the few. He opposed any system of exclusion; therefore he considered that concessions to the Roman Catholics were essential if Ireland was to be kept peaceful. He wrote to Lord Holland:

> Conciliation and kindness as general principles are those alone by which we can secure the attachment and affection of the People of Ireland, and when circumstances compel me for a time to depart from those principles, it will not be without feelings of the deepest regret mixed with serious apprehensions for the consequences.

During his time in office there was unrest among the Catholics in several Irish counties and the Dublin 'threshers' were organising agitation to resist paying tithes. The Grenville government launched an investigation into the tithe issue but because of the unrest the Duke was put under pressure to apply the insurrection acts. At first he refused because he had little faith in the Protestant magistrates dealing fairly with the situation. He feared that if they were given too much power they would use it to persecute the Catholic population. His policy alienated the Orangemen and landlords, who felt he was more interested in remaining popular with the Catholics than protecting their interests. His policy also failed to win over the Catholics because, although he was sympathetic towards them, eventually he was persuaded to permit an insurrection bill to be drawn up.

Increasingly, the Duke found himself caught in the middle of an insoluble problem. He wrote to Lord Holland: 'My aim is to steer an even course, regardless of the violence which is perpetually assailing me on one side or the other . . . my situation I assure you is not an enviable one.'

During this difficult time the Duchess provided the support the Duke needed. She was a charming consort but she also knew just how to make a political statement without saying a word. The Duke and Duchess pleased the Catholics by reviving the practice of celebrating St Patrick's Day at the castle with a ball and supper. At the dance Georgina subtly signalled her respect for Irish history by wearing in her hair a specially designed jewel modelled on one worn by an ancient Irish princess. She wanted to encourage 'Irish genius' so gave her permission to announce her name as the patroness of the jewel, hoping that other women would follow her example and buy a copy from James Bruth and Son, jewellers, in St Andrew Street. In another bid to boost the local economy, Georgina had all her clothes made in Ireland and encouraged all the ladies at her court to wear Irish clothes.

Even when she found herself in the most sensitive political situations, Georgina was not afraid to stand up for her beliefs. When Sydney Owenson, later Lady Morgan, was criticised for writing a nationalistic novel entitled *The Wild Irish Girl*, the Duke and Duchess decided to show their support for her publicly. They took their whole household to an opera she had produced called *The First Attempt*. Many years later, Lady Morgan recalled the effect of their public patronage:

> The vice-regal box and dress-circle were exclusively occupied by the Court, and officers of the garrison, who were headed by the Commander in Chief. The whole of the liberal part of the Irish bar, and their friends, filled the upper circle, and the pit and galleries were occupied by a popular Irish Catholic audience whose fun and humorous sallies filled up the intervals of the acts, while their frequent cheers for the Lord Lieutenant and frequent call for 'Patrick's Day' and for 'Kate Kearney' [a popular composition of the author's] produced a sort of national drama 'avant la scene' infinitely more amusing than that which was enacted on it. The Duchess of Bedford and all the ladies of her circle wore the Irish bodkin, and thus raised the price of Irish gold in the Dublin market of bijouterie.

Through her mother, Georgina had grown up immersed in politics, so being the wife of a politician was second nature to her. Although she did not emulate the Duchess of Gordon's overtly political role, she took an intense interest in her husband's work, asking for his speeches to be sent to her and acting as a sounding board for his ideas. She was often so over the top in his praise that it bore little resemblance to reality and she constantly assured him of her 'pride' in his achievements:

> Never was anything so pleasing and so gratifying as the accounts given by all your party and many others, of the universal admiration and attachment felt for you by all ranks. I hear your speech was the most beautiful in point of composition ever heard and delivered in a most feeling and impressive manner . . . I hope my letter gives you that just confidence in your own abilities that you always ought to feel. Continue darling Johnny to show the world what you

really are and rely on my word, that you will be the most brilliant character now living as you unite talents, honour and greatness of mind . . . you only require to be known to be adored.

The closeness of the Duke and Duchess's relationship is clearly illustrated in a series of letters written by Georgina to her 'best beloved' while he was away from her for a few weeks on an 'agricultural tour' visiting the magistrates in Sligo, Mayo and Connaught. Georgina wrote sometimes twice a day and complained if letters from the Duke were not equally frequent. They clearly hated being apart and Georgina could not wait for her husband to return to 'the longing arms of your darling little girl'. The tone of her letters is loving and flirtatious, as a letter written on 4 October 1806 reveals:

> What a happy day to all of us the day you return, the greatest pleasure I can experience in your absence is to know that you are very gay and happy, and I am then certain that you will be well. Remember darling old man that you tell a story better than any body, that when in spirits you are the most pleasing and most agreeable creature in the world and that I beg you will talk incessantly out of compliment to me – pray do and recollect that I am too much interested in your fame to recommend anything to you, that would not show you in the most advantageous light. Make love to all the ladies, but keep your dear heart for me, tell naughty stories to the Gentlemen, but keep their effects for me, handle all the cattle with pleasure, but keep the tender pleasure for me – God Almighty bless you.

While in Ireland, Georgina found she was pregnant again. This time it was not an easy pregnancy and she complained of looking ill and ugly. She suffered from bad pains in her head, spasms after eating and fainted several times. Her doctor thought the baby was taking all the nourishment from its mother and prescribed calomel, a strange choice as it is a purgative, but throughout Georgina's life she was a firm believer in its good effects on her health. She had to restrict her social programme because of her condition. On Christmas Day the Duke rode from the vice-regal lodge to Christ Church for the Christmas service but Georgina was too ill to accompany him. By the end of January she was well enough to go to a service in St Patrick's Cathedral to hear the 'Hallelujah Chorus' from Handel's *Messiah* performed with a 'sublime effect', but the celebration of the Queen's birthday had to be postponed until after the Duchess's accouchement. The *Dublin Evening Post* coyly explained it as 'her Grace being at present far advanced "in that state in which ladies wish to be who love their lords" '.

This time Georgina was sure she was going to have the baby daughter she so longed for. In her letters she talked about having 'the young lady' and 'little Georgy'. Her maternal instincts were wrong and at four o' clock in the morning on 10 February 1807, Georgina gave birth to a third boy. Dublin Castle was inundated with enquiries about the Duchess's health as the people of Dublin wanted to show 'the vast estimation' in which they held 'the amiable and accomplished Duchess of Bedford'. On 12 March the Archbishop of Dublin christened the little boy at Dublin Castle. The Duke, as a tribute to his political hero, insisted on calling his son Charles James Fox Russell. In fact, the christening turned into another excuse for a good party and the festivities began on Friday evening and finished the next morning.

The Duchess's popularity was further evident when she held her first drawing room after the birth. It was much more crowded than usual and all the avenues leading to the castle were entirely filled with carriages.

Although the Duke and Duchess were held in high esteem by the Irish people, their vice-regal rule was to be just a brief interlude. By the spring of 1807 the Duke found himself at the centre of the crisis over Catholic rights. At this time Dublin's Catholic leaders were threatening to petition Parliament for full Catholic relief. The Cabinet knew that opening up this debate was certain to divide the ministry, so Lord

Howick tried to find a compromise. He introduced a parliamentary bill which would have opened up all ranks of the army and navy to Catholics, but George III was vehemently opposed to the proposal, and asked for it to be withdrawn. Faced with a very difficult decision, Grenville agreed to drop the bill. However, this climb down was not enough to satisfy the King, and he pressed his case further, demanding an undertaking that the ministry would never again ask him to make concessions of this sort. Grenville would not give such an undertaking; nor was the Duke of Bedford willing to continue as Lord Lieutenant under such restrictions. On hearing the King's request, the Duke declared his intention to resign because he believed that with holding the concessions from the Catholics would make Ireland ungovernable. At the end of March, after the King announced that he intended to seek an alternative administration, Grenville surrendered his seal of office; his ministry that had started with such high hopes was at an end. Under the new administration, the Duke of Bedford was replaced as Lord Lieutenant by his brother-in-law, the Duke of Richmond.

The people of Dublin were sad to lose the Bedfords, both for the gaiety and the fair-minded political philosophy they had brought to Ireland. Georgina's final balls at Dublin Castle and at the Rotunda showed how respected she had become. The events were 'crowded by the attendance of almost every person of distinction and respectability at present in Dublin'. The couple's popularity was even more apparent when they left Dublin on 18 April 1807. The *Dublin Evening Post* described the emotional scene:

> It was through streets thronged with people agitated with such feelings, that on Tuesday their Graces of Bedford passed from the Castle to the water side, accompanied by all of rank, respectability and patriotism to be found in this city – At two o'clock the farewell Levee of his Grace commenced at the Castle; the number of Nobility and Gentry who attended were immense, we scarcely supposed the Union had left so many in the Country – their Graces appeared,

sensibly to feel the testimonial of Irish respect and approbation.

At four o'clock the procession left the castle; the Duke was in one carriage with the new Lord Lieutenant, the Duke of Richmond, while Georgina was in a second carriage with three friends. The *Post* continued:

> They had proceeded but a little way in Dame Street, when the generous affections of the Irish heart became visible, when the people, unable longer to master their feelings, insisted on taking the horses from the carriages of the Duke and Duchess: notwithstanding many intreaties [sic] to the contrary, they affected their purpose, and thus were their Graces of Bedford drawn by the people to the Pigeon House, a distance of two miles . . . All the streets through which their Graces passed were lined with the military, and the windows were filled with beauty and fashion, and they were gratified as they went along by waving of handkerchiefs, plaudits and cheers; the emotion and sensibility of her Grace was apparent, which spoke more eloquently to the Irish heart than words can possibly do.

At five o'clock the Duke and Duchess embarked on the royal yacht, *Dorset*. They were unable to sail that night as the wind was in the wrong direction so they held a dinner party on board for select friends. At eight o' clock the next morning they set sail for England.

The Duke and Duchess left Ireland with mixed emotions. Although their time there had been a public-relations success with the ordinary people, the Duke was not happy with the way his policy of conciliation had been undermined by the British government. He considered the government had been forced to make a humiliating concession to the King that would result in 'evil consequences' in Ireland. He felt that he could no longer face the Catholics after 'so manifest a breach of Faith' and he refused to become subservient to the Orange faction. His experience in Ireland had left him disillusioned with politics and demoralised. On his return to England he described himself as 'a dismissed and fallen viceroy'. He wrote to Lord Holland about his disenchantment:

> When I consented to go to Ireland I know not whether I estimated my own strength too highly, when I thought that I might successfully undertake a Government founded on measures of kindness and reconciliation, but sure I am that I was wholly unfit to conduct one of severity and coercion – my habits of life and a debilitated state of health, but above all my feelings and my principles, disqualify me for the Task – every act emanating from such a system would be repugnant to those doctrines moral and political which my mind has ever been accustomed to esteem, to cherish and to venerate.

The Duke was to champion causes such as Catholic emancipation and parliamentary reform behind the scenes but he never again took an active role in politics. Although Georgina had been the perfect vice-queen, combining political subtlety with style, her dream of being the consort of a political leader was permanently dashed.

CHAPTER FOUR

Laying the Foundations

T he Irish interlude had been a formative experience for both the Duke and Duchess as it had put their political views, social skills and marriage to the test. When they returned to England it was a time for reflection and reassessment. In August 1807, John wrote an analysis of the 'meaning of life' in a long essay exploring his views on religion, marriage and Georgina's character. Evidently, he discussed his beliefs with his wife and he was influenced by her opinions:

> There is a fixed principle of right and wrong, or as G [Georgina] very justly expressed herself there is one great unerring standard, by which we must all govern our conduct – that standard is undoubtedly the doctrine of Christ as recalled by his divine mission.

His essay emphasises that he was a humane man and shows that although his philosophy had not succeeded in Ireland he had not become cynical: 'I entirely agree in the opinion that cruelty or rather barbarity towards those who are in subjection under us is a real want of virtue – it is indeed odious and unprincipled – kindness and humanity are among the first of Christian virtues.' His opinions about women and marriage show some surprisingly modern attitudes, but with Georgina for a wife perhaps his views are less unexpected. She had been brought up by her mother to believe that women were as talented as men; therefore in her marriage she expected to be treated as an equal partner. The Duke wrote:

> Men are too apt to treat women as mere children . . . Man should consider woman as his equal in point of intellect and judgement, as his superior in many of the best feelings of nature and as his inferior only in strength of body, in fortitude of nerves and contempt of personal danger – a man should conduct himself towards the softer and more amiable sex not only with affection, but with kindness, not only with kindness but with confidence, and that, not common place ordinary confidence but an unlimited and unreserved reliance in all her ties of Love, Friendship and Esteem.

The Duke moved from general principles to a detailed analysis of Georgina's personality, and his description suggests that their time in Ireland had strengthened their marriage. John had been made fully aware of his wife's multi-faceted character and clearly he had been impressed by her performance both in public and private. After four years of marriage, he was still very much in love with Georgina. His reflections give a real insight into both her character and their relationship:

> Of all women existing, I know none more capable of enjoying happiness than Georgiana. Her heart and mind

are excellent and she feels and appreciates the true value of virtue . . . She has a just sense of the blessings of religion, when her natural flow of animal spirits will allow her to think seriously on a subject . . . her mind warmly and actively benevolent is incessantly seeking the welfare of others and the interests and comforts of those she loves become the perpetual pursuit of her life – never did I see a woman so full of accomplishments of talents and all the requisites which constitute the charm and polish of society, so far from vanity she seems unconscious of her own powers of pleasing; and without a grain of selfishness in her whole composition, if she sees those around her pleased, happy and content her whole soul seems satisfied with the good which results whilst she appears scarcely sensible it is of her own creating.

However, although the Duke adored the Duchess, he was not completely uncritical. He was aware of her faults but he understood her well enough to be able to excuse them. He blamed them on her 'warm and ardent nature, and a too exquisite sensibility'. His description of the effects of her quick temper conjures up a picture of a couple that had heated arguments but soon forgot them:

Her imagination full of vivacity, she sometimes betrays a degree of impatience inseparable from a warm Temper, if others are more torpid in their ideas, or in their powers of apprehension than herself; but the moment she sees she gives pain, she checks herself, as nothing is more repugnant to her nature than to hurt the feelings of even the most blest individual.

John concluded his reflections with a declaration of love and a promise to Georgina: 'She is beloved by all who know her intrinsic worth, by none more than by myself, and if I can make her happy whilst God gives me health and strength, she shall be so.'

For both Georgina and the Duke their marriage was the cornerstone of their lives and because that foundation was secure they were able to build on it to reach out to other people. On their return from Ireland, the couple began to establish the friendships and social routines that were to continue for the rest of their marriage.

The Bedfords' greatest friends were Lord and Lady Holland. Henry Richard Fox, who became the third baron Holland when he was just a year old, was very close to his uncle Charles James Fox. The older man's political principles were to guide him throughout his life. The Duke of Bedford shared this commitment to Fox and his policies and this was the reason for the initial bond between the two men.

When he was twenty-one, Lord Holland met and fell in love with Elizabeth, Lady Webster. The daughter of a Jamaican planter, she was married at the age of sixteen to an aged Sussex baronet but became deeply unhappy in her marriage to the dull, older man. When she met Lord Holland the attraction was instant and powerful; inevitably, the young couple became lovers. After a divorce was granted by the House of Lords they married, but the social stigma attached to a divorcee was great and not everybody accepted the new Lady Holland. One of the first people to go out of his way to welcome her into society was the Duke of Bedford. His support when they were at their most vulnerable was never forgotten by the Hollands.

The dynamics of the foursome were complex; the Duke was closer to Lady Holland and the Duchess to Lord Holland. The Duke wrote constantly to Lady Holland for more than thirty years, confiding in her everything from his concerns about Georgina to a bout of boils he was suffering from. Lady Holland was said to resemble his first wife, although it seems she was a more attractive version. Mrs Wyndham wrote to Lady Holland: 'I think nobody can now mistake Lady John Russell for you. All the rouge that is possible to put on can never give her that degree of beauty necessary to produce a resemblance between her and you.' However, in personality, Elizabeth was more like Georgina and her feistiness evidently appealed to the Duke.

While Lady Holland's relationship with the Duke was almost maternal, the Duchess's friendship with Lord Holland was flirtatious.

It was a sophisticated, subtle relationship. He wrote flattering poems to her and in their letters they exchanged innuendos. His literary skills were widely recognised; Lord Brougham described his style as 'luminous, animated and flowing'. He was a writer and translator with a wide classical knowledge and 'a poetical felicity'. As well as homages to the Duchess, he wrote political sonnets in the style of Milton for a wider audience.

His charm and complete unselfishness won him many friends, but none were closer than Georgina. She relished spending time with him, perhaps because whenever they met, he made her laugh with his wit and skilful mimicry. Georgina wrote to him early in their friendship: 'When will you come and see us? I hope soon as I assure you, there are very few people's society in the world, that I think so agreeable as yours and Lady Holland's.' Lord Brougham's description of Lord Holland makes it easy to understand why the Duchess so enjoyed his company:

> It was in his private and domestic capacity that Lord Holland's principal charm lay. No man's conversation was more delightful. It was varied, animated, passing from grave to gay, from lively to severe; full of information, chequered with the most admirable vein of anecdote . . . His advice was excellent; he viewed with perfect calmness the whole circumstance of his friend who consulted him . . . he threw his whole soul into the discussion . . . The great delight of those who approached him was certainly in his amiable disposition of his heart, and of a temper so perfectly sweet, so perseveringly mild, that nothing could ruffle it for an instant.

The two couples gave generously to each other, not only of their time but also in frequently exchanged presents. The Duke sent a stag shot at Woburn to Lady Holland and in return received a turtle from her Jamaican estates. The theatres at Covent Garden and Drury Lane were on Bedford land, so the Duke and Duchess received complimentary tickets. As both couples enjoyed the theatre, the Duchess often made her box at the opera or theatre tickets available to her friends. As time went on, the Hollands and Bedfords found they had more and more in common as they were equally uninhibited in their enjoyment of the good things in life. They all shared what Lord Brougham described as 'a kind of indolence' and when they got together copious amounts of champagne were drunk and rich food was eaten. Sometimes they paid for their over-indulgence; Lord Holland suffered from gout while the others experienced headaches or biliousness.

The friendship was so close that the Duke and Duchess trusted the Hollands to take charge of their children. Since his mother's death, Lord John Russell had treated Holland House like a second home and Lady Holland like a mother. In 1808 the Hollands asked if they might take John with them on their trip to Spain.

Although taking a sixteen-year-old boy into a war zone might seem an unusual request, his father had few qualms about sending John. He trusted his great friends to look after his son and perhaps he thought it was worth risking an element of danger for John to have the chance to see history in the making. The Duke wrote to Lord Holland in October 1808:

> Your offer [to take John with them] is so flattering and I feel
> so thoroughly persuaded that you would not have made it if
> it had been in any wise inconvenient to you, that I have no
> hesitation in accepting it – in your society the expedition
> will I am sure be instructive and it cannot fail to be amusing
> to John and I trust you will find him not unworthy of your
> kindness.

Georgina was also delighted, believing it to be 'a plan in every respect so beneficial to him'. Her judgement was right; it turned out to be a stimulating journey for the future politician. In 1808 the Spanish had revolted against the French occupation of their country. Animosity had started the year before when Napoleon marched large numbers of French troops through the country to invade Portugal. In February of the following year French troops seized Barcelona and Pamplona and the next month the French Marshal Murat entered Madrid. The King of Spain was coerced into abdicating in favour of Napoleon's brother Joseph Bonaparte and when the Spanish in Madrid rebelled they were violently crushed by Murat.

Rebellion spread across the country. The Spanish won some victories and Joseph Bonaparte was forced to evacuate Madrid. Revolt also broke out in Portugal. When Arthur Wellesley (the future Duke of Wellington) arrived with the British expeditionary force in August, the French suffered a defeat at the Battle of Vimeiro. The French then negotiated a convention at Cintra that involved surrendering Lisbon. The British army led by Sir John Moore was sent to help the Spanish insurgents. The campaign was not clear cut; at one stage one side seemed to be winning while at another the other army seemed to be advancing. Moore was to lose his life during the fighting but eventually Wellesley drove the French out of Portugal and Spain.

The Spanish campaign caused controversy in Britain. Many of the Whig leaders, led by Grenville and Grey, disapproved of the action, but Lord and Lady Holland disagreed with their friends. They believed the battle in the Peninsula was a fight for the soul of Europe, with the British representing moderate parliamentary democracy against the French extreme democracy and military despotism. The Hollands had travelled widely in Spain and now they wanted to show solidarity with their Spanish friends' fight for liberty by joining them in their hour of need. It was a risky but exciting experience as they found themselves very close to the fighting. Their party arrived at Corunna in November 1808, but the French advance stopped them from going to Madrid so they went to Lisbon instead and then spent the winter in Cadiz. It was a fascinating experience for Lord John, seeing as he did the effects of a political crisis at close quarters.

As Georgina's family increased in size she was equally happy to leave her own children in Lady Holland's capable hands. Her eldest child, Wriothesley, was the first to stay with Lady Holland for two or three days when he was seven years old. Georgina's letter sent in preparation shows just how over-protective she was of her first born, and reveals her life-long tendency to hypochondria:

> I have sent his maid with him which will astonish you as I think him too old to be taken care of by women, his health has always been delicate, and I have been obliged to ask many questions, which I could not so well put to a man, this will explain what I fear will shock you. Pray when we meet tell me if you think that he has got the hooping [*sic*] cough. I have no doubt of it, but you will be a better judge as I do not recollect ever having had it. You will find Wrio at first very shy and frightened at everything but he is very sociable and entertaining.

Occasionally, over the years, Georgina and Lady Holland would temporarily fall out, but rows were always resolved because, in essence, they understood each other. Like Georgina, Lady Holland was beautiful, intelligent and domineering. Charles Greville wrote of her:

> She was certainly clever and she had acquired a great deal of information both from books and men, having passed her whole life amidst people remarkable for their abilities and knowledge ... She was often capricious, tyrannical and troublesome, liking to provoke and disappoint, and thwart her acquaintances, and she was often obliging, good natured and considerate to the same people.

Both Georgina and Lady Holland were used to being queen bees in their own circle, and although this could lead to clashes, it meant they developed a deep mutual respect. Greville explained:

> [Lady Holland's] love and habit of domination were both unbounded and they made her do strange and often unwarrantable things ... and though she liked to have people at her orders and who would defer to her and obey

her, she both liked and respected those who were not afraid
of her and who treated her with spirit and freedom.

The Hollands often visited Woburn and the Bedfords were equally
frequent guests at Holland House in Kensington. Lady Holland's salon
was famous for the fascinating mixture of people it brought together.
Lord Brougham wrote that the liberal hospitality of the house made it
'the resort not only of the most interesting persons composing English
society, literary, philosophical and political, but also of all those classes
who ever visited this country from abroad'.

The drawing room was dominated by a very vicious, fat cat who on
occasions was known to lash out at visitors, giving them a savage
scratch; apparently, the only effective deterrent was a pinch of snuff.
Its mistress's temperament was equally unpredictable; the reception
Lady Holland gave her guests depended on her mood. In contrast, her
servants were always treated with caring consideration so it was often
said that her staff were much better off than her guests. Charles Greville
described what it was like to visit Holland House:

> The tableau of the house is this – Before dinner Lady
> Holland affecting illness and almost dissolution, but with a
> very respectable appetite, and after dinner in high force and
> vigour; Lord Holland, with his chalk-stones and unable to
> walk, lying on his couch in very good spirits and talking
> away; Luttrell and Rogers walking about, ever and anon
> looking despairingly at the clock and making short
> excursions from the drawing room; Allen surly and
> disputatious, poring over the newspapers ... Such is the
> social despotism of this strange house which presents an
> odd mixture of luxury and constraint, of enjoyment physical
> and intellectual, with an alloy of small desagrements ...
> Though everybody who goes there finds something to abuse
> or ridicule in the mistress of the house, or its ways, all
> continue to go; all like it more or less; and whenever, by
> death of either, it shall come to an end, a vacuum will be

made in society which nothing will supply. It is the house of all Europe; the world will suffer by the loss; and it may with truth be said that it will 'eclipse the gaiety of nations'.

The Duke and Duchess were not the only regulars at Holland House. John Allen, the Hollands' librarian, was 'an essential and remarkable ingredient' in their circle. He had first joined the household as a young Scottish physician in 1802, when the Hollands were travelling to Spain. He soon became a permanent inmate of Holland House as the librarian. A very learned man who wrote regularly for the *Edinburgh Review*, he added to the intellectual stimulus of the salon, his strong powers of argument and his 'certain irritability of temper and impatience of contradiction' guaranteed heated debates.

Although Macaulay claimed Lady Holland treated Allen no better than 'a Negro slave', he became so much part of the family that he carved at her dinner parties. Charles Greville wrote: 'Lord Holland treated him with uniform consideration, affection and amenity, she [Lady Holland] worried, bullied, flattered, and cajoled him by turns.' He was known as 'Lady Holland's Atheist' because he was a fierce unbeliever and if faith was discussed he gave an irreligious turn to the conversation. Lady Holland preferred to keep the conversation on politics, poetry and philosophy and off religion. Although the Hollands were sceptics, all views were tolerated around their table and under their roof no one was ever insulted for having a different opinion.

The Hollands and Bedfords saw even more of each other when Lord Holland inherited Ampthill, the neighbouring estate to Woburn. Catherine of Aragon had lived there after her divorce from Henry VIII, and now a visit to the Hollands' house became an integral part of a stay at Woburn.

In an era when filling your leisure time was treated as a full-time job, the Duke and Duchess's year was broken up by visits to other aristocrats. House parties could last for weeks with different visitors coming and going. The Duke particularly enjoyed shooting parties at Lord Coke's home, Holkham Hall in Norfolk, commenting, 'In all Europe I found nothing like England; and in all England nothing like

Holkham.' Coke was a delightful host and he invited many interesting guests to his 43,000-acre estate. Perhaps the most striking feature in his elegant house was the large pink marble hall decorated with pink and white marble fluted colonnades. As a connoisseur of the arts, the Duke enjoyed his friend's superb collection of pictures, sculptures and antiques that rivalled his own growing gallery at Woburn.

The Bedfords were also regular visitors at Lord Grey's estate at Howick and almost every year, on their way to Scotland, the Duke and Duchess stayed with the Whig politician and his wife. The Greys, like the Bedfords, had a large family; Charles and his wife Mary Elizabeth had eight sons and five daughters. The two families enjoyed each other's company, and the children as well as their parents became great friends.

Georgina relished her visits to Scotland. Sir Walter Scott described her enthusiasm:

> I have seldom seen any person so happy at revisiting their native country. She was quite ready with the damsel in the old song,

> 'To throw off her gallant shoes
> Made of the Spanish leather,
> And to put on the Highland brogues
> To skip among the heather.'

When not staying with the Gordon family, the Duke and Duchess visited the Duke of Argyll at Inverary. Known as 'the Castle of Indolence' it was a decadent place to stay. Lady Holland wrote after a visit:

> Upon the whole it is a most princely domain . . . the only objection to the mode of life is the extraordinary lateness of the hours and the consequent inability of doing anything . . . As late as half past seven in the morning, I have heard the billiards at work by T. Sheridan and Mr Chester.

Although each aristocratic house offered different attractions, Woburn house parties were judged to be particularly luxurious and lively. Lady Holland wrote that Woburn was 'both grand and comfortable', and during a visit guests could expect a mixture of politics and pleasure. After the Duke's return from Ireland, his home became an unofficial headquarters for the Whig party. The leading politicians – Grey, Lauderdale, Whitbread, Brougham and Tierney – could often be found discussing the issues of the day at Woburn. The Duke, although no longer active in politics, was still influential and he had it in his power to allocate parliamentary seats. He gave advice to the Whig leaders on men and measures, particularly on the Irish problem as this remained his main political concern. He wrote to Lord Grey in 1808: 'It is essential that the Catholicks [*sic*] of Ireland should know that they have a firm, zealous and united body of friends among the leading men in this country.' A year later, he wrote: 'Do me the justice to believe that there is no object nearer to my heart than to see re-established that harmony of co-operation in Ireland.' The Duke enjoyed getting together 'real friends of liberty and Reform' and he was soon lobbying for parliamentary reform as well as Catholic emancipation.

At Woburn, politicians, actors and aristocrats were thrown together and all were expected to take part in the many activities on offer. The Duke took his shooting seriously and invited other keen sportsmen, including Lord Spencer and Lord Jersey, to join him. After a day's shooting, the whole party would get together in the evening for 'rows, festivities and masquerades'. The champagne and the conversation flowed endlessly. After a particularly splendid dinner for Georgina's birthday, Lord Holland's sister Caroline Fox wrote a poem to the Duchess that captures her personality and the atmosphere she created:

> Laureats for one poor butt of sack
> Yearly are forced their brains to rack
> To praise some worthless King, and
> We on this auspicious Day
> Tho' flushed with bright Champagne delay
> Our beauteous Queen to sing.

And yet to perfect form and face
To all that o'er this cheerful place
Sheds joy and ease and mirth
To wit that every hour beguiles
To fairy feet and heavenly smiles;
This very Day gave birth.

No form without a soul is thine
No face without a heart,
The Gods who worthy goods dispense
To use them gave thee youth and sense
And goodness to impart.

The Muses fondest Dreams are true
For twenty years age, when you
Lay smiling on her knee
What more than beauty, rank and wealth
And to enjoy them heart and health
Could she have hoped to see?

Then oft mid sessions and debates
Contending parties, falling states
May Bedford's day record
So may we leave our toilsome life
Fore go our cares, forget our strife
And turn a time on her.

And if indeed year after year
One much disposed to Woburn cheer
Your Grace desires to see;
If one be wanting in your train
To guzzle Turtle, swill champagne
Pray send in haste for me.

Despite Miss Fox's fulsome praise, Georgina's entertaining was not to everyone's taste. Frances, Lady Shelley, certainly did not enjoy her visit to Woburn, complaining that the Duke lived 'in the languour created by the dearth of intellectual amusement'. She wrote critically to Lady Spencer about her stay:

> We were very late, and a formal reception prepared the way for a silent dinner of twenty people. You will guess from this that I now know what your 'Noah's Ark' is, for they were all in pairs, and I the solitary snipe. During dinner everyone whispered to his next neighbour, and I was obliged to do the same, from the dread of hearing my own voice. But when evening came, God knows, I had no longer the same fear, for a scene of such vulgar noise and riot, I never beheld!

Once dinner was over, the Duchess went to breast-feed her baby after an uninhibited discussion on the subject with her guests, both male and female. Everyone then divided into different groups; in one room some of the gentlemen played billiards while in another Lady Asgill reclined on a sofa with Sir Thomas Graham (the future Lord Lynedoch, a soldier and neighbour of the Bedfords) at her feet. In the next room guests played whist while Lady Jane and Miss Russell (Georgina's nieces) destroyed 'The Creation' by playing it out of tune on a harp and piano. Lady Shelley continued:

> Alas! It was chaos still! And, in the long gallery, a few pairs were dispersed on sofas; others sauntered from room to room. I joined the latter, and talked of furniture, china and ormolu, till the subject was exhausted. I was bored to death, and 'triste à mourir'; the tête à tête forming a barrier to the billiard room [Lady Asgill and Sir Thomas]. At last I established myself at a writing table in the card room. Scarcely was I seated, when the Duchess entered; and collecting her romping force of girls and young men, they

all seized cushions and began pelting the whist players. They defended themselves, by throwing the cards and candles at her head; but the Duchess succeeded in overthrowing the table, and a regular battle ensued with cushions, oranges and apples. The romp was at last ended by Lady Jane being nearly blinded by an apple that hit her in the eye! Shelley, before that, had been almost smothered by the female romps getting him on the ground and pomelling him with cushions.

The party continued with Blind Man's Buff but the innocent horse-play was far too rough for Lady Shelley's delicacy and she slipped off to bed in disgust. She was as shocked by the morals as the manners of the house party because Georgina allocated bedrooms to make liaisons as easy as possible for her more promiscuous friends. Lady Shelley complained to her mother about the

> . . . disgusting familiarity of Lady Asgill and Sir Thomas Graham, who though in the field a hero, is in love a dotard. To give you a specimen – Lady Asgill yesterday said to me, in speaking of the house at Woburn: 'We have the apartments next yours. They all communicate, which is extremely comfortable. Sir Thomas's is next yours, I have the next and my sister, Mrs Wilmot the third.' . . . You have seen too much of the world to be surprised at anything, but to me this parade was both new and disgusting.

Georgina had to juggle life as a leading hostess with frequent pregnancies. It was not always easy and sometimes she suffered from tiredness or even fainted during long dinners. In 1808 a fourth son, Francis John, was born, adding to the burgeoning brood. She doted on all her children and like most mothers thought her offspring were exceptional. She wrote of Wriothesley: 'His disposition is really heavenly and his upright and strictly honourable feelings are really wonderful at so early an age and give fair promise of what he will be should he be spared to us.'

Although Georgina loved her sons, she desperately wanted a daughter so it was a time of great celebration when in 1810 she gave birth to a baby girl. Georgiana was born at five o'clock in the morning on 23 June; it was an easy birth so the Duke was not detained from his shooting for too long. The day after he wrote: 'The Duchess is now quite well and my mind is so perfectly at ease that I shall go to Holkham tomorrow and return the middle of the week.'

As usual, the Duchess insisted on breast-feeding her baby but by December constantly nursing her daughter was affecting her health. The Duke wrote to Lady Holland: 'She has been far from well and . . . fainted dead whilst we were at dinner, but rallied again with her accustomed spirits and came back into the room, only to faint a second time – she is still very languid, but I cannot prevail upon her to wean her little girl.'

Coming from such a matriarchal family, it was natural for Georgina to become closer to her daughters than her sons. The happiness she felt about having a daughter of her own is evident in a letter written to Lady Holland when little Georgiana was eleven months old: 'I never saw Woburn in such beauty the scenery really is like my idea of fairy land and my little girl to me represents Mistress of those fairies, she is so elegant, lively and beautiful; forgive this rhapsody.'

Although Georgina appreciated Woburn's beauty, its stately grandeur and centuries of Russell history meant that it was not a place where she could make a lasting impression. She needed another outlet for her creative, home-making talents. Perhaps remembering her own happy childhood holidays in Scotland, Georgina and the Duke decided to create a rural retreat where they could escape formality and live a 'simple life'. Despite their extensive estates in Devon and Cornwall, the Russells did not have a family house in the West Country, and the Duke and Duchess decided it was time to build one. In 1809 Georgina found the perfect place near Tavistock in Devon. Deep in the Tamar valley, bordered by a river and wooded hills, she decided it was here they should create a shooting and fishing lodge in the latest picturesque style. Although miles from her beloved homeland, the view was reminiscent of the Highlands and no doubt this was part of the appeal for the Duchess.

In the autumn of 1810, Georgina and her four young sons laid the foundation stone for Endsleigh House. The inscription reads:

> Endsleigh Cottage was built and a residence created in this sequestered valley by John, Duke of Bedford, the spot having previously been chosen from the natural and picturesque beauties which surround it by Georgiana, Duchess of Bedford. The first stone of the building was laid by her four eldest sons, Wriothesley, Edward, Charles Fox and Francis John, Sept 7, 1810.

This home, more than any other, was to become the Duke and Duchess's special place. In its creation the Duke indulged Georgina, allowing her to let her imagination run wild to create the ultimate picturesque landscape. The result was an enduring success; Endsleigh is considered to be one of the finest examples of the picturesque movement in England. This picturesque was a standard of taste lying between beauty, which was just pretty, and the sublime, containing qualities of awe and danger. William Gilpin, in his *Three Essays on the Picturesque*, defined it as that which stimulates the imagination to reverie or admiration. Endsleigh, with its rugged rocks and fast-flowing river, conformed to this ideal of a landscape needing a certain irregularity and roughness to offset the prettiness of a cosy cottage.

The most fashionable landscape gardener Humphry Repton, who had already worked for the Bedfords at Woburn, and the top architect Jeffry Wyatt (later Wyatville) were employed to turn Georgina's ideas into reality. It was one of Repton's last works and he devoted a chapter of his *Fragments on the Theory and Practice of Landscape Gardening* to Endsleigh.

Wyatt had already made his reputation with his period restorations and additions to historic mansions. He had worked at Longleat and Wollaton but later he was to become even more famous for his romantic remodelling of Windsor Castle for George IV. The success of that project was to earn him the suffix 'ville' and a knighthood.

Although at first there was competition between the two men – Repton and his sons had hoped to design the house as well as the garden – the end product was a perfect combination of both their talents. Repton later wrote:

> With respect to the manner in which the design has been executed, I shall only say, it is such as will do credit to the name of Wyatt when time shall have harmonized the raw tints of new materials. The design and outline are so truly picturesque that I must regret my inability to do them justice.

Endsleigh is a cottage orné (a building consciously imitating the careless rustic style of the vernacular), reflecting the fashion for cottages that had begun at the end of the eighteenth century. During the Napoleonic Wars, aristocrats imagined that living in a cottage was a romantic way to escape the stresses of formal society by getting back to nature in an idealised, sophisticated way. I.C. Loudon observed in the *Magazine of Gardening*: 'It is one of the enjoyments of those habituated to live in a style of high art and refinement to take occasional refuge in the contrast produced by comparative artlessness and simplicity.'

The house took four years to complete and work on the garden and other buildings was to continue for many more years. When the Bedfords first visited the site, the original thatched farmhouse was there; although it was very basic it was in the right position so it was decided that the new house would be on the same site, thus capitalising on the spectacular view of the Tamar. Repton wrote:

> The first question that obviously occurred was, what style will best accord with the landscape (embosomed in all the sublimity of umbrageous majesty) . . . the good taste of the noble proprietor was directed by what he saw. An irregular

cottage backed by a hill and beautiful group of trees presented an object so picturesque that it was impossible to wish it removed or replaced in any other style of building that architecture has invented, viz., a castle or an abbey or a palace, and so applicable to the scenery as this cottage, or rather group of rural buildings.

The house was planned to suit the Bedfords' lifestyle and was specially designed to accommodate a large family. It was made up of two 'cottage' blocks, one for the Duke and Duchess and their guests and the other for their children. Built of Portland stone and local wood, the main house and the children's wing were linked by a curved terrace and rustic colonnade. Reflecting Georgina's hands-on attitude to motherhood, her study overlooks the nursery wing, with its own terrace and pond fed from a pair of lions'-head fountains. While the Duchess wrote letters, she could watch her growing brood sailing model boats on the pond.

Every detail of the house had to be perfect, from the sheep's knuckles used to form the cobblestones on the terrace to the oak tree trunks acting as rustic colonnades. Again there were echoes of Scotland; gatehouses in a similar style could be seen near the Duchess of Gordon's farmhouse at Kinrara. Ornate but attractive, Wyatt added low eaves, gables and dormers to enhance the outside of the house. In Neale's *Views of Seats* the effect is described in detail: 'The woodbine, the ivy and honeysuckle grow along the walls and form natural festoons above the windows: under the shelter of these plants birds build their nests and cheer the scene with their notes.' The inside of the house was intended to be equally harmonious with the landscape: 'The furniture corresponds in all respects with the exquisite simplicity of the habitation. The internal decorations are perfectly appropriate.' The entrance hall had three large maps of Devon, Cornwall and the Bedford estates, a fireplace with polished brass shields of the Russell arms and a bust of the fifth Duke presiding over the scene. The ante-room and drawing room faced south and looked out over the grass terrace. To create the impression of the inside and outside merging, there were doors on to the verandah and the rooms were painted green, stone and white. The drawing room had a large looking glass over the fireplace and Glover watercolours on the wall. In the cabinet the Duchess kept her china collection. Homeliness as well as style was important to the Bedfords. Around the room chairs, couches and ottomans were arranged with chintz cushions scattered on them; there were work tables for the day and satinwood card tables for the evening's entertainment. Double doors from the drawing room opened into the book room that was stocked with books in many languages; guests could read their chosen volumes sitting in the bay window looking over the garden. Over the fireplace was a picture by Mrs Wilmot of 'The Fall of Phaeton' and in the middle of the room was a fine octagonal Gothic table.

Throughout the house, decorations reflected the Russell family and the area's history. In the small room within the library were the armorial bearings of Ordulph, Earl of Devonshire, founder of Tavistock Abbey, and the arms of the Abbot of Tavistock. The dining room was panelled to two-thirds of its height and the upper walls were painted in *trompe l'oeil* to continue the panelling effect, with small shields of the arms of the aristocratic families linked to the Russells decorating the walls. The ancestral theme was echoed in the mullioned windows that had stained-glass representations of the armorial bearings of different Earls of Bedford and their wives.

In the upstairs bedrooms, Georgina's feminine taste could be seen in abundance. The Duke and Duchess had separate bedrooms with their own dressing rooms, decorated in delicate rosebud chintz and simply furnished. There were four more bedrooms for guests, including the Chinese room with its own dressing room. It had hand-painted chinoiserie wallpaper and a daybed upholstered in a Chinese pattern placed next to the large window so that guests could enjoy the view along the grass terrace. The other visitors' rooms were the canopy bedroom, green room and pink room.

Like the house, the gardens combined style and comfort. A carriage accident in 1811 which left Repton in a wheelchair made him particularly aware of practical as well as aesthetic requirements. He wrote that he regretted

> . . . that the most picturesque site to which I have been
> professionally consulted should have been reserved to so
> late a period of my life, that I could only become acquainted
> with its recondite beauties, by being carried to places
> otherwise inaccessible to a cripple.

He had to rely on a local surveyor, John Hutchins, to prepare a plan,
and his final design at Endsleigh was affected by his changed view of
the world:

> Having provided against the rigours of winter I will not be
> unmindful of that winter of life which must alike assail the
> cottage and the palace . . . Having myself lost the power of
> gathering a flower or picking up a fossil from the ground, I
> have found great comfort in banks raised to the height of
> three or four feet on a face of ornamental pebbles to bring
> nearer to the eye those lesser rock-plants or delicate blossoms
> which are too minute to be seen on the ground.

The house's rustic verandahs opened out on to a long grass terrace
edged by a huge herbaceous and shrub border, backed by flowering
and evergreen trees. Nearby were the Upper and Lower Georgies,
scenic walks named after the Duchess, where she could stroll with her
family and friends. There was an arboretum where every tree was
carefully chosen by the Duke and Duchess to enhance the landscape.
It still contains more than a thousand specimen trees of arboricultural
and historical importance. A rose walk was created by a straight gravel
path, edged with slates and enclosed by a series of ironwork arches
supporting climbing roses and wisteria. At the end of the rose walk a
shell house was built. Overlooking the Tamar, it was used as a summer-
house but it also served as a 'grotto-like receptacle for specimens of the
fossils and ores abounding in the neighbourhood'.

Across the river, nestling in Wareham Wood, a boatman's cottage
was created. Although it was not regularly inhabited, every morning a
woodman lit a fire so that there would be smoke coming out of the

chimney. It was purely for picturesque effect; Repton believed the smoke was essential to enliven the view.

Like Marie Antoinette, Georgina wanted to play at farming so a miniature thatched dairy, complete with a bubbling fountain in the middle, marble slabs and marble troughs for holding the milk, was built by the Dairy Dell pond. Further away from the house, to recreate the romance of nineteenth-century Alpine travel, a Swiss cottage was constructed on a hill overlooking the Tamar. It had 'a sort of Alpine garden' and Swiss furniture and tableware made of wood so that visitors could sit and enjoy a splendid view back towards the house.

No expense was spared in the house or garden as the complete set of bills for the building of Endsleigh reveal. The twenty-eight sheep's leg bones alone cost £3 10s. (approximately £100), while bringing all the stone from Portland involved major expenditure. Some critical contemporaries estimated that the overall cost of creating Endsleigh was £120,000 (nearly £4 million).

Over the years, Georgina and the Duke were to use Endsleigh when they wanted to escape from the stuffiness of stately home life. From the moment they drove in their carriage down the drive, beneath a canopy of oaks and rare conifers with rhododendrons and camellias on either side, they were entering a private, magical world. It was an enchanting place to share with only the most intimate of their friends.

The house and gardens soon became famous and were known by contemporaries as 'the garden paradise of the west'. Stockdale in his *History of Devon* wrote: 'The singular beauties of this plan, its sequestered situation and distance from the busy scenes of life excite universal admiration.' A poem in Neale's *Views of Seats* was written in praise of its attractions:

> The beauties, ENDSLEIGH! In the lonely vale,
> Allure the heart to love thy blest retreat,
> Of noble dignity and grace the seat,
> Fann'd by the pinions of the western gale,
> Thy winter smiles, serene in mantle green,
> And earliest birds of spring resume their lay;

Cheer'd by the vernal show'r and sunny ray,
There the first blossom of the year is seen.
Thy herds and flocks in fertile pasture rove
On Devon's hills, near Cornwall's sylvan bow'rs;
And down thy banks, the lovely queen of flow'rs,
The summer-rose breathes odours round the grove:
Beneath whose borders echoing Tamar flows,
And sooths the weary mind to calm repose.

Although a visit was supposed to involve living the simple life, Georgina expected the standard of food and comfort to be the same as at Woburn. We get an insight into the lifestyle she created from the surviving detailed bills for the running of the household. A retinue of servants travelled down from Bedfordshire to ensure a seamless service for the Duke and Duchess. Travelling on subscription coaches, boasting a speed of seven miles an hour and 'hills avoided and distance saved', it took them just over a day to arrive in Plymouth. It was an expensive exercise, costing £7 2s. 6d (about £231) for one kitchen maid to travel from Woburn. Nor was it cheap paying the local staff; the salary of one gamekeeper was forty guineas (£1,320) a year while it cost 14s. to employ a man for three days to shift feathers in the beds to ensure a sound night's sleep for the residents.

Although Georgina was extravagant, she was a thoughtful mistress. Bills show that she was the one, not the Duke, who ordered a pair of boots for the shepherd and gamekeeper at a cost of £2 (£66) and she also made sure that the shepherd was seen by an apothecary and given medicine when he was ill.

During a stay at Endsleigh, guests could look forward to sumptuous meals. Salmon, oysters, duck, lamb, beef and veal were on the menu accompanied by white and purple broccoli, savoy cabbages, early stone turnip and early Cornish cabbage. There was certainly no shortage of fresh fruit, with nectarines, peaches, melons, plums, gooseberries, raspberries, pears, blackcurrants and redcurrants bought in large amounts. The theme of making the most of fresh produce was continued in the china; meals were served on a specially designed dinner service in the shape of bunches of asparagus, cauliflowers, cabbages and other fruit and vegetables. To enhance the convivial atmosphere, wine, port and Madeira were brought in from Plymouth to wash down the delicious dinners.

Days were spent fishing in the river or shooting, while on some afternoons boat trips were organised with six boatmen hired to take the party down the Tamar to Plymouth. If the weather was bad, plenty of reading matter was needed. On one visit, the Duke bought two volumes of the *History of Cornwall* while Georgina joined the Tavistock subscription library – evidently the Duchess borrowed books as she was fined for having several overdue. The Duke kept in touch with what was going on in the outside world with local newspapers, including the *Exeter and Plymouth Gazette* and *Western Luminary Weekly*. In the evenings the party would play cards or listen to music. Usually guests entertained each other but one year an organist, Mrs Robson, was invited for a week to play for the guests.

Over the years, Endsleigh became a regular part of the Bedfords' seasonal migration. They usually visited their Devon estate in the spring and early summer when the garden was at its most lush and verdant. At Endsleigh, Georgina created a place where she could relax in an environment reminiscent of her beloved Highlands, but she also left an eternal monument to her faultless style.

CHAPTER FIVE

Travelling with Death

O n the surface, Georgina's life was the epitome of Regency glamour, but beneath the frivolous façade the Duchess was experiencing challenging times. In her thirties she faced death close up for the first time, but the way she coped with a series of losses revealed a resilience and strength of character which proved there was depth beneath the apparent superficiality of her life.

In April 1812 Georgina's mother died; her end matched the flamboyance of her life. She had fallen from grace because of her support for Napoleon, while her separation from her husband had left her without the status and finances she was used to. With Gordon Castle closed to her, she lived in hotels or stayed with her children in their stately homes. One of her regular haunts was Pulteney's Hotel at 105 Piccadilly and although it was not a real home it did have a certain charm. It was one of the most luxurious and fashionable hotels in London and foreign royalty stayed there when visiting the capital.

Although her political power was taken away from her, the

Duchess never lost her matriarchal position. Her children and grandchildren remained the *raison d'être* of her life and they returned her affection. They enjoyed spending time with their eccentric grandmother who, even in her early seventies, showed a determination to live life to the full. Her grandson Lord William Lennox described her last weeks:

> One evening when paying a visit to the Duchess of Gordon in her box I met the Honourable Edmund Phipps who asked me if I would like to go behind the scenes and be introduced to Madame Catalini with whom he was on the most friendly terms. I, then a Westminster boy, was delighted with the idea, and the moment the Opera was over we hastened to pay our respects to the Queen of Song. Upon returning to the box the Duchess, my grandmother made the most tender inquiries after the great singer whom she was anxious to engage for a concert about to be given for charitable purposes. A few weeks afterwards the Duchess was attacked with a serious illness from which she never recovered. She was staying at the Pulteney Hotel, Piccadily . . . where the day before her decease she requested to see as many of her grand-children as were within reach. I and my brother Frederick were taken from Westminster to bid her a long farewell; up to the last she was the kindest-hearted creature imaginable, and as we shook hands with her, she with a faint smile placed a couple of guineas in our palms and uttered a prayer for our welfare.

For the three days before her death, Jane lay in state, playing out her dying scene with all the careful costuming and stage management of a true drama queen. Like a dying monarch, she received family and friends for the last time dressed in crimson velvet. During these difficult days Georgina tried to continue as normally as possible, and instead of grieving by her mother's death-bed she filled her time with distractions. She intended to go to the theatre with the

Duke to see *The Hypocrite* but she did not want the play's title attached to her, so her visit was kept secret to prevent critics from calling her callous.

The Duchess of Gordon seems to have died at peace with herself and the world. In her final hours she had an old Scots Presbyterian minister with her and a few hours before her death she received the sacrament. Always a woman who planned ahead and never a person to underestimate her own importance, she left detailed instructions for what was to turn into virtually a state funeral. Her hearse was drawn all the way from London to Scotland by six jet-black horses; then, once it reached the Duke's Highland territory, every opportunity was provided for her faithful 'subjects' to pay their last respects. Her body lay in state first at Dalwhinnie Inn and then at the Inn of Pitmain. She had made it clear that she wished to be buried at Kinrara, in a field she had planted out herself, on the banks of the Spey, and a huge crowd followed the hearse from Pitmain to this final resting place. In death, as in life, she was proud of her greatest achievements – her daughters' marriages – so carved on the obelisk, above the plain marble slab of her grave, were the names of her children and their illustrious partners.

Although her mother's behaviour must have at times caused Georgina acute embarrassment, her nerves were severely shaken by the loss of the woman who had so dominated her early life. The Duchess of Gordon had been an overpowering character but she had always been supportive of her children and there was no doubt that she adored them and took a genuine pride in their successes. Her death must have left a massive vacuum for all her children, but perhaps particularly for Georgina because there were so many similarities between mother and daughter. They were on the same wavelength, which meant that although other people might misunderstand them, they rarely misunderstood each other. Ever sensitive to his wife's needs, the Duke took her away to Brighton for a change of scene.

Georgina was not the only person who was very distressed by the Duchess of Gordon's death. Her brother George also found the world a very different place without his possessive mother but, in a way, he was liberated by his loss. A few months after the funeral he finally married a suitable young woman called Elizabeth Brodie.

In his mid-forties, George was no longer the handsome man of his youth. Elizabeth Grant described him as 'now in the decline of his rackety life, overwhelmed with debts, sated with pleasure, tired of fashion'. His bride, although young, was no beauty, but her wealth and good nature provided the emotional and financial stability he needed. Her father, Alexander Brodie, a wealthy India merchant, paid off George's debts and his new wife managed his finances skilfully. Although Elizabeth was shy and at first socially inept, she was a good wife and her strong moral principles and devout religious faith kept George under control. The only thing she did not give her husband was an heir and, as the marriage was childless, Lord Huntly was to be the last Duke of Gordon.

Jane had been a very involved grandmother, and some of her grandchildren were also greatly affected by her death. Lady Jane Montagu had lived with her grandmother since her mother, the Duchess of Manchester, had run off with the gamekeeper. Now the Duchess of Gordon was dead, Jane returned to her father's house at Kimbolton to live with her sisters and their governess, but she was not happy in her old home and suffered from depression which she called 'the blue devils'. When Georgina became aware that her niece was suffering, she came to the rescue and took Lady Jane into her care. The young girl enjoyed the informal fun of her aunt's home and evidently got on well with her cousins and her uncle, whom she called 'Johnny Duke'.

Jane was a very attractive young woman and Georgina's stepson William soon fell in love with her. He described her as 'Beautiful as the morning sun – with a temper more heavenly sweet than ever was known. I never met her equal. But she is destined for a Duke at least.' In fact, her destiny was to be a tragic one. A year after her grandmother's death she started to cough up blood and consumption was diagnosed.

Georgina was 'under the greatest distress of mind possible' at the news. She was physically unwell herself at the time because constant child-bearing and caring for the latest additions to 'the rabbit warren', as the Duke called it, was taking its toll. In 1812 she had given birth to a second daughter, Louisa, and within a year she was pregnant again. This time all did not go smoothly. In a bid to boost their health, Georgina and her niece spent some time in Devon and then travelled to the Isle of Wight, where they stayed for several months at St Boniface, Ryde. During that time, neither woman was well. Jane had an 'alarming and serious attack', while the Duchess was so ill that she was forced to give up walking.

In September the Duke spoke to the Duchess's London doctor, Clarke, about her difficult pregnancy. Her husband and her physician wanted her to travel to London for the birth so that she would have the best medical advice nearby but Georgina refused because she liked the Isle of Wight. She wrote to Lady Holland: 'This is a most delightful spot but would not suit you, the roads are bad and excepting the butcher once a week I have not seen a soul since we have been here. I never saw a place I liked better.'

In early October Georgina began to haemorrhage. The bleeding continued for more than twenty-four hours and became increasingly violent. On 6 October 1813, after a severe and painful labour, she gave birth to a son but the following day he died; he had survived for just forty hours. During that time he suffered from repeated fits but his constitution was so strong that he kept reviving, which prolonged his suffering and made Georgina distraught. The doctors said that although he was more than two months premature he was very large for his age. The Duke consoled himself that under the circumstances 'it is best as it is' and he wrote: 'I rejoice for the Duchess' sake that he was released from his sufferings.' However, Georgina was physically and mentally weakened by his death and as the Duke explained to Lady Holland, seeing his suffering had been 'too much for her anxious mind to bear – she is much affected and very low'.

Instead of wallowing in self-pity for long, the Duchess was soon channelling her energies away from grieving for her son and into planning a trip abroad. It was hoped that a warmer climate would improve Jane's health and so the Duchess wanted to go to the south of Europe, particularly Spain. As Lady Holland knew the area well,

Georgina turned to her for advice on everything from what clothes to take to what travelling beds they would need. The Bedfords travelled well prepared. Although the Duchess could not resist buying a glamorous black astrakhan travelling cape, she also made many practical purchases, including four Wellington beds and cots for the children, complete with lace mosquito nets. Always concerned about her family's health, Georgina invested in a large mahogany medicine chest, which was stocked with a range of lethal-sounding concoctions worthy of a travelling pharmacy; there were bottles of 'James' Fever Powder', 'Ague of Ammonia Juice', sulphuric acid and even a vial of quicksilver with chalk. Wary of foreign water supplies, the Duke ordered hampers of Bristol mineral water to take with them.

The Bedfords decided to take their daughters with them, but to leave their young sons behind, so Lord Tavistock, the Duke's eldest son, was left in charge of his stepbrothers. The excitement of the trip was just what the Duchess needed to distract her from her loss. The Duke wrote to Lady Holland:

> The Duchess is going on well. She has gone thro a great deal, poor soul! More than I thought her strength would be able to bear, but I trust she will now do well . . . I think before the expiration of a month we shall be on our way to Spain – the thoughts of this seems to give the Duchess spirits.

The Duke and Duchess took with them on their travels an entourage of nineteen people including a cook, a doctor, a tutor for the children and a companion, John Nicholas Fazakerley, an MP who was a friend of Lord and Lady Holland. They also took a cow because Georgina insisted upon giving her children fresh milk. To make sure the children were kept entertained during this Grand Tour, Georgina ordered dolls, a doll's house, an alphabet and a pack of cards for her daughters. The Duke bought a mini-library of books to take with them. There were the latest volumes about the political situation in Spain and Portugal for him to read, while *Don Quixote*, the latest poem by Lord Byron and Inchbald's books on the theatre and *Farces* were for Georgina.

The party set sail from Portsmouth in November 1813. The Napoleonic Wars were still raging and ships were in short supply so they had to travel on one of the King's ships, the *Volunteer Frigate*. The Captain, Waldegrave, was faultlessly considerate to them throughout the journey and Georgina wrote to Lady Holland that his 'never ceasing attention to us from the moment we arrived at Portsmouth till we landed . . . is beyond expressing and indeed can never be repaid'. After a good passage lasting eight days they arrived in Lisbon where Lord William joined them. William had grown into a handsome and charming young man. Choosing to become a soldier, he had fought in the Peninsular War and served as the Duke of Wellington's aide-de-camp in Spain. After a few days' rest they set sail again for Cadiz; although it was a calm journey, the whole party were very sick except Lady Jane and little Georgy.

An epidemic that had killed 1,500 people had been raging in Cadiz for the last three months, but by the time the Bedfords arrived it had subsided. The Duke believed there was no longer a risk of contagion so they were able to land and then travel to the small town of Chiclana nearby. Although the climate was 'heavenly', mild and sunny with little rain, they were not impressed with the area. Georgina wrote 'the country is very ugly and this place most melancholy'. Situated on the south of the Gaditanian Bay, Chiclana's landscape was made up of sandy beaches, pinewoods and salt marshes. The quiet town of whitewashed buildings and ancient churches offered scant intellectual or cultural stimulation for the Duchess.

With British and Spanish troops working together in the Peninsular War, the French were facing defeat. Since the beginning of 1812 Wellington had been advancing through Spain. Although there were fewer British than French troops, Wellington was able to push forward because the Spanish regular and guerrilla forces were engaging the French armies in battles elsewhere in Spain. During the summer, Wellington won a decisive victory at the Battle of Salamanca. Over the winter events moved further in Britain's favour since Napoleon's disastrous invasion of Russia meant that he did not have extra troops to send.

In the early summer of 1813, Wellington returned to the offensive and in June he won a vital battle at Vitoria. By mid-July he had reached the Pyrenees where he achieved another victory. By the time the Bedfords arrived in Spain the Peninsular War was drawing to a close. The last battle was fought in April 1814 and on the twelfth of that month news reached Wellington that Napoleon had abdicated.

It was a controversial but fascinating time for the Duke and Duchess to visit the country. It seems the Bedfords had heard a great deal about the politics of Spain from Lord and Lady Holland and, as a leading Whig, the Duke was interested to visit the country at this time of change, even if it was potentially dangerous. He was in the right place at the right time to see the beginning of the Spanish tradition of liberalism. From the start of the war against France, juntas of army commanders, civilians and guerrilla leaders had been set up in areas outside French control to oppose the foreign enemy. A central junta was established in Cadiz as a surrogate for the absent royal government. In 1810 the Cadiz junta called together representatives from others to create the 'Cortes of All the Spains', which would be the single legislative body for the country. Liberals were in the ascendant in this assembly and in 1812 they formulated a constitution which became the 'sacred codex' of liberalism. It was to serve as a model for the liberal constitutions of many Latin countries. Its main aim was to prevent corrupt royal rule by allowing a limited monarchy to govern through ministers subject to parliamentary control. The 1812 constitution was seen as a revolutionary document by some conservatives. When King Ferdinand was restored to the Spanish throne in 1814, he would not recognise it and he dismissed the Cadiz Cortes.

No doubt the Duke was interested to see how the situation developed, but staying in the country did involve risks. Crime was rife as once the country was free of the French the guerrillas turned their attention to plundering houses.

Staying near Cadiz may have satisfied the Duke's political curiosity but it did not live up to Georgina's expectations. Used to a hectic social life in England, the Duchess was disappointed with Spain. Although the Bedfords' old friends Lord and Lady Hinchingbrook stayed with them in Chiclana, Georgina found few interesting people with whom to socialise. The company became even more boring when William left them to join Wellington's army. She complained: 'It is the most abominable, dull, frightful place imaginable, nothing but the delightful climate and the hope of it doing dear Jane good could make me visit there.' With little to entertain her, Georgina dwelt on Jane's deteriorating health and was constantly anxious about her niece. The Duke wrote to Lady Holland:

> Although she [Jane] appears occasionally to rally most wonderfully I confess I have no hopes whatsoever of her ultimate recovery – a Spanish Physician at Cadiz who has been called in, pronounces most boldly that she will recover, but I fear his opinion is grounded on ignorance, rather than a rational view of the nature and character of her complaint.

After two months in Chiclana the party travelled to Gibraltar and then Malaga because it was hoped that the sea air and change of scene would improve Jane's health and the Duchess's mood. The Duke travelled by land to Gibraltar as he did not enjoy sailing, but the ladies went by ship on a journey that provided the Duchess with the element of exotic adventure she craved. During their voyage they looked in at Tangiers and Georgina was highly amused to see a Moorish wedding taking place; this splash of colourful local custom appealed to her sensuous nature. Back on board the ship the Duchess, maternal as ever, took care of all the passengers as if they were family. She took her nursing responsibilities seriously and once in Gibraltar she was unable to go on sight-seeing expeditions with the Duke because she would not leave Jane.

Unfortunately, the move did not help as the climate did not suit Jane and she became increasingly ill. However, the Duchess's spirits improved and it seems the depression she suffered after losing her baby began to lift. On 6 March the party sailed for Malaga and with a fair wind they reached the port on the following morning. Georgina particularly liked Malaga, saying that it was the only place in Spain where she would like to live. Her *joie de vivre* restored, she began to throw herself into Spanish life with her usual exuberance, learning Spanish dances and performing them with such grace and style that the local people assured her she could be taken for a Spaniard. She also learned Spanish and showed a natural aptitude for the language. Spurred on by her success, she would try it out on anyone she came across.

At the end of March, the Duke travelled across the mountains to Granada, leaving the Duchess in Malaga with her niece and Mr Fazakerley. The Duke jokingly mentioned to Lady Holland that the Spanish might suspect Georgina was having an affair with their travelling companion 'with the necessary approbation of her husband'.

Mr Fazakerley was certainly entertaining and was proving to be a great addition to the party. The Duchess, starved of good company, enjoyed flirting with him. She wrote to Lady Holland that he was 'a most agreeable, amicable creature . . . I fear Naples will seduce him from us, tho I assure you he has had three sultanas trying to please him but without much effect'. The Duke complained, with a hint of jealousy, that 'there is a nonchalance and a deouvrement, if I may use the word, about him, which is sometimes provoking – he is however a great favourite among the ladies and they all seem to consider him as a good, obliging, useful creature'.

When they returned to Gibraltar, the Bedfords experienced trouble with their staff. Two Spanish servants had to be dismissed as they fought like cat and dog and were 'worse than useless'. This left the household short-staffed and, except for an Italian cook, whom the Duke described as 'a great rogue', they were left with only English servants.

After a month in Gibraltar, the party travelled back through Cadiz to Lisbon where the Bedfords' sons were due to join them. By now Georgina could not wait to leave Spain. 'I confess I depart from this country without any regret,' she wrote to Lady Holland. Her disenchantment with the place was interwoven with her unhappiness about her niece's condition; by this time, Jane was very ill:

> Her's is a disheartening and melancholy state. She every now and then has violent attacks which consist in increased pain in her shoulder and chest, amounting quite to agony, constant cough and great difficulty in breathing, these last a week, sometimes ten days, she then rallies again and the disease appears to stand still, but after these attacks I can always observe some aggravation to her old symptoms . . . she is in excellent spirits and does not look as ill as you would expect . . . I have no hopes of her ever getting well, yet I think she will get worse very slowly.

In contrast, Georgina's daughters were thriving and in a letter to Lady Holland, the proud mother shines through. 'Georgy is really as beautiful as it is possible to imagine,' she wrote. 'Louisa the image of her Mama, with the same spirits and the same happy turn for mischief.' The letter also reveals what a hostage Georgina was to her fertility because she was delighted that for once she was not pregnant. She wrote with relief that it was 'wonderful to add none on the stocks at present'.

The journey from Cadiz to Lisbon was tempestuous. The party once again sailed on the *Volunteer* and their ship fell in with the *Niobe*, which had sailed from Cadiz five days earlier. On the afternoon when the two ships met, the *Niobe* ran aground off Cape St Mary, so the *Volunteer* had to go to her rescue. Both ships survived but the foul weather made the rest of the journey extremely unpleasant.

Once in Lisbon, Mr Fazakerley left them to sail to England. The Duke and Duchess waited anxiously for their sons, who were sailing from Portsmouth. Their arrival was delayed, partly due to bad weather and partly because of John, who, after the boys had waited for him for three weeks, had changed his mind at the last minute and decided not to come.

While in Lisbon, Georgina went to a grand ball given by the Spanish consul, but she was no more impressed with Portuguese society than Spanish. She complained that in Portugal 'society appears to be as scarce as beauty', and she wrote to Lord Grey that the Portuguese were 'so proud, ignorant, inhospitable and dirty that no amusement can be derived from any intercourse with them. They are an odious Nation, after all our country has done for them. They distrust us.'

The family spent the summer in Cintra. For a while, Lady Jane seemed to be better, but then on 9 July she had a relapse, suffering from pain and fever for several days. The weather in Cintra became increasingly hot, reaching 84 degrees, and in the stifling heat Jane became more breathless. The only positive event was when, on 12 September, after weeks of anxious expectation, the Duke and Duchess's four sons arrived in Portugal with their tutor Mr Roy. Ten days later, Lord John joined the party, but he seemed almost as frail as Jane; the Duke described his son as 'on the whole, weak and far from well'. Throughout his life John was prone to ill-health, suffering from frequent colds, coughs and hay fever. On this occasion his father was not sympathetic towards him. He resented the fact that John had delayed his other sons' arrival and told Lady Holland: 'I the more regret it [the delay] on his account, as I am persuaded it would have been of the greatest service to his health.'

After a few months in Portugal, the Duchess was delighted to leave for Italy, but the voyage across the Mediterranean was not easy. First they encountered gales, then they were condemned to forty days quarantine at Leghorn because there was a fever epidemic in Gibraltar and the authorities were afraid of it spreading. The Duke appealed to the Governor and eventually their quarantine was halved to twenty days. After such a prolonged journey it was a relief to step ashore. The main purpose of the trip was to meet up with Lord and Lady Holland in Rome for Christmas, but it was also an opportunity for the Bedfords to see Italy. On their way to the capital they visited Pisa, where they were 'highly gratified by the Cathedral, the Baptistry, the falling Tower, and the Campo Santo, the last of which has been much decorated by Bonaparte, by placing round the Cloisters, an immense quantity of ancient Sarcophagi, Statues, Vases etc, etc, collected from various parts'.

The next day they travelled to Florence through 'a beautiful and highly cultivated Country'. During a fortnight in the city the Duke and Duchess 'were much pleased by the numerous interesting objects to be seen there'.

Lord John travelled with his family as far as Florence and while there took the opportunity of crossing to Elba to meet Napoleon, who had been in exile there since his abdication in April 1814. Lord John was one of many English aristocrats who visited Bonaparte during this time. Apparently, sixty-one English visitors crossed to Elba from Livorno to see him and more travelled from Naples or Genoa. The former Emperor had become a curiosity to British tourists, so much so that alabaster busts in his image sold out in Florence's shops.

Even though in 1807–8 the Hollands had supported the Spanish, they were two of Napoleon's greatest admirers. Lord Holland had met Bonaparte in Paris in 1802 and he now headed a group of Whig politicians who opposed the restoration of the Bourbon monarchs in France. Many of Napoleon's English visitors were members of the Holland House set. Hugh Fortescue, Viscount Ebrington, a friend of the Bedfords as well as the Hollands, visited in December 1814, followed by the Duke and Duchess's travelling companion Fazakerley, who was lavish in his praise of Bonaparte: 'I would rather have crossed the Alps twenty times for this scene, and would rather give up the recollection of anything I saw, than of these four hours.' Lord John was also impressed. He wrote that 'his manner seems studied to put one at one's ease by its familiarity; his smile and laugh are very agreeable.'

Evidently Napoleon enjoyed his audiences with British visitors. Not only did they keep him entertained, they also provided him with useful information about what was happening in Europe. At this stage Napoleon still thought he would be recalled to the French throne and that the Bourbons would not reign for long. He knew any successful return to power depended on Britain's attitude, as in Paris many people held the British responsible for the restoration of the Bourbons. It was helpful to him that the British Whigs opposed renewed hostilities on the Continent, partly because of the cost to Britain of continuing the war, but also because conservatives at home and abroad supported the return of 'legitimate dynasties' such as the Bourbons. Napoleon was keen to hear what British politicians thought and once questioned Lord John Russell about the Hollands:

> He inquired if I had seen at Florence many Englishmen who came from there [France]. And when I mentioned Lord Holland, he asked if he thought things went well with the Bourbons. When I answered in the negative he seemed delighted and asked if Lord Holland thought they would be able to stay there.

After John's visit the Duke of Bedford hoped to see Napoleon with Lady Holland in the spring, but their plans were upset when the former Emperor escaped from Elba. Lady Holland played a part in his escape – she had sent Bonaparte a copy of the *Courrier* which first put forward the idea of exiling him to St Helena; fears of this move were instrumental in encouraging his escape from Elba.

English aristocrats like the Bedfords and Hollands admired Napoleon partly for political reasons – as Whigs they disliked powerful monarchies – but part of their fascination was due to the sheer charisma of the man. The Duke explained: 'Everything I hear of this most extraordinary man increases my desire to see him.'

After their arrival in Italy, Lady Jane suffered a severe haemorrhage and became weaker than ever. Watching her gradually die was taking its toll on the whole family. The Duke wrote:

> By William's last letter I imagine he will be here in about a week and the scene will be a most melancholy one to him poor fellow! I have persuaded John to go to Naples for a short time and I rejoice that he has, tho' reluctantly suffered himself to be persuaded; for he has visibly suffered both in mind and body from his increasing anxiety about this poor girl.

The Duchess coped with the depressing situation by not thinking about it too much and by focusing on the positive side of life. Perhaps her greatest asset during this time was her sense of humour; it meant that she could see the funny side of even the most irritating situations. For instance, some of the Italian boarding houses they stayed in were infested with fleas but when Georgina became food for these mites, instead of complaining about the inconveniences of foreign travel, she turned it into a joke. She wrote to Lady Holland:

> Since Mr Faz left Portugal I have not seen one creature worth talking to nor any living thing showed me any attention but the Fleas, who prefer ME to everyone else and think me so hospitable that they live upon me sometimes to the number of thirty . . . I am such a complete scarecrow from being thinner than I have ever been since I was married . . . that I grudge the fleas their diet.

The Hollands arrived in Rome before their friends so the Duke wrote detailed letters to Lady Holland asking her to prepare for their arrival. He was very specific and demanding in his requirements, stating that he wanted 'a good, comfortable, clean house in a warm situation and with a southern aspect'. To emphasise the point, he added, 'do not take a house for us in a dark situation – it must be airy, cheerful and SUNNY. I would not have the best Pallazzo in Rome if it were in a narrow street and gloomy, for independent of the state of our invalid, I am an old man and like the cheering rays of the sun.' In a later letter, he asked Lady Holland to make sure the house was ready when they arrived with 'all the necessaries of life, such as fuel, provisions, wine for the servants etc and pray take some means to furnish us with dinner on the day of our arrival as my cook will not be able to reach Rome much before us. I shall want stabling for two saddle horses and standing for four carriages.' What Lady Holland thought of being treated like a paid agent is not recorded, but the Duke excused himself for taking advantage of his friend by saying, 'I am afraid you will find me very troublesome but I am so much accustomed to good nature from you.'

Once safely arrived in Rome, the Duchess relished at last having some entertaining company, especially Lord Holland. During their stay, the Hollands and Bedfords made friends with Guiseppe Binda, a bright young Italian who had been connected with the governments in Rome and Naples. From 1796–9 Napoleon's army had taken over the whole Italian peninsula and installed French-controlled governments, but Italy had been thrown into turmoil by Bonaparte's fall from power in the spring of 1814. The states established by Napoleon were dissolved and French laws were systematically abolished. Although many of the judicial reforms introduced under Bonaparte remained in force, the change in regimes affected many people's careers, including Guiseppe Binda's. At the end of their stay, the Hollands took Binda back to England with them and he became another permanent inmate at Holland House and a regular visitor to Woburn.

As well as good company, Rome offered excellent art, and the Duke found it was the perfect place to add to his growing collection. He was a great patron of the arts and like other contemporary collectors he thought nothing of buying large objects abroad and shipping them home at great expense. While in Spain he bought 'a little gallery' of exquisite figurines dressed in accurate Spanish costumes, but Italy offered artistic attractions on an even grander scale. Rome was the centre for some of the greatest sculptors of the era; Antonio Canova, Carlo Finelli, Lorenzo Bartolini and Adamo Tadolini all had studios there.

Antonio Canova, in particular, dominated European sculpture with his promotion of the Neoclassical style and while in Rome the Duke and Duchess visited him in his atelier. He was quite short and stocky with a fine face. He spoke French badly and was much happier speaking in his native Venetian patois. From early in the morning until late at night, he worked in his studio, but whatever the time of year there was no fire because he insisted on keeping the studio cool, believing that hot rooms would give him a cold.

During one visit the Duke commissioned a statue of the Three Graces from the great sculptor. These were popular subjects throughout Ancient Greece and Rome; they were the beautiful daughters of Zeus and represented Gracefulness, Friendship and Gratitude. The Duke was not the first patron to commission the Three Graces from Canova. His first version was commissioned by the Empress Josephine at a cost of 60,000 francs. Unfortunately Josephine died in 1814 before the work was finished so Canova wrote to her son and Georgina's former admirer Eugene Beauharnais, to see if he still wanted the figures. Eugene replied that he had no intention of giving up his claim to them but by 5 January 1815 Canova had still not received a payment. By this time the Duke of Bedford had appeared on the scene, fell in love with the Three Graces and was determined to have them. It seems Eugene was not willing to relinquish the statue as easily as he had given up Georgina more than a decade before, so the Duke asked the sculptor to make another version of the Graces for Woburn. Evidently Canova knew about Georgina's relationship with Josephine's son; when by July Eugene still had not paid any money, Canova wrote to him asking if he might allow the Duchess of Bedford to have the finished first version and accept the second version for himself. There was no nostalgic gallantry in Eugene's response: he immediately sent one of his agents to pay for the statue.

During their stay in Italy the Duke and Duchess became friends with Canova. They enjoyed informal dinners together and one evening Georgina felt so relaxed and happy that she waltzed and danced with castanets in front of the sculptor. The relationship between Canova and his English patron was to continue after the Bedfords left Italy. When he visited England later that year Canova was invited to Woburn to meet the architect who had built Endsleigh, Jeffry Wyatt, and the sculptor Richard Westmacott.

It is likely that it was through Canova that the Bedfords were introduced to Elizabeth Rawdon and her mother. Although it was clear from the start that Georgina and Elizabeth were very different types of women, the Duchess could not have imagined the destructive role this younger woman would play in her life. Bettina, or Bessy as she was also known, was the daughter of the Honourable John Rawdon, brother of the Earl of Moira. When her father died in 1808, Elizabeth and her mother moved in with her uncle at Donnington

Park in Leicester and also used his town house in St James's Place. Elizabeth was an intellectual beauty and her formidable academic achievements included a detailed knowledge of the classics and the ability to read in eight languages. Never a woman to hide her erudition, Elizabeth even wrote letters to her friends in Greek as it was a convenient way to conceal her often bitchy comments from less learned acquaintances.

Through her uncle she became a friend of Princess Charlotte and began to mix in the highest society. When the Tsar Alexander of Russia visited London, he singled her out as the most delightful woman in the city and chose to waltz with her. Byron was equally captivated and wrote of her in his poem 'Beppo':

> I've seen some balls and revels in my time
> And stayed them over for some silly reason,
> And then I looked (I hope it was no crime)
> To see what lady best stood out the season;
> And though I've seen some thousands in their prime
> Lovely and pleasing, and who still may please on
> I never saw but one (the stars withdrawn)
> Whose bloom could after dancing dare the Dawn.
>
> The name of this Aurora I'll not mention;
> Although I might, for she was nought to me
> More than that patent work of God's invention;
> A charming woman, whom we like to see;
> But writing names would merit reprehensions,
> Yet if you like to find out this fair She,
> At the next London or Parisian ball
> You still may mark her cheek, out blooming all.

Elizabeth's healthy bloom was a poignant contrast to Lady Jane's deathly pallor and evidently Georgina's stepson William was attracted to this challenging young woman. It seems William and Elizabeth met several times in Rome and a few times in Naples and then went their separate ways, but they kept in touch. Gradually a relationship developed between them that two years later was to end in marriage.

The sociable interlude in Rome had done Georgina's spirits good, but by the spring that happier time was coming to an end. The Duke and Duchess and their party were planning to move to Naples and the Hollands were soon to return to England.

Naples was a controversial place to be in 1815, and inevitably Georgina got caught up in the turmoil. But the Duke and Duchess were never nervous of risk-taking and seemed to relish being at the centre of world events. Nor were they the only English people to disregard the danger. Elizabeth Rawdon, her mother, and Lord and Lady Oxford were also prepared to join the English colony in Naples at this unstable time. In 1808, Joachim Murat and his wife Caroline (Napoleon's youngest sister) had become King and Queen of Naples. They established a lavish court and brought in important reforms including measures for breaking up large landed estates and the introduction of the Code Napoleon. Advancement became by merit and measures were taking to control Neapolitan brigands. In 1812, Murat fought in Napoleon's Russian campaign, but as things began to go wrong, he had to rush back to Italy to try to save his own kingdom. In 1813, he wavered between loyalty to his brother-in-law and negotiating with the Allies, but eventually signed a treaty with the Austrians in the hope that they would allow him to keep the throne of Naples when Napoleon fell. However, the former Bourbon rulers of Naples objected to this and his position was still uncertain when Napoleon returned to France in 1815 after escaping from Elba. This time Murat decided to stake his hopes on an appeal to Italian nationalism but his gamble failed and his Neapolitan soldiers were defeated by the Austrians at Tolentino on 21 April. He was forced to escape to Corsica, while his wife, Caroline, was left to surrender their kingdom and see the Bourbons regain the throne. Later that year, Murat made a final attempt to recover his kingdom, but was taken prisoner and shot.

The Duke and Duchess were planning to travel to Naples in the middle of this crisis. With her customary spirit, it was Georgina, not her husband, who went ahead to see if it would be safe for the family to stay there. The Duke explained:

> The extraordinary political events which occurred about this Time made it absolutely necessary that we should decide upon some plan for the Summer, which determined Georgiana to set out for Naples on Tuesday the 28th [of March], proposing that I should follow her with Jane, if she found all things quiet there, and a fair prospect of our being tolerably secure under the Protection of King Joachim through the ensuing Summer . . . The accounts which I had from my Wife, after she had made every enquiry into the political state of Naples, and the security which the English might expect to enjoy in the Event of hostilities, determined me to leave Rome as soon as practicable.

The Duke and the rest of the family joined Georgina in Naples at the beginning of April. As the crisis escalated, a British squadron was sent to monitor the situation in Naples until the Austrians arrived, and the Duke and Duchess became deeply involved in the negotiations between the Queen of Naples and the British. It is likely Georgina knew Queen Caroline from her stay in Paris in 1802 during the Peace of Amiens. The Duchess remembered this time fondly and it seems she still thought about Eugene Beauharnais as she wrote to Lady Holland at this time: 'I envy you having seen my old friend Prince Eugene, I cannot understand why he has never answered two letters that I wrote to him last year.' Georgina had been friends with the whole Bonaparte clan and with characteristic loyalty she refused to let international hostilities get in the way of her friendships. Caroline was in trouble so Georgina showed her some 'common kindness and attention in the difficult situation in which she was placed'.

Queen Caroline played on this connection and carefully courted the Bedfords. The Duke and Duchess arrived in Naples just weeks after Napoleon's escape from Elba. Caroline knew that if she was to hold onto the throne of Naples she would need English support. She was well aware that the Bedfords were close friends of the Hollands, who were ardent supporters of the Bonapartes and had influence in British politics. Caroline knew just how to manipulate the Duke. As he was a keen art collector she invited him to a breakfast at Pompeii and told him he could keep any 'find' he made among the ruins. The Duke discovered part of a small bronze satyr which no doubt had been planted for his delight by the Queen.

The Duke and Duchess realised that their support for Queen Caroline might be seen as unpatriotic and so the Duke kept in contact with the British squadron and also recorded detailed minutes of exactly what happened during those historic days in Naples. On 26 April 1815, five days after Murat had been defeated at Tolentino, Captain Campbell arrived at the Bay of Naples with part of the British fleet under his command. The Captain wrote to the Duchess to inform her that his instructions were to cooperate with the Austrians in an attack on Naples. The Duke went to the palace to see Queen Caroline and to pass on this important information. On hearing the news she expressed 'great anxiety still to preserve Peace between the two countries [Naples and Britain] and to avoid every thing on her part that could bear the slightest appearance of hostility'. But her wish for peace seemed unlikely to be realised; Captain Campbell was already preparing his squadron to enter the Bay of Naples and bombard it with shells and mortars. The danger was so imminent that the Duke received a warning note from the Captain expressing his hope that the Bedfords' house was 'not in the range of shot and shell'.

As time was running out to prevent the onslaught, the Queen sent an envoy to negotiate with the British and terms were agreed. The Queen had to give up her warships and naval arsenal to the British, but in return 'every protection' was offered to the Queen, her family, private property and all individuals who claimed the protection of the British flag. Captain Campbell even agreed to convey Caroline and her family to France.

After this agreement was reached, the Queen asked to see the Duke at her palace because she felt that there had been some misunderstanding between herself and the British. She asked him to mediate between them and he arranged for Captain Campbell to visit the Queen. The Duke, who was also present at this meeting, described their interview as 'frank and good humoured' and thought it 'seemed to give perfect satisfaction to both parties'. The next day the Duchess had a long audience with Caroline and was very impressed with her grace under pressure. Talking as one mother to another, the Queen admitted that she would be able to act 'with more firmness and resolution' when she knew that her children were safe because 'she could not help feeling all the weakness of a woman when she saw her children daily and hourly exposed to danger'.

Her anxieties increased when an English fleet under the command of Lord Exmouth, Commander in Chief in the Mediterranean, appeared in the Bay. The Queen again asked to see the Duke. She explained to him that she had no fears for herself but she was afraid that her people might be attacked. Then the Austrians arrived in Naples and it became obvious that the Queen would have to go into exile. She was left with no choice but to board Captain Campbell's ship, leaving her kingdom to her enemies.

That night the Duke and Duchess were invited aboard the ship to dine with Caroline. The Duchess was determined to minimise the suffering of her brave friend and offered to accompany Caroline to France, 'that she might render the voyage less irksome to her'. The Queen wrote back to Georgina 'full of gratitude but declining to accept so great a sacrifice'. The Duchess, however, would not accept no for an answer and it was agreed that she would travel with the Queen, provided a ship was made available to guarantee Georgina's return to Naples.

The Duke went to see Lord Exmouth to finalise the arrangements and during this first interview the Commander in Chief was very helpful. He said that the Duchess's return voyage could be easily arranged; reassured, Georgina began preparations for her journey. However, Lord Exmouth's attitude changed after a meeting with the Austrians. On 22 May, Captain Campbell visited the Duke and

Duchess and told them there were difficulties about Caroline going to France because the British and Austrians were determined none of the Bonaparte family should act as a potential rallying point there. No doubt they were concerned as Napoleon was still enjoying his brief return to power, known as the Hundred Days, before his final defeat at the Battle of Waterloo.

The Queen was very distressed by the news and wanted to see her friends to discuss what she should do. When the Bedfords went on board the ship they found her 'under much apprehension as to the uncertainty of her Fate'. After the meeting, the Duke went to champion her cause with Lord Exmouth but this time the Commander's attitude was antagonistic. It was clear that he did not wish the Duchess to travel with the Queen and that no ship would be made available for her return if she did decide to make the voyage.

The Austrians wanted Caroline to go to Trieste or Venice, while the British suggested that she should go to Gibraltar or Malta and then possibly on to England. Eventually, the Queen decided to be taken by the Austrians to Trieste. The day before she left, the Bedfords went to say goodbye to her. She told them that 'she could no longer trust to the good Faith of the English' as she feared that if she went to England she would be taken prisoner. She explained that the Austrians 'at least treated her with civility, which the English did not'. Caroline was, however, very grateful to the Duke and Duchess for all they had done on her behalf and she appreciated their selfless support during her hour of need. The Duke wrote:

> She then took an affectionate leave of the Duchess and myself, with many expressions of kindness and gratitude and we left her, with a full conviction in our minds that good Faith had not been kept with her and that she had not received the treatment from us, which her exemplary conduct in a very difficult and arduous situation justly entitled her to.

The Duke and Duchess were disgusted by the British commander's behaviour, while in contrast, they were full of admiration for the Queen, respecting 'the patience, good humour and resignation with which she submitted to her fate'.

The Bedfords' experience in Naples echoed their experiences in Ireland. Once again, they had behaved with a basic humanity that seemed to be absent from the British authorities. They judged people as individuals, not as enemies because of their race or religion, and, unlike many members of their class, they were unwilling to support the British establishment view, right or wrong. The Duke was very disillusioned by the way Queen Caroline had been treated and never forgot the lack of compassion shown towards her. In many ways, he had more admiration for the Bonapartes than the British royal family. Two years after the Neapolitan incident, he sent a parcel of books and a case of medals to Napoleon while he was on St Helena, hoping they would provide some entertainment. To Lady Holland he wrote: 'I hope he will accept these as a trifling testimony of the many civilities I received from various branches of his family whilst I was in Italy.'

After the departure of Queen Caroline, the Duke no longer wished to stay in Naples, and on 1 June he returned to England with his sons. On his journey home, he visited Waterloo and walked over the battlefield, just days after the momentous battle had taken place.

Although the Duke showed the highest principles in public life, he could be selfish in private. While back in England he was able to resume normal life, visiting Holland House and inviting guests to Woburn to enjoy 'unquestionably the finest [summer and autumn] I ever remembered in England', the Duchess remained stranded in Naples because Lady Jane was too ill to travel by land. The only alternative was to wait for a ship to take them home. Left in a foreign country during turbulent times, with a dying girl to care for, the Duchess described herself and her niece as 'forlorn beings'. Not only had the Duke left them, so had her favourite stepson, William. He had gone to Paris to advance his military career and enjoy the hectic social life available in the city. Georgina's sense of isolation was increased by the fact that the Duke's letters from England were not getting through. Eventually, he had to resort to using a private courier to keep in touch with his wife.

By August, both Georgina and her niece were desperate to get home, but still no ships were available. Unfortunately for the Duchess, Viscount Exmouth was in charge of these arrangements and, despite her pleading letters, he failed to find a place for Georgina and Jane. It seems he was suspicious of the Duchess because of the kindness she had shown to the former Queen of Naples. Georgina was placed in a very vulnerable position, at the mercy of a man who had no intention of showing more compassion to a Duchess than he had to a Queen. Georgina wrote to the Commander telling him about Lady Jane's terminal illness and the Duke sent delegations to the Admiralty but none of their appeals worked. The Duke wrote to Lady Holland: 'She [the Duchess] is suffering every possible anxiety of mind, and that to see poor Lady Jane is sufficient to melt the most obdurate heart – Lord Exmouth's however is not to be moved.' The Duke's anger increased when he discovered the lengths the Commander would go to in order to block the Duchess's return. He told Lady Holland:

> I have a letter from Captain Campbell – he says when he was on the point of sailing he wrote a letter to Lord Exmouth, asking permission to take the Duchess home, when to his astonishment the commander in chief sent his Captain on board to desire that the letter might not be sent to him, adding that the Duchess had repeatedly written to him on the same subject! What an unfeeling brute this man must be! But this is all to punish the Duchess for her civility to poor Mademoiselle Murat.

As Jane became more unwell, her anxiety to get home to England increased, but Georgina realised that if no ship became available by the beginning of September, she would have to remain in Naples until Jane died. They could not risk sailing long after that date because they would have encountered the equinoctial gales.

Time was running out for Jane to make any journey. By 8 September she was 'reduced and enfeebled almost to nothing'. She was confined to bed and so close to death that she had received the last sacrament, but to the Duchess's great surprise she suddenly rallied, got up, dressed herself and went out in the carriage. It was only a very brief respite and her almost supernatural energy was a sign of the last stages of her disease, not her recovery. It was a very bleak time for the Duchess, separated from her husband and friends and left alone to watch her niece die a slow and painful death. She wrote: 'It is so dreadfully melancholy, attached as I am to her and valuable as she is to me and would be to the world as a bright ornament of everything good, amiable and superior to most of her sex, that I cannot bring myself to give up hope.' But there was no hope, and just a few weeks later, on 27 September, Jane died. The whole family was devastated by the news, as the Duke explained: 'Altho' I was fully prepared for the event, my nerves are so much unstrung by it that I cannot go out to day.' Although Georgina was shattered by the loss, she was at last free. The Duke wrote:

> My poor Wife who loved her with real warmth and Tenderness, and whose attentions to her were unremitting to the last, sent me word that as soon as her earthly remains were consigned to the Grave, she should set out with William for England.

No longer dependent on Lord Exmouth for a ship, Georgina prepared to travel by land to Paris to meet her husband. William came from Paris, where he was working for the Duke of Wellington (now Commander of the Allied Forces of Occupation), to escort his stepmother on her journey from Naples. The Duke could not wait to see his exhausted wife, and to cheer her up he planned a three- or four-day stay for her in Paris, 'not only to rest herself but by way of a little break for she will have much need of resuscitating her body and mind, poor soul!' But even this meeting was delayed and the Duke was disappointed and worried not to find the Duchess in Paris when he arrived; in fact, her journey had been held up by a shortage of horses. When eventually she did arrive, Georgina did not have the strength or spirits to enjoy the city. All she wanted to do was to get back to England and see her family and friends.

CHAPTER SIX

The Society Hostess

*B*ack in England after an absence of almost two years, Georgina resumed her role as a leading hostess. The Bedfords had the money and contacts to be at the centre of Regency society and they entertained with style, organising grand house parties for a mixture of old friends and interesting acquaintances. The Duke and Duchess were unashamedly hedonistic and provided a luxurious stay for their guests. Charles Greville wrote:

> The Duke of Bedford is a complete sensualist and thinks of nothing but his personal enjoyments, and it has long been part of his system not to allow himself to be ruffled by the slightest self-denial. He is affable, bland and of easy intercourse, making rather a favourable impression on a superficial observer; caring little, (if at all) for the wants or wishes of others, but grudging nobody anything that does not interfere with his own enjoyments, and seeing with

complacency those who surround him lap up the super-fluities which may chance to bubble over from his cup of pleasure and happiness, while he alone drains it to the dregs.

Woburn was run like the most exclusive hotel. Bedrooms were large and well furnished, unlimited water was available and three types of soap and soft towels provided every day. Breakfast was served between ten and eleven in a state room between the Van Dyck dining room and the Venetian drawing room, which was filled with Canalettos. The breakfast room was richly ornamented, with old English masters hanging on the walls and a bookcase filled with small editions of Shakespeare, British poets, French classics and Italian writers.

At Woburn, breakfast was a substantial meal, including a range of cold meat such as venison, beef, fowl and tongue. Fruit was in abundance, with grapes, figs, strawberries, peaches and nectarines on offer. There was white bread, two kinds of brown toast, buns, rolls and muffins, while to drink there was a choice of cocoa, coffee or tea. Everything was of the best quality and very fresh; in a step well ahead of her time, the Duchess insisted that the eggs served were marked with the date on which they were laid.

The food was presented with great attention to detail, each person's place being set with exquisite and distinct Sevres china. Preserves were found in earthenware dishes made to look like fruits; split the peach in two and a guest would find marmalade, open the walnut and they would discover powdered ginger. Even the cutlery was carefully crafted, with the handles of the knives made of beautifully cut Scotch jasper while forks and spoons were shaped like snakes or branches.

After breakfast, Georgina often spent the morning in her room writing letters, but she made sure her guests had plenty to entertain them. The American George Ticknor wrote:

> Considered as a whole, Woburn is sometimes called the finest estate in England. As I went over it, I thought I should never find an end to all its arrangements and divisions . . . [the house] is the largest and most splendid I

have seen ... I could have occupied myself in these apartments for a month.

Inside the house there were the picture and sculpture galleries and an extensive library. Henry Holland had originally built the gallery as a greenhouse, but a decade later the Duke had considered it to be the ideal place to display his growing art collection. In 1813, Jeffry Wyatt designed the new greenhouse or camellia house and it was joined on to the sculpture gallery. The library was also designed by Holland. Divided into three parts by screens with fluted Corinthian columns, it was lit by an elegant chandelier which showed off to advantage portraits by Rembrandt and Van Dyck. The Duke was still a great collector of books and his interest in botany was reflected in the many volumes on the flora and fauna of the Bedford estates. His library housed some rare volumes, including books from the Cabinet du Roy and the works of Pierre-Joseph Redoute, and his map-reading room was stocked with rare maps.

Outside the house, guests could enjoy three thousand acres of parkland. The estate offered some of the best shooting in England. At one house party lasting five days, 645 hares, 835 pheasants, 59 rabbits, 10 partridges and 4 woodcocks were shot. The Duke prided himself on the success of Woburn shoots as George Ticknor's description of his visit reveals:

> It was a day of no common import at a nobleman's country seat, for it was the last of the shooting season. The Duke was anxious to have a quantity of game killed that should maintain the reputation of the Abbey, for the first sporting-ground in Great Britain; and therefore solemn preparations were made to have a grand battue of the park, for it was intended in order to give more reputation to the day's success, that nothing should be shot out of it; nor indeed was there any great need of extending the limit, for the park is twelve miles in circumference ... The first gun was fired a little before twelve, the last at half past five.

If shooting did not appeal, the more active guests could go to the riding school or tennis courts, while the less energetic could visit the menagerie and aviary to see rare deer, tortoises, peacocks and pheasants. They could walk around the rare plant garden and see the Duke's collection of cacti, or get lost in the maze. During the afternoon a stroll to the grotto made a pleasant walk. It had originally been designed as an open loggia; in the centre there was a fountain while the stonework was carved to resemble stalactites and seaweed and the walls were inlaid with shells; the furniture was carved with seashells, and sculpted dolphins supported the tables and chairs. Another walk was to the 'ruined' folly, built by the Duke to add a picturesque element to the landscape. The folly was close to the Chinese dairy where poignant echoes of pre-revolutionary France were emphasised by two Sevres china pails made for Marie Antoinette and given to the Duchess. Once they had completed their tour of the estate, guests could enjoy a picnic at the Thornery, served on fine Wedgwood caneware (a refined earthenware introduced by Josiah Wedgwood in 1779).

Usually lunch was a ladies-only occasion; known as a second breakfast, it was a light meal. The formal dinner in the evening was the main meal of the day, often attended by twenty people. Guests were expected to dress smartly and be punctual; the meal began at half past six instead of the usual hour of seven. Dinner at Woburn was a stylish occasion. The opulent dining room was full of fine paintings and heirlooms, each with its own fascinating history. The gilt bronze wall lights, for instance, decorated with acanthus leaves and berries, had been created by the goldsmith to Louis XV. The table was always beautifully set with the family silver and an exquisite Meissen dinner service painted with a variety of birds and insects. On the grandest occasions, another dinner service, presented to the fourth Duchess by Louis XV in appreciation of her husband's role in negotiating the Treaty of Paris in 1763, was used; it had 183 pieces, each painted with a different design.

The food was as exceptional as the setting. The Bedfords employed one of the best French chefs to create new and exciting dishes for their guests. Unfortunately, there was a logistical problem in delivering this haute cuisine to the table because the dining room was a long way from the kitchens. Serving platters had to be kept warm by using covers and stands with burners underneath, or dishes with an inner and outer lining between which hot or cold water was placed. In the Regency period, entrée dishes were placed on the table while the soup and the fish were being eaten; then roast meat including pork, venison, beef and mutton were served. Sweets were put on the table at the same time as the roasts and once these courses were eaten all the dishes were cleared away for the serving of dessert, which included a wide variety of fruit such as pineapples, grapes, peaches and raspberries. The copious amount of food was washed down with endless wine and champagne. To reflect this indulgent atmosphere, Lord Holland sent the Duke his statue of Bacchus from Ampthill with the following poem:

> The Honest God of wine and joy,
> Who rules o'er Woburn cheer,
> Whom I, perhaps too long a boy,
> Invoked so often here;
> To thank you for your bright champagne
> I now in person send,
> Hoping he may for aie remain
> The offering of a friend.

Reflecting the Duke's pride in Woburn's shoot, dinner often ended with the gamekeeper appearing, dressed in all his paraphernalia, to say what had been caught that day. After the meal, the ladies departed to the state saloon or the blue drawing room, while the men stayed drinking port. Later in the evening the sexes would be reunited to play cards, listen to one or several of their number perform music, or gossip. Small-talk did not come easily to the Duke because he was a shy man and among the guests at Woburn there were often many hangers on, more interested in enjoying his hospitality than his company. Charles Greville wrote:

He is a good-natured, plausible man, without enemies, and really, (although he does not think so) without friends ... there are many who like Brougham pretend a strong affection for him and some who imagine they feel it. Vast property, rank, influence and station always attract a sentiment which is dignified with the name of friendship.

In contrast to her quiet husband, the Duchess was an extrovert hostess whose conversation was bold and racy. As an excellent mimic who could impersonate many of the well-known characters of the day, Georgina often had her guests in fits of laughter. Using the social skills she had learned from her mother, she tailored her topics to interest her guests and turned flattery into an art form. An Irishman, Thomas Moore, recorded that she talked to him of farming technicalities and the price of pigs; then with the charm she saved for those guests she liked, Georgina complimented him: 'she expressed a wish that I could transfer my genius to her for six weeks; and I answered, "most willingly, if Woburn was placed at my disposal for the same time." '

At the end of the evening, guests were often treated to a game of charades, an amateur theatrical production or an informal ball, in either the ballroom or the theatre that had been specially created for these events. The ballroom was fashionably decorated with Chinese wallpaper designed with willow trees and birds, while a portrait of the Duke's father, Francis, Marquess of Tavistock, painted by Pompeo Batoni in the early 1760s, imparted a sense of history.

Woburn's theatrical performances were put on with all the polish of a professional production. The scenery was carefully painted, costumes skilfully made and elegant programmes printed on white satin. Professional actors from London often joined the amateur thespians but not all guests were as keen as the Duchess to take part. Emily Eden wrote: 'We have been on the point of acting, but the Providence that guards "les fous et les ivrognes" evidently keeps an eye on Amateur actors and preserves them from actually treading the board.'

Aristocrats, poets and artists were frequent guests at Woburn but perhaps the most important visitor was the Duke of York. As he was a member of the royal family, the preparation for his visit in 1816 had to be like a military operation. Afterwards, Bedford admitted that 'altho' the Duke of York is the best humoured man in the world a "partie de campagne" is always full as pleasant without royalty'. All the hard work paid off; the King's son was very successful in the shoot and enjoyed his stay so much that over the next few years he paid annual visits to Woburn.

As well as visiting celebrities, by this time the Bedfords had established a circle of close friends who were regular guests. Lord and Lady Holland remained the most frequent visitors and the relationship between the foursome was essential to both couples. As an expert flatterer herself, Georgina appreciated being the focus of Lord Holland's over-the-top adulation; fortunately, both their partners treated their smooth-tongued repartee with wry amusement. The Duke wrote to Lady Holland in February 1817: 'As Holland is so fond of the Duchess as to be positively dying to see her, we must not let him die, and the sooner he comes to see his life the better.'

It seems that one courtier was not enough to satisfy Georgina's vanity and soon the future Prime Minister Lord Grey was added to her list of admirers. The Whig politician and his family paid regular visits to Woburn, but the Duchess expressed her annoyance in no uncertain terms when Lady Grey's ill-health meant they had to cancel a visit in 1817. It seems she expected her friend's life to revolve around her wishes not his wife's needs, but perhaps on reflection Georgina realised she had been unreasonable because the Duke apologised for her rudeness. 'The Duchess . . . was very sorry for the cross letter she wrote you on her disappointment at not seeing you all here,' the Duke explained, 'which you must have received at a moment when your mind was necessarily full of feelings far different from our nonsense – your kind message to her proves to her however that you have forgiven her.'

Georgina's quick tongue and candid expression of her feelings could get her into trouble. The experience guests had at Woburn depended on her mood and she gained a reputation for being particularly capricious with other women; sometimes she would exude charm to them but at other times she could be haughty. Emily Eden wrote of her visit:

> It was clever of me to expect the Duchess would be cross, because of course that insures her being more good natured than anybody ever was. I am only oppressed by being made so much of. Such a magnificent room, because she was determined I should have the first of the new furniture and the advantage of her society in the mornings, though in general she makes it a rule to stay in her own room. In short you may all be very, very good friends, but the only person who really values my merits is the Duchess of Bedford, and once safe with her the house is pleasant enough.

On another occasion, Lady Granville received a less warm reception:

> The Duchess appeared. She was to me just what I wish her to be, uncommonly cold and uncommonly civil . . . I am not very much charmed here. I declare I do not know why I am not more . . . I have a delightful room and find the day too short for all I have to do in it . . . Why then do I count the days till I can go? Why do I feel that I shall not be able to refrain from screaming for joy when I drive off. It is no affront to Woburn. I do justice to its comforts, ease, splendour and society. It is simply a strong, unconquerable wish to go, and I am inclined to say to everybody with the utmost sincerity: 'Yes, it is delightful, only can't I possibly get away?'

Georgina seemed to get on best with other outspoken women who shared her free-spirited approach to life. Another society hostess, Lady Jersey, became a friend and regular guest. She was the daughter of the wealthy banker Robert Childs, and when her family and Lord Jersey's refused to consent to their marriage, they eloped to Gretna Green.

'Sally' Jersey's wealth meant that despite this scandal the couple were accepted back into society and Lady Jersey was soon entertaining in style at her houses, Middleton and Osterley. A domineering, opinionated woman, she was nicknamed 'Silence' because she never stopped talking. George Ticknor met her at Woburn and described her as 'a beautiful creature with a great deal of talent, taste and elegant knowledge'. However, although many men and a few women, including Georgina, liked Lady Jersey, many women hated her. Lady Granville described her behaviour during a visit to Woburn in scathing terms:

> Lady Jersey is too absorbed to think who is for or who against. She sits netting and raving and it sometimes comes across my mind that she will go out of hers. Her countenance is become so stern and political that it affects her beauty. She occasionally stands up and gesticulates with unfeminine vehemence. Yesterday she seized Lord William by both sides of his coat, I believe what is called 'collaring' a man, exclaiming, 'Why should we have Germans to reign over us?'

Another controversial woman, Princess Lieven, also became a friend of Georgina's. As the wife of the Russian ambassador and Metternich's mistress she had an inside knowledge of international politics. Metternich was the leading Austrian statesman who played a crucial role at the Congress of Vienna (1814–15), shaping the future of Europe. Through him the Princess gained an unrivalled insight into the affairs of the Continent. She was highly intelligent but she had a bitchy streak and it was certainly wiser to make her a friend than an enemy. Charles Greville wrote:

> The contempt she has for the understandings of the generality of her acquaintances has made her indifferent to please and incapable of taking any delight in society . . . She carries ennui to such a pitch that even in the society of her most intimate friends she frequently owns that she is bored to death.

Georgina did not spend much time cultivating or nurturing female friendship because she responded better to men and preferred their company. She could easily fall out with even her closest women friends and in 1818 she rowed with Lady Holland. The argument occurred because Lady Holland had been openly critical of the rooms she was given during a visit to Woburn; this led to a rift in the friendship lasting several months. The clash became public knowledge and one wit compared it to the feud between Queen Elizabeth (Lady Holland) and Mary, Queen of Scots (the Duchess). As usual, it was the Duke who eventually repaired the breach by writing to Lord Holland:

> As soon as the Duchess found that inconvenience existed when she [Lady Holland] was last here, she endeavoured to put a stop to it, and I will tell you truly and candidly that when the Duchess heard that Lady Holland had been complaining to others of the treatment she received at Woburn by being so ill lodged, she [the Duchess] felt a good deal of hurt, because one single word from Lady Holland to the Duchess in the first instance would have remedied everything. I have no doubt that expressions were much exaggerated as they always are in these cases, by 'some dear and good natured friend or other,' and here is an end of the subject.

Soon the two couples were back on their usual intimate terms. Both husbands, in their different ways, played their part in repairing the damage done by their intransigent wives. With a mixture of erudition and courtly love, Lord Holland knew just how to charm the Duchess and at about this time he wrote a particularly flattering poem about her role in his life:

> Gladden his days prolong his life
> Has been the study of his wife
> And I look back on winters spent
> Survey my works and say Content

She says – in vain we winters seek
In such smooth skin and damask cheek
That ivory neck with graceful curves
That glow, the present source forgoes
All give such hearts of truth to thee
And swear, few years have yet gone by
Her age is in her beauty seen
Say what she will she's but nineteen.

Not content to leave his friend to pay all the compliments to Georgina, the Duke replied with his own verse, in a similar vein. It reveals just how much he valued his wife and provides an insight into their relationship after almost twenty years of marriage.

Her Youth, is in a warm and lively heart,
A mind at ease must also bear its past;
Tis in her active form, her roundest limbs
Her laughing eye, that ne'er all her years dims.
The dimpled cheeks where loves disport and play
Her bonnie cheerful look, so blithe and gay
The merry girls, and jumping, sporting boys,
Make the old Abbey echo with their noise
To me their loved, and ever varied charms
Form the bright spell, which gloomy care disarms,
Whilst she in sickness soothes the aching pain,
In sorrow, comfort bids return again –
This is the portrait you've with skill portrayed,
The vivid colours that can never fade –
Premiums such as these, claim double worth,
However to those – to her who gave them birth,
Bedford the theme of thy inspired lays,
Tis Holland gives – tis she receives the praise.

The Duke always acknowledged the Duchess's feminine appeal and although over the years she aged and put on weight, in his eyes she remained the beautiful young woman with whom he had first fallen in love. When the Duchess was in her late thirties, he wrote to Lady Holland: 'Your description of the sleeping Nymph in Landsdowne House reminds me of the Duchess' proximity and I think I see Landsdowne with his glass to his eye doing the honours of her nymphean charms!'

He readily admitted that 'I never do well without her' and relished the lively family life she gave him; the growing band of boys and girls seemed to be never ending. Almost every year Georgina provided a new addition to the family. In February 1816 Henry was born and by the end of the year she was pregnant again but this time she was unwell. She was confined to her room, or 'prison' as the Duke described it, for several months with a threatened miscarriage, but in July 1817 Cosmo was born. At first she was 'a little disappointed at another boy' but she soon reconciled herself to the child's sex and was describing him to friends as 'a beauty'. Eighteen months later she had another son, Alfred, but he survived for less than a month. As she grew older her pregnancies became more difficult and after the birth of Alexander, when she was forty, she took a long time to regain her strength.

The Bedfords lived before the Victorian view that 'children should be seen and not heard' became fashionable. Their children were at the centre of their world and often included in their social life, but from an early age they were also provided with a sophisticated social life of their own. Georgina put on a 'child's ball' for her brood and their well-connected friends, which the Duke of Wellington's confidante Mrs Arbuthnot described as 'the prettiest thing I ever saw. They were quite little children; most of them danced very well and one little girl of the Princess Esterhazy's waltzed quite beautifully.'

As a doting mother, Georgina expected guests to watch performances by the young Russells and Twelfth Night plays became an integral part of the family's Christmas celebrations. Performances were aimed at showing off the children's talents; for instance, one year a ballet was put on specially to display Louisa's dancing prowess.

Georgina was practically involved in her children's care; she was too protective a mother to leave their welfare purely in the hands of nurses and nannies. When they were ill, she would sit up day and night with them and anxiously nursed them through the childhood illnesses of measles, scarlet fever and croup. She had strong views about medical treatments, and it seems likely that she had her children immunised against smallpox because she supported the Royal Jennerian Society for the Extermination of Smallpox by paying a subscription of three guineas a year.

The closest friends got to know the whole Bedford family well and were encouraged to bring their own children to stay. The chosen few were included in the Duke and Duchess's circle not just at Woburn but in their other homes. During the London season they stayed in their town house, first in Hamilton Place and then St James's Square. The Duke was a member of many clubs, including Almack's, Boodle's and White's, but perhaps his most appropriate membership was of the Dilettante Society. While the Duke visited his clubs, the Duchess organised formal balls and dinners for their many friends and acquaintances. She also put on impromptu parties; sometimes she took guests on steam-boat trips up the Thames and to the pleasure gardens at Vauxhall.

Many people were invited to Woburn and London but few received an invitation to Endsleigh. In this home, away from the stiff formalities of society, the Bedfords could really relax in what the Duke described as his 'ultra retirement' in Devon. 'Endsleigh is anything but triste,' he wrote, 'and as a locale I know no place so gay, and we are occupied and interested from morning till night.' In another letter he described the weather as 'uninterruptedly beautiful' and the atmosphere as lively as ever, 'tho' there is much humour/ too much/ and some cleverness; but the slip-slop and malapropism too incessant'.

One of the activities the Duchess enjoyed most at Endsleigh was fishing. After a particularly successful expedition she wrote a flirtatious message to Lord Holland via his wife, about her impressive catch: 'I tell Lord Holland with my love that it is a delightful fishing day, and the trout that we have caught have been excellent – I wish I could send you some and that he could be my "compagnon dans le peche" [companion in fishing/sin] as my poor mother would have said.'

Behind the informal atmosphere, very formal arrangements were needed to keep all the Bedford houses running smoothly. At each establishment there was a set number of permanent staff but there were also other servants who moved with the Duke and Duchess from house to house, including six footmen and four gentlemen. The gentlemen were the Head Steward of the Household, the Duke's Valet, the Duchess's Valet and the Butler. Their important roles were recognised in their title – they had to be called 'Mister' by everyone except the Duke and Duchess. One of the footmen travelled with the Duke, another with the Duchess and a third served the children. At each house there was a head housekeeper called 'Mistress'. The same gradations of rank among the servants went from the coach box to the stable so the head coachman was known as Mister, as was the head groom, but lower ranks were known only by their surnames.

Perhaps as an outlet for Georgina's endless energy, the Duke and Duchess were constantly on the move. In March 1818 they went to Paris with their daughters to visit William and his wife Elizabeth. After Lady Jane's death, William had enjoyed flirtations with several women, including Elizabeth Rawdon, and beneath a demure exterior he had gained a reputation for being 'a gay deceiver'. When his engagement to Miss Rawdon was finally announced at a ball, another candidate for his affections, Emily Rumbold, collapsed in despair and it was said that a married French woman was equally distraught.

The couple married in 1817 and at first opposition came from Elizabeth's, not William's, family. The Duke and Duchess were delighted with the match, erroneously believing that it promised great happiness for William, but Elizabeth's devoted mother was afraid of losing her daughter and her view of marriage was very like Mr Woodhouse's in Jane Austen's novel *Emma*. Countess Granville wrote:

> Lord William looks quiet and pleased, but a little small between his accomplished bride and exigeante mother-in-law, who talks all the time as if Lady William was dead:

'From the time I lost my poor Bessy.' It is clear Lord William will not love Mrs Rawdon.

During their engagement, the young couple turned to the Bedfords for advice. The Duke's letter to his son, shortly before his marriage, is amusing to read; he advises William to do exactly the opposite of what he did when he married Georgina – even down to the form the wedding ceremony should take. Perhaps with hindsight the Duke had some regrets, or perhaps he just had one rule for himself and another for everyone else. 'Avoid all unnecessary expense in the first instance, and begin with economy,' he wrote. 'If you get involved in difficulties at the outset, you may never recover them; whereas if you live within your income for the first two or three years of your marriage you will benefit of it ever after.' And although he had married Georgina at Fife House instead of in a church he told his son: 'I am decidedly of the opinion that the marriage should be in Church. Those sort of private marriages which take place in houses never appear to me to carry with them the sanctity and solemnity of the marriage vow.'

The Duke and Duchess were looking forward to seeing William and Elizabeth in France. However, from the start the trip proved ill-fated. During their voyage from Dover to Calais they were 'all tolerably sick', then on their arrival on French soil, the Duke was annoyed by their treatment at French Customs. They kept the Duke and Duchess's luggage for nearly the whole of the day and then gave the Duchess's trunks the most rigorous examination, making her open her jewel box and 'exposing with the utmost rudeness and lack of delicacy all her wearing apparel on the floor'.

Their journey to Paris was slow; the weather was 'horrible and the roads execrable'. It had been raining in France for six weeks so all the meadows and marshes were under water and they could not be ploughed. During their journey the weather was dry but exceptionally cold.

Once in Paris, they stayed with Elizabeth and William, using their home as a base to see old friends and make new ones. The city offered a vibrant social life and William, with a hint of censure, claimed that his father and stepmother were soon caught up 'in a vortex of pleasure and amusement'. The Duke and Duchess attended several balls and dinners; at one event the Duchess especially enjoyed meeting the Duc de Berry. She wrote: 'The Duc de B was most particularly kind in his manner to me and the Duke who had retreated behind a row of men to hide himself, he sought him out, and was full of politeness.'

During their visit the Duke of Wellington was also in Paris preparing for a congress at Aix-la-Chapelle, and Georgina and the Duke arranged to meet him at Fontainebleau. The Duchess wanted to give a dinner for Wellington at Versailles, but he refused her offer and instead said that he would give a dinner for her at Le Petit Trianon. When he asked King Louis to allow this, the King refused, saying that *he* wanted to give the dinner. In the end, the monarch got his way and it proved to be a memorable evening, as Lord William wrote to Lady Holland: 'Le peuple said a great many sweet and sour things; on seeing the Hero's vain efforts to pluck some roses in the gardens for the ladies, they called out thro the grille "qu'il savait cueillir des lauriers mieux que des roses" [he knows how to pick laurels better than roses].'

While the Bedfords were in Paris, Elizabeth was pregnant and at the beginning of April she gave birth. It was a difficult labour and the doctor was afraid Elizabeth might die. As an expert in childbirth, Georgina stayed with her throughout her ordeal, sitting up with her for twenty-four hours. The Duke told Lady Holland that Georgina was very impressed with the doctor:

> The Duchess commends him in the highest terms, his skill, judgement and presence of mind – I understand he on his part says he really knows not what he should have done without the Duchess's assistance . . . He was so much overcome when he left the house that he declared he would never undertake another accouchement.

A daughter was born to Elizabeth but the little girl died when she was three months old.

Shortly after this worrying time, the Duke and Duchess became anxious about their daughter Louisa's health. She had been ill for four or five weeks and had lost weight and strength. When it was discovered that she was suffering from the croup all the doctors offered were strong emetics. Little Georgy was also unwell and the Duke and Duchess felt Paris did not agree with their children, so it was decided that the Duchess would take her two daughters back to England.

The trip home was no hardship for Georgina. She was unimpressed with Paris and welcomed the excuse to go home and see all her children. While in London she visited Lady Holland, who thought she was looking very well and slimmer than usual. The Duke, with an uncharacteristic lack of gallantry, wrote to Lady Holland:

> What you say of the Duchess is very gratifying to me; though she must have lost flesh considerably by her rapid journey for she was certainly very 'gorda' when she went from hence – I trust however that she has got rid of her stomach, as she calls it and always accuses me of calling it by a more coarse name.

After a brief stay in England, the Duchess placed Louisa and Georgy, both now recovered, in Lady Holland's care while she returned to the Duke in Paris. While they were separated from their girls the Duke and Duchess sent presents and loving notes with 'a thousand kisses'. On Louisa's birthday the Duke wrote, 'be a good child, always obedient to the wishes of your mother, love your brothers and sister and believe me your very affectionate father,' while Georgina added her own playful note: 'How do you do Mistress Pussy Cat? How are all your dolls – I hope they talk French with Mademoiselle Clarisse, et qu'elles sont tres sage.'

In June, the Bedfords travelled through the south of France to Milan. Then, at the end of July, they returned to France and set sail for England. It was a bad crossing. They sailed from Calais on a Monday evening but the weather was appalling, with strong winds and rain, so after beating about the harbour for two hours the ship put back to Calais. The next day, although the sea was still rough, they sailed again and during the seven-hour voyage, four miles of which was in an open boat, they were both very seasick. It was a relief to land safely at Dover at one o'clock in the morning.

The main aim of the trip to Europe had been to see William and his wife but although Georgina had helped to save Elizabeth's life, the experience did not bond the two women. Over the next two years their relationship was to deteriorate. William and Elizabeth returned to England and were frequent visitors to Woburn but this just highlighted Georgina and Elizabeth's incompatability. Georgina became so concerned about it that she consulted Lady Holland, explaining, 'I am anxious to avoid every appearance of neglect or unkindness which as Lady William has been prejudiced against me, the slightest omission might confirm.'

William openly attacked Georgina and the Duke by writing critical letters to his father, accusing him of extravagance and blaming the Duchess. It was true that the Duke over-spent and even his vast wealth could not support such conspicuous consumption. At times he was forced to take out mortgages on his estates or make small economies. The famous Woburn sheep-shearing was cancelled at one stage, for instance, because the Duke had over-spent at Endsleigh. Nevertheless, the Duke resented his son telling him that he indulged in 'selfish and sensual amusements'.

Despite the constant criticism, Georgina continued to write warm letters to William. She did not want a family rift to develop because she knew that it would upset her husband. In 1819, after the birth of Elizabeth and William's son Hastings, she wrote:

> [I] rejoice more than I can express that everything has gone
> on so well, and that your dear and amiable wife is safe,
> happy and comfortable. I always feel delighted when I have
> it in my power to prove the unalterable affection I have
> from my first acquaintance with you; the coldness of your
> manner towards me is always a subject of regret, particularly

as I know it to be a great injustice to me, for if I have any
merits, sincerity is one of the many.

Rather than improving the situation, the Duchess's affectionate
letters seemed to exacerbate it. Elizabeth was jealous of the close
relationship her husband had had with the Duchess before their
marriage and she even insinuated there had been a sexual element
between stepmother and stepson. According to Elizabeth, her husband
had been

> Kept like a frightened schoolboy under the thumb of an
> artful and vulgar minded woman for so many years – who
> wished to cow him, my task was not easy; the greatest part
> of her spite has been my weaning him from her. His intimacy
> and communications to her before marriage were of so
> extraordinary and degrading a nature according to my
> notions of decorum that I hardly conceived it possible that
> such could exist except between a stripling and a
> 'complaisante' of the lowest kind.

Elizabeth dominated her husband at least as much as Georgina
controlled the Duke. The rift between the two women became so bad
that William took his wife to live abroad in 1821. He gave up his seat
in the House of Commons and harmed his close relationship with his
father to please Elizabeth. Over the next few years they travelled
through Germany and Italy, but absence did not make William's heart
grow fonder and he continued to write censorious letters home from
abroad.

Although at this stage Francis and John did not get involved in the
argument, the three brothers had always been very close and they
remained so after William's marriage. It seems they both preferred
Elizabeth to Georgina for different reasons. Francis had never been
close to his stepmother and it seems he felt jealous of the influence she
had over his father. While Lord and Lady William were abroad he kept
them in touch with news from England by letter. John got on well

with Georgina but he had no intention of falling out with his attractive sister-in-law. In fact, he felt more than a brotherly affection for Elizabeth as he had courted her at the same time as his brother. While William was flirting with many women, John had turned his attentions on Elizabeth. Apparently he even asked her to marry him but by then he was too late as she had just accepted William's proposal. Perhaps John was still a little in love with his sister-in-law; certainly his letters to her were flirtatious and flattering. He enjoyed calling her his 'belle-soeur' and he told her that he kept meeting her admirers. But at this time Lord and Lady William did not try to make the rest of the family take sides.

Although the Duke and Duchess were hurt by William's behaviour, they did not let it alter the way they lived, and with their wealth and social position they were beholden to no one. They behaved as they wanted and said what they thought to everyone, no matter how important the person. In the acrimonious battle between the new king, George IV, and his wife Caroline they took the side of the underdog, as usual, and supported the Queen.

The royal marriage which had started so inauspiciously became increasingly bitter as the years went by. George found Caroline repulsive, particularly as she showed scant regard for her personal hygiene. After the birth of their only child, Princess Charlotte in 1796, the couple lived apart. Once separated both husband and wife lived debauched lives. George reverted to the plump, married mistresses he had always preferred, but Caroline was equally libidinous. There were rumours of her taking lovers and even having an illegitimate child. In 1814 Caroline left England and scandalised the Continent with her behaviour. There were stories of her dancing naked to the waist at a ball in Geneva, and flaunting a lover in Naples.

On the death of George III in 1820, the Prince Regent became King. Although the government offered her money to stay away, Caroline returned to England from Italy determined to claim her rights as Queen. The new King persuaded Lord Liverpool's government to bring an Act of Parliament to deprive her of the title of Queen and to declare their marriage void. A highly embarrassing trial was then held. In August the House of Lords demanded that the Queen appear before them. They intended to dissolve the marriage on the grounds that she had been involved with Bartolomeo Pergami, 'a foreigner of low station', in the most degrading intimacy.

The Whigs, including the Bedfords, opposed the measure and there was much public support for Caroline. Every day as she attended the House of Lords her coach was surrounded by a cheering mob. Lord Brougham spoke so brilliantly in her defence, stating that to punish her would be to jeopardise both crown and constitution, that he won over many opponents. In November 1820 the bill passed its first reading in the Lords, but the majority was small. A few days later it passed its third reading with an even smaller majority. Liverpool announced that they were postponing the measures for six months, which in effect meant the bill was being dropped. The Bedfords, like many other Whig aristocrats, rallied around the Queen.

The Duke and Duchess were savagely attacked in the new satirical newspaper *John Bull* for their stand as passions ran high between crusaders for the Queen and supporters of the King. In December 1820 the paper launched a vitriolic tirade against the twenty-six ladies who they claimed had visited Caroline during the seven months since she had returned to England. The character assassination of Georgina they published opened old wounds and although there was certainly an element of truth in their comments, it was a snide attack:

> The Duchess of Bedford is a lady of the most refined sensibility. She was in mourning for the late Duke of Bedford (to whom her hand was engaged) when she accepted the offer of his brother. In this, however, let the world think as they may, there was no inconsistency; the young lady had vowed to herself and mother that she would be married to a Duke of Bedford; and if the mortality had spread in the family, her ladyship would probably have transferred her affections to all the branches of the illustrious House of Russell, till she had found one.

By January, many of the twenty-six ladies retaliated by denying they had paid a visit to the unruly Queen, but the explanations of just what had happened became a joke. Apparently, Lady Jersey was forced to go by the Whips of the Whig Party while the Duchess of Bedford, Mrs Hume, Lady Hood and Lady William Russell were 'forced to go by their Husbands', although they did not go further than the door. The idea of Georgina or Lady William being made to do anything against their will by their husbands is hard to believe, but a letter written to *John Bull* from 'True Blue', further explaining the situation, was even more incredible:

> The Duchess did visit the Queen, with sorrow do I say it, but her Grace is not in the smallest degree to blame: it was to my certain knowledge, with reluctance, but by his Grace's command that the visit was paid – we all know a wife must obey . . . The Duchess of Bedford is not the only Peer's wife to whom it has happened to have a husband who has compelled her to do what was most repugnant to her high feelings of propriety and what injures her reputation of those who are ignorant of such base tyranny.

John Bull was hardly consistent in its portrayal of the Duke. One week he was a tyrant dominating his submissive wife, the next week they poked fun at his 'unconquerable diffidence'. Their description of his oratory, cruel as it was, certainly bore more resemblance to the reality than the image of him as a controlling husband:

> It is notorious that the Duke of Bedford cannot speak two sentences and that on the only occasion to which he is remembered to have made the attempt in the House of Lords, neither his oratory nor his memory could help him to more than the first words of an intended speech. And after blushing, stammering, and blowing his nose, he sat down suddenly, to the great distress of all the spectators, and the great relief of himself.

Georgina, like her mother before her, was used to malicious attacks and did not let a few libellous comments inhibit her actions. In 1821, she took great delight in gate-crashing a ball given by George IV at Carlton House to celebrate his birthday. Mrs Arbuthnot wrote:

> [The King] invited the Duchess of Bedford because she went to the Drawing Room and sent the card an hour before the ball with 'duplicate' written upon it to make believe it was a mistake her not having got it before. Of course, the Duchess laughed at him and told it to everybody as a good joke and proof of his duplicity.

A month later, Georgina was equally irreverent in her treatment of the Duke of Wellington. Mrs Arbuthnot again: 'I went to a ball at the Duchess of Bedford's it was very good, but she was very cross because, by mistake, she had not asked the Duke of Wellington and she abused him to me because he had not come without an invitation.' As with Lord Holland and Lord Grey, Georgina seemed to see the Duke of Wellington as one of her courtiers, and so she was very indignant when he left Woburn early to go to another house party at Wherstead. He used the excuse that business in the cabinet obliged him to go to London, but Georgina thought his motives for leaving were less pure and she wrote to him tersely: 'Dear Duke, – for Cabinet read boudoir. Yours GB.'

At the time of George IV's coronation in July 1821, the Duke was still very open in his criticism of the new monarch. The King made the first move to re-establish a relationship by making the Duke one of the pages at his coronation. He also agreed to meet him with the Duke of Devonshire and Lord Jersey at the Duke of Wellington's house. Mrs Arbuthnot did not approve:

> I said [to Wellington] I thought it a great shame that he should join the King in paying so marked an attention to the most bitter amongst the Opposition, especially the Duke of Bedford and Lord Jersey who had done everything to be

personally obnoxious to the King. The Duke defended himself by saying they had been remarkably civil to him, were constantly asking him to their houses and that he had been glad to make some return.

Although the new King wanted to be reconciled to the Whig supporters of Caroline, he had no intention of pacifying his wife. When she asked the Prime Minister what dress to wear to the coronation she was told that she would not be taking part. However, on the day of the ceremony Caroline arrived uninvited at Westminster Abbey and was repeatedly refused entry by the guards. Later she crossed to Westminster Hall, where the doors were unceremoniously slammed in her face. Caroline's unhappy life was to have an equally sad end: she died just nineteen days later.

The Duke of Bedford had strong principles but sometimes standing up for his beliefs got him into more difficult situations than he intended. This was certainly the case in a political argument that developed between him and the Duke of Buckingham in 1822. Apparently, Bedford had 'bestowed opprobrious epithets' on Buckingham at the Bedford County Meeting, saying that the government 'purchased' Buckingham's support and services by offering in return high offices to his friends. The implication was that Buckingham was corrupt and, understandably, he was unwilling to ignore this slander so he called for a duel. At first Bedford tried to back-track by saying that he had meant 'nothing personally offensive'; as a gentle, peace-loving man in his fifties, he was quite happy to shoot game but not other dukes. However, his opponent continued to demand satisfaction to clear his name and Bedford was left with no choice but to accept the challenge.

In fact, the duel turned out to be more farcical than frightening. The two slightly decrepit dukes met at seven in the morning in Kensington Gardens. Both fired at the same moment, but Buckingham missed and Bedford fired in the air. Bedford then came forward and assured the Duke of Buckingham again that he had not intended anything personal against him and this time his opponent was satisfied.

When Georgina heard what had happened she was 'very much flurried'. The Duke had kept it secret from her because he was concerned that she would worry. The night before, when he returned from his club, he asked to see Georgina under the pretence of seeing her dress, then he kissed her and wished her goodnight. In the morning she thought he had left early to breakfast at Holland House and had no idea he had gone to fight a duel. The Duchess did not expect such risk-taking behaviour from her usually calm, rational husband. It showed that although the Duke was a reluctant hero, he did have the courage of his convictions and, after almost twenty years of marriage, he could still surprise his wife.

CHAPTER SEVEN

The Family in Crisis

During the early 1820s Georgina faced one of the most testing times of her life when the Duke became seriously ill and nearly died. The Duchess was made aware of her own vulnerable position and found herself exposed to her enemies; for the first time in her life, her usual resilience left her and she experienced serious depression.

In June 1822, while the Duke and Duchess were at Endsleigh, the Duke suffered a paralytic stroke that affected his face badly, damaging the nerves and changing his appearance. His doctor was Sir Henry Halford, physician to George IV and later William IV and Queen Victoria. Sir Henry made a detailed diagnosis of the Duke's condition for the Duchess, explaining that although the paralytic seizure involved the muscles of the face only, it was 'as complete attack in its nature . . . as if it had incapacitated half the body' and that after such a severe attack there was always a 'stronger propensity' for another seizure. The treatment he suggested was aimed at preventing a second stroke and also at restoring proper action to the muscles that had been damaged, although he doubted the Duke's face would ever return to normal and any progress would be very slow. He concluded, with the smooth bedside manner for which he was famous:

> I feel sanguine in my hopes that more disorder may be prevented by a process of treatment to which the Duke submits himself with all that good sense and manliness for which he is remarkable – and as no injury appears to me to have been done to the mental faculties I trust he will live in comfort though in a less assured state, and deprived of some of those powers of enjoyment which are compatible only with perfect health.

Used to her husband always being there for her, like a rock in her life, Georgina was completely traumatised by her husband's illness. She wrote to Lady Holland: 'It would make your kind heart ache to see his poor dear distorted face and his whole sickly appearance.' After a couple of months, the Duke began to recover slowly, but Georgina was sure her husband would have another stroke and die:

> There is always a little pain either in the head, the eyes or the neck, tho' not sufficient to be considered as illness, yet enough to irritate and keep up constant anxiety in my mind. The paralysed side of the face remains immoveable . . . God knows what we shall do, but wherever I am, I must ever be in a wretched situation.

Instead of being supportive at this difficult time, two of her stepsons, Francis, Lord Tavistock, and William, were critical of her, believing she was exaggerating the extent of the Duke's illness. Georgina was painfully aware of what they thought:

> [Lord Tavistock] will not see how ill his father is and writes favourable accounts of his health to all enquiries. Do not

mention this as neither Lord or Lady T was kind to me, and this observation of mine would only make bad worse. Lord John is all kindness to me and all attention and affection to his father.

Having spoken to his brothers about the situation, William delayed his visit to England and rather than take responsibility for his decision himself, as usual blamed the Duchess. He wrote to Lady Holland: 'Unhappily the Duchess has taken such a hatred for Bessy and myself, and has so poisoned my father's mind against us, that I fear our presence gives him no pleasure. This is a great source of unhappiness for me, for you know how I love my father.' In another letter he explains:

> Notwithstanding the anxious longing I have to see my father
> (whom I love with all my heart and soul) after his terrible
> illness. In my eyes he has but one fault in the world – which
> is not loving and admiring Bessy enough, but it is natural
> he should be biased by the feelings of his wife.

In August the Duke and Duchess returned to Woburn. As soon as they were settled, Georgina dedicated herself to nursing her husband, often sitting up with him for twenty-four hours a day. As Halford had warned, the Duke's progress was slow and the only medical intervention available at this time was cupping him to drain blood every ten days. As the days dragged by Georgina's depression deepened. She told her friends that seeing her husband in such a frail state was 'a melancholy and heart-breaking sight'. When eventually William paid a visit to England in September he saw for himself that the Duchess was not over-reacting. He wrote in his diary: 'I found my father in a melancholy state of health, tho' I hope not dangerous, his mouth distorted, the muscles on one side of his face unnerved.'

To try to improve the Duke's health, in November 1822 the Bedfords went to Hastings. The Duke showed a stoical attitude to his suffering, explaining to Lady William:

I am come in search of that most desirable and enviable of all blessings health. Whether I shall find it or not, God alone knows, but the progress I have made since William left us is very slow – if I could persuade myself that it was sure I should be content. At all events the old remedy *patienza* is always at hand, and to that with a grateful and cheerful mind I submit.

During this time, William sent many letters and presents to his father, but the Duke was more concerned about Lord and Lady William's attitude to the Duchess than material tokens of affection. Tensions between the people he loved best distressed him. He urged his son and daughter-in-law to re-establish harmony for his sake. He wrote to Lady William:

I cannot help wishing that you had named the Duchess in your letter. It is an object near to my heart that all misunderstandings should be done away and I cannot help feeling anxious, most anxious about it – should I not get over this protracted illness, it will smooth the pillow of a dying man on his way to the tomb.

Despite the Duke's plea, Lord and Lady William continued to put the blame for the feud on Georgina. The Duke wrote to his son:

The concluding sentence in your letter gave me great pain. Why should you suppose that the Duchess dislikes you? I can assure you that the very reverse is the case, and I think I know every feeling of her heart. She is ever anxious to show every possible kindness and attention to you and your brothers, but her spirits are sometimes depressed, and this I think you may readily account for without any great stretch of the imagination. She indeed, imagines that neither you nor Tavistock nor John like her, and in this I am sure that she is wrong, but the feeling arises from an excess of sensibility and I cannot blame her.

Gradually, over the winter, the Duke regained his strength, but he was still not his old self and nine months after his initial illness the situation was made worse by a severe attack of gout in his leg and hand. The Duke was confined to his room for more than a month; over-anxious and depressed, Georgina was sure the pain in his leg was due to a recurrence of his illness and not gout. 'Constant watching and miserable anxiety has subdued the gaiety of my mind,' she wrote. 'But there is enough left to be always cheerful before him, and I thank God, also, for the power of making him quite happy.'

During this time the Duchess never left the Duke. She did everything possible to make him comfortable, wheeling him from his bed to the sofa and back again at night and writing his letters for him as he was not able to write for himself. She described her spirits as 'like a thermometer, and they rise and fall according to the Duke's feelings'.

Although she tried to put on a brave face in front of him, inside she was feeling totally isolated. The Duke was her security both emotionally and financially and, as only the stepmother of the future Duke, she worried about what would happen to her and her children if he died. At this time, she saw Woburn as a prison, and claimed this 'captivity' was unbearable to her Highland blood. Unable to travel, and in no mood to entertain, she did not even see her father and brother, who were in Scotland, or her sisters, who lived in different parts of the country. As her letters reveal, her emotions were very raw and near the surface:

As long as I do not hear music or meet anyone very kind to me, (which I am not very liable to) I appear cheerful and calm. But I cannot tell you what a desolation takes place in me when exposed to either of these things, I then feel all the horror I must go thro' and the tears are a relief, the thoughts that accompany them are too dreadful to dwell on, and I fly out on to something or other to drive away thoughts.

In her unhappiness Georgina turned to Lord Grey for support. He had for many years been a friend of both the Duke and Duchess, but at this time Georgina's letters showed a dependence on him that suggests a very intimate friendship. She asked him to 'write to me now and then, it is a great comfort in affliction to hear from those who we love and esteem', and in another letter she told him:

> To you I would say anything if you were in reach of me, should I be visited by the heaviest calamity you are the person I should above all wish to see, to consult, to be guided by, for in you I have complete faith and for you the greatest affection and highest respect, there are some things that cannot be written, tho' they could be said.

Georgina always had time for flirtation, and even during these dark days she could switch from being morbid to coquettish. She always cared about her appearance and relished the flattering compliments of her admirers:

> You are very kind my dear Lord Grey, to say that you shall be happy to see me, I am certainly not worth looking at, but perhaps that attraction may make me a little more valuable to those who like yourself are amicably and affectionately inclined towards me.

The other stalwart friends at this time were Lord and Lady Holland and they cheered up the Duke and Duchess by visiting Woburn. The Duke looked forward to their visits and said that he was well enough 'to laugh at your jokes and feel your kindness'. Knowing Georgina well, Lady Holland could see that the Duchess was deeply unhappy, and seemed to understand her suffering. Feeling exposed, Georgina wrote to her: 'You are very kind towards me, I more seriously ill than anyone is aware of, all I hope is that I may not fail till the Duke no longer wants my love, then, whatever happens is of little consequence.'

However, although Georgina appreciated Lady Holland's friendship, her depression made her question all her relationships and for a brief period of time in early 1823, she believed even her greatest friend had turned against her. She thought Lady Holland was trying to exclude her and turn their foursome into a *ménage à trois*. The Duke explained to his friend:

> There is a passage in your letter which has very much hurt the Duchess – she thinks you propose to me to go abroad with you and Holland and leave her in England! – it is in vain that I endeavour to persuade her that it is morally impossible that such a proposal could come from you, so you must write to her yourself and set her too sensitive mind at rest.

It seems likely the Duchess was suffering from nervous exhaustion and was on the verge of a breakdown; certainly the Duke seemed to think she was showing signs of paranoia. He told Lady Holland:

> You must forgive the Duchess – her spirits are worn down by constant watchings and anxieties during ten hideous months, and her sensibility is acutely alive to every trifling occurrence, too frequently imagining things which have no existence in truth and perpetually worrying her own mind by imagining evils – most anxiously do I wish that her good and generous heart were relieved from a purpose which seems to overwhelm all her comfort and happiness.

The real problems lay not with Georgina's friends but with her stepsons and, by being wary of them, the Duchess was not being paranoid; their animosity was real. At first Georgina tried to be magnanimous towards them and although they had been cruel to her when the Duke was taken ill, she tried to put her hurt feelings behind her. When Lord William came to stay at Woburn in April 1823 she was very welcoming and William had to admit to his wife: 'The Duchess received me with the greatest affection and appears anxious to please me . . . She also talks of you as if she intended to be civil if not kind to you, expresses a desire to hear you sing etc.'

After his visit, Lord William received a letter from the Duchess saying she wished to get on well with him and his wife. Trying to bring the problem out in the open and get at the heart of it, she wrote emotionally about the genuine pain Lord and Lady William's unfair attacks had caused her:

> Notwithstanding all you have heard to the contrary, that my feelings towards you have never varied . . . The total change in Lady William's opinion of me, and her affection for me, is very mortifying, and what I sincerely regret, but as my conscience is perfectly free from having said or done anything against her, her husband or her child, I can only trust time will convince her that she has been misinformed. You may ask those you have perfect faith in, if ever they heard me express anything but the strongest attachment to you, and the greatest possible admiration and liking for Bessy . . . Lady Tavistock in particular knows how often to her I have lamented that all my attentions and wish to please Lady William had failed and how much I took to heart everything I meant kindly, being received differently and differently stated. My prospects for a great length of time have been very melancholy. Probably dearest William, I shall ere long be separated from you all and we may never meet, but I do swear most solemnly that I have to all of you, been a steady, true and attached friend, and that I am ready to face anyone who will bring any charge against me either of speaking unkindly of you or Lady William. Your father, if ever you will speak to him upon the subject will state the same thing, he knows how often I have grieved over my unfortunate fate of never pleasing where I took most pains to do so.

After reading his stepmother's letter, William's attitude softened towards the woman who had once been his trusted friend and he told Elizabeth: 'I have accepted the stretched out hand – and squeezed it.' Echoing the words of his father a few months earlier, he begged his wife to put the old arguments with the Duchess behind her for the sake of the Duke:

> . . . remember dear love your part in the great drama of life is to play the daughter-in-law of a wicked, envious step-mother and your reward if you play it well (and no small one either) will be to smoothe the pillow of a dying man – to say nothing of contributing to a husband's happiness.

But it seems the fine sentiments of both sides did not transfer into actions because when William met the Duchess in London he claimed she 'was cold and distant to me, I could not make her out, but she was playing some game too deep for my simplicity'. Despite his stated good intentions, William could not resist taking every opportunity to undermine the Duchess's vital role in his father's life. When the Duke complained to his son that he did not feel he was making any progress in his recovery, William blamed Georgina for his father's low spirits, claiming that she depressed the Duke's mood by constantly recalling his illness. The Duchess's faithful defender, Lord Holland, was furious at this attack and told William exactly what he thought:

> [Your father] neither is, nor can be, in a state which a reasonable man can take anything but a gloomy view of his condition, and my wonder is that he contemplates it with so much evenness of spirits and calmness of philosophy as he does . . . What there is therefore of melancholy in his letters I attribute to his sense of his true situation, to the disease, and to the lowering remedies, certainly not to the Duchess. She is despondent in her own mind and in her conversation with others, but quite the reverse with him, unremittingly attentive, and full of conversation, exertion and fun before him. Believe me, upon long, very long

experience, that the health and in greater degree, the spirits of your father as far as they are good, are due to the Duchess, and if she does now and then worry any of you about trifles and tracasseries you will, I am sure, make some allowances for the painful and anxious attendance she has gone through, which is really enough to overcome the spirits of anyone much less disposed than she is want to be mentally and by nature, to torment herself with foreboding calamity.

Although beneath the surface the feud was not resolved, for a time there was at least the appearance of a rapprochement. The Duke asked his son to get a lady's watch for the Duchess as a twentieth wedding anniversary present, and when Elizabeth first returned to England the Duchess made a real effort to be friendly. When they visited Woburn, even Elizabeth had to admit 'the Duchess was full of every kind of attention'.

Like Georgina, Elizabeth preferred the company of men to the friendship of women and she was much more forgiving of the faults she saw in the opposite sex than in her own. In fact, Elizabeth liked her father-in-law and found it much easier to get on with him than with Georgina. Many years later, she wrote:

> Mon beau père était grand Seigneur (qualitiés et défauts), fort genereux, aimant la bonne chère et aimant à la partager avec ses amis ... Un peu Céladon mais pas avec les servants, il n'était pas crapuleux, quoique gourmand et gallant; fort liberal en politique ... il était philosophe. [My step-father was a great man (in his qualities and his failings), very generous, he loved the good life and liked to share it with his friends ... A bit of a sentimental lover, but never with the servants, he was not villainous, although greedy and gallant; fiercely liberal in his politics ... he was a philosopher.]

She did not feel the same respect for the Duchess. Both Elizabeth and Georgina were very attractive and expected to be the centre of attention. When they were together, each felt the presence of a rival and neither of them enjoyed such close competition from within the family. They also had completely different approaches to life. Elizabeth was an intellectual while Georgina was instinctive; the Duchess was fun-loving and flirtatious while Elizabeth was high-minded and moralistic. It is also possible that Elizabeth was jealous because, as a Duchess, Georgina enjoyed much greater wealth and social prestige than she would ever possess as the wife of a second son.

In July 1823, William and Elizabeth came to stay at Woburn for nine months. Fortunately, the Duke and Duchess were away for much of this time visiting London, Scotland and then Brighton. Although the Duke claimed he was short of money, he found sufficient finances to buy Campden Hill, an estate in Kensington. The house was elegant and simple with large windows and an attractive verandah, but Georgina soon employed Jeffry Wyatville, the architect who had designed Endsleigh, to remodel the house in a more fashionable style. To give an Italianate feel, four large terracotta vases were ordered for the garden, a new drawing room was designed and the dining room was enlarged. As at Endsleigh, the plan of the house reveals the Duchess's desire to be near her children. On the first floor, Georgina's dressing room is next to the children's sitting room so that her sons and daughters could spend time with her while she was dressing for dinner. Over the years, the Bedfords turned the house into a comfortable family home, adding two water closets to make the most of the latest modern conveniences. Another great advantage of Campden Hill was that it was next door to Holland House, so the Duke and Duchess looked forward to having the Hollands as their neighbours not just in Bedfordshire but also in London.

While in London, Georgina continued her charm offensive on Elizabeth by offering to help Lord and Lady William find and decorate a town house. However, although her letter to her stepdaughter-in-law was friendly, she could not resist the odd barbed comment aimed at the couple's past criticisms of her. Beneath a veneer of friendship, it was a cleverly coded way of letting Elizabeth

know that Georgina was well aware of the rude comments her
adversary made behind her back:

> I have just heard a most excellent sermon the effects of
> which are to make me feel in charity with all man and
> womankind, to do unto others, as I would be done by . . . I
> have looked at the outside of Cavendish Square. I like the
> appearance much and should have great satisfaction in being
> allowed to assist in your comfort, let me paper the quarter
> gallery, by way of something Duchess like, and magnificent,
> don't say I am stingy after such a distinguished mark of
> extravagance . . . I will try to see everything en rose, instead
> of en noir, but do you think I have any reason to be full of
> joy or hope . . . I flatter myself your suggestions have been
> attended to as they always will be, by a sensible woman like,
> Georgy Bedford.

In a letter to Lord William after Elizabeth had suffered a miscarriage,
she wrote in a similar, slightly sarcastic tone, showing that she was
trying to forgive but she would not forget the past:

> I hope Bessy will take care of herself, and she has proved
> that she is not past childbearing. I hope for some time she
> will rest upon her 'lauriers'. My kind love to her. I think we
> get on, tho' slowly de part et d'autre; dear, then my dear
> Lady William, now come to dear Bessy, je tremble de mon
> audace.

At the end of August, the Duke and Duchess went to Scotland. The
Duke enjoyed the Highland air and was able to get plenty of exercise;
one day he managed to spend seven and a half hours outside, on his
pony or 'striding over the rivers, gun in hand, and killing nearly all
that I saw'. The Duchess amused herself by fishing and was rewarded
with a good catch; one day she hooked a fifteen and a half pound
salmon with a fly and the next she caught a seventeen and a half

pound one. In the relaxed Highland atmosphere, the couple were happier than they had been since the Duke's illness began.

Once back at Woburn with Lord and Lady William, the Duchess's good mood soon evaporated. She became as concerned as ever about her husband's health, telling Lord Grey:

> The return of his face to its natural form and powers would be evidence that pressure no longer remains. As his face is immoveable I cannot consider him as better . . . I do not think him stronger that he gains flesh, living as he does as well as possible, meat one day game the other – It is useless for people to try and persuade me out of the evidence of my own sense, believe me I see clearly and my fears are but too well grounded . . . I have no human being near me to who I can say anything on the subject nearest my heart and I am told I have many enemies.

Halford had suggested that the Duke and Duchess should consider spending part of the winter in Brighton as he thought taking the waters and the milder climate might do the Duke good. From the late eighteenth century, Brighton had grown up as a fashionable resort due to the belief that seawater had medicinal properties. A Sussex doctor, Richard Russell, set up practice in the town and wrote a book on the good effects that not only bathing in but also drinking seawater could have on a patient's health. Brighton became known for its louche and lively society, particularly when the Prince Regent became a regular visitor, building his decadent Pavilion in the resort.

After looking at several houses, the Duke and Duchess rented two in Regency Square because they needed an overflow house for their staff and children. One of the main attractions of the town for the Duke was being close to the Hollands who also came to stay in Brighton. Georgina told Lady Holland: 'to be near you really and sincerely is my first object as I think the Duke's happiness abroad depends chiefly upon you and your dear kind Holly.' The Duke agreed, writing to his friend: 'Our intercourse will I trust be frequent, and I think I shall always find myself in your house on a fine day, when I wish to look at a gay Canaletto, or any other pleasing picture. You must moreover pass our door every day in taking your airings.'

The Duchess was also particularly dependent on the Hollands at this time and was grateful to Lady Holland for advising her to get away from Woburn for a change of scene. Georgina wrote to Lady Holland in fulsome tones about how much she missed her friends when they were apart. Her letter also showed how much the Duke's illness had changed her, revealing how vulnerable and insecure she was feeling at this time; for once, she was more interested in securing female affection than attracting male attention.

> Absence from those we love for a short time is bearable. But what is life worth without the charm of their society. It is dreary indeed and I thank you for having got me away from the Abbey for no one can imagine how completely wretched my life was there . . . By your kindness through life my dearest Lady Holland it will ever be a comfort to you to expect that your affectionate attentions smoothed the declining days of a being as full of gratitude to you as I am. Forgive my little trite note, but when I think how slight the tenure of any happiness is, you cannot wonder at my being at least serious. I hope I am established in your heart for ever and ever.

While in Brighton the Duke bathed every other day, but overall neither of the Bedfords were particularly impressed with the town. It had recently expanded with the population doubling and the number of houses increasing almost threefold. Georgina described the scene as 'very triste. Many houses built and no one to live in them, the place ill kept and what was once a little quiet village has made an unsuccessful attempt to become a rival place to Worthing.' Like the older generation in every era, the Duke was critical of the type of trendy young men attracted to the resort and he complained about 'the shoals of City Dandies walking, riding and driving there'.

In fact, there were few people with whom the Duke and Duchess wanted to socialise, but although there was a lack of friends there was also an absence of enemies and Georgina admitted, 'it is a relief to me to be without those who so evidently dislike me'. During their stay, George IV invited the Duchess and her children to a child's ball at his Pavilion. The King was 'engrossed' with the Bedford brood and when he saw one of the boys looking at his Order of the Golden Fleece George asked him what he thought that order was. 'Chinese, I suppose,' replied the self-possessed little boy, to his monarch's amusement.

Louisa, looking beautiful, like a miniature version of her mother, was an instant success with the King. All her many performances at Woburn's theatre had been a preparation for this moment when she danced a solo, 'The Spanish Shawl Dance', before George and one hundred other thoroughbred children and their doting mothers. Afterwards the King went up to her and said, 'You are a very pretty little girl and you dance charmingly. Now is there anything I can do for you?' Showing the boldness of both her mother and grandmother, Louisa answered, 'Yes there is. Your Majesty can bring me some ham sandwiches and a glass of port wine negus, for I am very hungry.' Never a man to disappoint an attractive female, George promptly did what she asked.

In December, the Duke and Duchess returned to Woburn for Christmas. Georgina's spirits were low and the Abbey seemed very dark and empty without any of her children staying. Her friend Lord Grey was visiting Endsleigh and it seems she would rather have been there with him than at Woburn with her husband. She wrote:

> As to the Duke I have nothing satisfactory to say, he has been very weak since we returned here . . . and I do not think he improves particularly in his walking. He is very weak on his legs. We have been quite alone, which in this large house is very melancholy . . . I wish I could have a comfortable chat with you, a quiet walk at my dear Endsleigh by the side of the River, or on the other side of

the river on a wild common with the rapid Tavy running through it, as bright as any Scotch stream, alas, I fear no such comfort is in store for me and I must content myself with my Mausoleum where all the inhabitants are cold and the splendid magnificence is very depressing and chilling.

The Duke was concerned about the Duchess; he knew her usually sky-high self-esteem had plummeted to an all-time low, and that in her early forties she was feeling her age. Portraits of her at this time reveal she had begun to look middle-aged and matronly, her once fine complexion now florid, her sensuous mouth turned down and her large blue eyes having a wary expression. The Duke told Lady Holland: 'The Duchess looks miserably thin and worn but in my eyes her Beauty, which you enquire about, is not at all impaired by it. She talks of herself as a worn fragment fit only for antiquarians to admire.'

Her mood was not helped by a renewed row with William and Elizabeth. They were rude about her behind her back, describing her as 'our red faced vixen' and 'an ill-conditioned mad woman', but when they were insolent to her face, the Duchess finally refused to put up with any more of their disrespectful behaviour. After a visit to Woburn, Lady William sent an angry letter about her treatment, accusing the Duchess of 'mischief making, duplicity and falsehood'. The Duke was furious and took his wife's side, explaining to Lady Holland:

I confess I cannot comprehend William's conduct to the Duchess, he does not treat her with the common decency and decorum due from a man to a woman; much more from him to his father's wife . . . Surely the Duchess cannot be expected to make an apology for an offence denied and not committed! Whilst William and Lady William continue to behave in this extraordinary manner, I cannot consent (painful as it may be to me) to go again to her before I leave town. I never name the subject to the Duchess. It has been one of great anxiety and vexation to her, and would to God she had been spared the pain of it from my own son!

He also wrote a letter to William defending Georgina, telling him candidly where he believed the fault lay:

> The Duchess and I have always felt and acted the same towards you and Lady William, and I can venture to affirm, from a thorough knowledge of the fact, that the Duchess's conduct towards you and yours has uniformly been kind, generous and affectionate, therefore she can have no 'sins' to lay to her conscience in that respect. I am unwilling to say anything which may appear in the least degree harsh, and will therefore content myself with observing that the Duchess has been abundantly tolerant and forbearing, and now let the matter drop and be buried in oblivion. It has been the cause of too much worry, both to the Duchess and myself, and in my state of health I feel it to be more than my head will bear.

By the summer of 1824 the situation was so bad that the Duke banned Elizabeth from Woburn. Open conflict broke out in August when Elizabeth was supposed to be going to the Abbey to take her leave of the Duke and Duchess before they went to Scotland and she went with William to Dorset. According to Georgina, her stepdaughter-in-law let them know the day before that she intended to come and the Duke considered this impertinent.

Elizabeth was just about to leave London when she received a letter from her husband saying that his father had sent a note begging him to stop her coming. The Duke wrote in his letter that although he could not demand affection for Georgina from his children, a certain 'decorum and respect was due to her as mistress of the house'. He went on to say that Elizabeth had been rude and ungrateful to the Duchess, especially as Georgina had saved her life when she gave birth in Paris. The letter finished by saying that unless Georgina was treated with respect, Lady William was banned from the Abbey.

Elizabeth was furious and saw her banishment as a declaration of war between the two women. The feud became so public that even the

King heard about it. In a damage-limitation exercise to try to protect the Russells' reputation, Lord John acted as a go-between. He wrote to his sister-in-law:

> I own I think it a great pity to make the world talk about our family quarrels . . . I have a great love and even reverence for my father which nothing will shake. I am very sorry that he is under the influence of a wicked woman, but I see some of my best friends under the influence of their wives and it is more their luck than their merit if those wives turn out to be well principled and virtuous. Whatever you do, pray do not abuse my father to the world.

He encouraged Elizabeth to end the quarrel or 'be prepared for the worst that a powerful, vindictive and unscrupulous enemy could do'. His letters reveal the jealousy and suspicion felt by the Duke's first family towards his second. Even Lord John voiced his concerns that the Duke might change his will in favour of Georgina's children:

> It is very bad policy to quarrel with Woburn. Only suppose that T [Tavistock] and I were to do so likewise, as we might without being very quarrelsome. Do not you think my father would hear less truth? That he would lead a more unhappy life and even that he might be led to do Tavistock a serious injury? In fact she throws stones at us to get back nuts and any expression of resentment on our part must strengthen her influence.

To take his advice would have been out of character for Elizabeth; even her husband acknowledged she had a 'haughty, proud, unbending and unforgiving mind'. As no neutral ground could be found, father and son were estranged, but although there were no meetings, the Duke kept in touch with his son by letter. He did not want to have to choose between his son and his wife but Georgina was more important to him than even William, and he admitted that she 'contributed so

large a portion of my happiness thro' life'. He was also a just man and
believed that Georgina had been unfairly treated, so he was determined
that his daughter-in-law not his wife should compromise. The Duke
wrote:

> I wish she [Lady William] could be persuaded for the sake
> of further peace and comfort to us all to make some advances
> towards the establishment of harmony – no-one is more
> alive than I am to the comforts of a happy and united
> family, but I fear/entre nous Lady William . . . is unwilling
> to own herself in the wrong.

William was equally intransigent and wrote to Lady Holland that if
the Duke felt it was his duty to protect his wife, he felt the same duty
to defend Elizabeth:

> . . . that being the case I cannot, nor will I enter the house
> of a woman, who turns out my wife on false grounds . . .
> What do you mean by repentance? I have nothing to repent
> of. The person who acts must repent, not the person who
> suffers, it was an act of revenge and hatred on the part of the
> Duchess of Bedford towards Lady William.

The argument was not resolved and proved to be very divisive, not just
among the Bedford family but also among their friends because they
were forced to take sides. Lady William was particularly scathing of
anyone who did not declare unquestioning loyalty to her. She wrote of
her brother-in-law John: 'Little Johnnikins always repeats everything
he hears to our disadvantage (to keep up our spirits) and on either of
us exclaiming "dear me, why didn't you contradict," he laughs violently
and answers, "Oh, I said nothing." '

Fortunately, the two warring couples were separated when William
and Elizabeth went to Dorset, and there were no meetings with the
Duke and Duchess for more than a year. Eventually, the Duke and his
son put the disagreement behind them, hoping their wives would

follow their example. The Duke was very relieved and evidently wanted to forget the whole explosive episode. In September, he wrote to William:

> Whilst I regret that we should be compelled to think and feel differently on the unpleasant subject we have recently discussed, I agree with you that any attempt at explanation must be perfectly useless. In every other respect, your letter has given me the most heartfelt satisfaction, and I cordially thank you for it. Let everything on so painful a subject be now forgotten and completely blotted from our memories.

CHAPTER EIGHT

The Art
of Loving

Georgina was emotionally destabilised by the Duke's illness and the feud with her stepchildren. As her letters to Lord Grey reveal, she was looking for a male protector, someone to give her the solace and support she needed. In fact, she found what she was looking for in an unexpected quarter, not with a mature statesman but with a young artist, Edwin Landseer.

Landseer was just eighteen when he first entered the Bedfords' circle in 1820. As a patron of the arts, the Duke was a keen supporter of contemporary artists and was introduced to Landseer, who was already recognised as outstandingly gifted. Born into an artistic family, Edwin had been a child protégé. His father, John Landseer, was a famous engraver, while his mother had modelled for Sir Joshua Reynolds, appearing in 1788 as a reaper in his picture of 'The Gleaners'.

Edwin started drawing at the age of four. His paintings of animals were so brilliant that he won the silver medal of the Society of Arts for a drawing of a hunter when he was thirteen, and also exhibited his first drawings at the Royal Academy. He had been studying art and the anatomy of animals in Benjamin Haydon's informal school for several years when, in 1816, he entered the Royal Academy, studying under the Keeper, Johann Fuseli, a painter fascinated with the weird and grotesque. Fuseli became particularly fond of the young man, calling him 'my curly headed dog boy' because of Edwin's curling hair and skill at painting dogs.

Landseer's first major success came in 1818 when his 'Fighting Dogs Getting Wind' was exhibited at the Society of Painters. The critics admired his work and he was soon acknowledged as 'the first animal painter of the day'. His early fame gave him celebrity status and he began to move in literary as well as artistic circles, mixing with the leading writers of the era. After a lecture by Hazlitt he met Keats, and Leigh Hunt became a frequent visitor at the Landseers' house.

The Duke became Landseer's first major patron and through his connection with the Bedfords, Edwin got an insight into the world of the aristocracy. The glamour and extravagance of the Duke and Duchess's lifestyle must have been quite intoxicating for the young man. When he first saw Georgina she was sexually confident and beautiful; as the Reverend Sydney Smith said of her: 'I am forced from time to time to read over my papers of holy orders to prevent myself from admiring her too much.' She evidently gave off an air of flirtatious availability and Elizabeth described her as 'une coquette comme la lune'.

No doubt Landseer also made an instant impression on Georgina, and not just through his art. Although not a tall man, he was very good-looking, with dark hair and brooding romantic features. The Duchess and the artist had much in common; he had a good voice and enjoyed singing and he was also a very good mimic, full of anecdotes. Lady Leslie wrote:

> His eyes sparkled when he told a good story, and as easily welled out tears by the narration of anything sad for he was a man of intense impressionability. He was witty and brought forth wit in others and the very Prince of story

tellers, with a dramatic power of narration and an incomparable mimic of both human beings and of animals. He would take one on imaginary walks in the Zoological Gardens imitating the birds and beasts wonderfully well.

Unlike Georgina's usual circle of aging aristocrats offering courtly love and smooth manners, beneath Landseer's urbane social veneer there was a hint of danger and violence. Some of his paintings showed a sadistic streak; for instance, his famous painting 'Cat's Paw' shows a monkey forcibly holding on to a cat and using one of the animal's paws to pick up some piping hot chestnuts that are roasting on top of a stove. The cat's two kittens, in the clothes' basket, are protesting at the cruelty to their mother. Another example can be seen in one of Woburn's game lists: each division is headed with a little etching of an animal in the agonies of death.

When they first met, a relationship between the Duchess and the artist must have seemed improbable. Landseer was twenty-one years younger than the Duchess and only slightly older than her eldest son. Although Campbell Lennie in his biography of the artist suggests that an affair between Georgina and Landseer began almost immediately, and that the Duchess's son Alexander, born in 1821, was the artist's child, it seems more likely for both logistical and psychological reasons, that the relationship developed later.

Landseer's first recorded visit to Woburn was in 1823 and at about this time he was commissioned by the Duke to paint a portrait of his wife. Inevitably, this meant Georgina and Landseer spent much time together at a moment when the Duchess was feeling at her most vulnerable and isolated. She feared that the Duke would soon be dead and after he had gone her life would 'become a cheerless blank'. The resulting portrait suggests Landseer managed to penetrate her isolation and to empathise with her mood. His painting, far from flattering, reflects the effects of depression on Georgina's appearance and perfectly captures her unhappiness. It appears this portrait was very special to Landseer because he kept a sketch he did for it for the rest of his life. It was an unusual work for the animal painter and afterwards he said it was the only 'regular portrait' he ever intended to paint. It seems he did not wish to take much money from the Duke for it, perhaps because his emotions about it were not purely commercial. However, the Duke insisted, explaining to Landseer:

> You must excuse me for saying that I think the price you have named for the portrait of the Duchess is quite ridiculous, and you must allow me in this instance to place my judgement in opposition and consequently to pay fifty pounds to your account . . . instead of the sum you named. Had you proposed a still larger sum than this I should not have been dissatisfied . . . the sum I have paid can neither be thought too much nor too little as it cannot be bought with precedent one way or the other.

Landseer and Georgina's courtship was through art rather than letters. The progression of their relationship is captured in the dozens of sketches and paintings Landseer did of her. Wherever they went, Landseer's sketchbook went too, and there are pictures of the Duchess on a pony, with a chimney sweep, arriving at a ball, gardening and picnicking. Some of the most touching sketches evocatively recreate the intimacy of their relationship. Perhaps the most subtly erotic is a sketch of the Duchess from the back, featuring her alluring swan neck, beautiful shoulders and curvaceous figure. Another more blatantly sexual picture shows the Duchess reclining with a blissful expression on her face and one breast bared. Landseer's sketches were like a modern photo album, aimed at capturing precious moments between them; they were not intended as a serious record, but the tenderness and love felt by the artist for his subject is plain for all to see.

Landseer also painted or sketched Georgina's children and animals. Lady Louisa was painted feeding a pony while Lord Alexander appeared with a pug dog and a spaniel. Art gave the lovers an excuse to spend many hours alone together and Edwin helped Georgina to explore her potential as an artist. As a girl, she had had a natural aptitude for art but her talent had not been developed; now Edwin taught her how to etch. It is clear that she was good – Grave's catalogue of Landseer's works shows that the Duchess etched most of his pictures of the middle 1820s. Working together on a common project, sharing enjoyment from the same simple pleasures, gradually a relationship developed between the older woman and younger man that was to last for the rest of their lives.

The romance that seems to have been built on several levels, physical, emotional and spiritual, added a new quality to every aspect of the lovers' lives. Georgina was Landseer's muse. Before meeting her he could draw animals brilliantly but his backgrounds were lacklustre. He was conscious of this deficiency and in 1822 he persuaded the accomplished landscape painter Patrick Nasmyth to put in the background of his painting 'The Bull and Frog'. He also asked permission to postpone painting the background of 'Lion', the Alpine mastiff, until after his first visit to Scotland in 1824.

Landseer's journey to Georgina's home country provided just the inspiration he required. He discovered that he loved the Highland landscape as much as she did and it was to provide the perfect background for his art. On this visit he travelled with fellow artist C. R. Leslie by steamboat to Edinburgh, then on to Loch Lomond and Loch Katrine. From there they walked across the mountains to Loch Earn to be present at an annual meeting of the Highlanders. Leslie's recollections capture the romance of their visit:

> It was a bright fresh autumnal morning when we left Loch Earn head for the other end of the lake, a distance of seven mile, in a large row-boat in which, besides ourselves were a number of Highlanders, – men, women and children. As we passed down the lake, the rowers amused us with stories of the fairies that inhabited the shores; these stories being matters of serious belief for them. Occasionally we heard the distant sound of bagpipes, and as they neared us the hills were enlivened by the appearance of parties of Highlanders in full costume each headed by a piper and all bound for the place of rendez-vous. The little voyage

afforded us an enjoyment of the Highlands, with all that is native to them, in perfection. The amusement of the games which we afterwards witnessed was nothing to the delight of gliding gently down the clear smooth lake with such accompaniments.

Although there is no official record of Landseer staying with the Duke and Duchess, they were in Scotland staying at Invereshie near Kinrara at the same time as his visit. Although Georgina now had Endsleigh as a rural retreat to remind her of the Highlands, she still craved the real thing. Staying at Invereshie she could enjoy the landscape and see her brother George and his wife Elizabeth. After the Duchess of Gordon's death, George had taken on Kinrara and most years he would spend a month there during the shooting season. In the 1820s Georgina and her family were often in the area at about the same time. As Elizabeth and George had no children of their own, they took a keen interest in their nieces and nephews, particularly the Duchess of Manchester's children, who were frequent guests at Kinrara. For both George and Georgina, surrounded by the next generation, there must have been many happy memories of their childhood holidays to share. According to the Duke, Georgina was full of energy and enthusiasm, preparing trips into the mountains, and it seems likely that Landseer did visit them. His painting of Lord Cosmo Russell on his pony at about this time shows the young boy in Highland dress with a Scottish landscape in the background. A letter from the Duke to Lady Holland confirms his son wore traditional garb while they stayed in the Highlands. He wrote: 'Your little friend Cosmo, looks very well in his Tartan dress and kilt, and seems to enjoy his freedom as a native Highlander.'

Before returning to England, Landseer revisited Edinburgh, where he met Sir Walter Scott, who took him to his home at Abbotsford. 'I am sure,' C. R. Leslie wrote, 'he will make himself very popular, both with the master and mistress of the house, by sketching their doggies for them.' In fact, they got on so well that Landseer was later chosen as one of the illustrators of the Waverley edition of Scott's novels.

Between them, the leading author and artist did much to make Scotland fashionable by giving artistic expression to the romantic view of the Highlands. English aristocrats were just starting to take hunting lodges in Scotland for the autumn, but soon the arrival of the railways would open Scotland up to a tourist boom. The Victorian tourists came in search of the simple Highland life displayed in Scott's novels and Landseer's paintings.

The transformation his discovery of Scotland brought about in Landseer was noted by his literary contemporaries, and it is hard to believe that the change was not as much linked to his feelings for the Duchess as the landscape. Scotland became their special place and as the years went by it was to be where they spent most time alone together. Monkhouse wrote that Landseer's visit to Scotland had given 'a new impulse to his work' and that it 'had for his art effects which amounted to little less than a regeneration. Fond of nature and animals as he always was, that fondness became now a more living and concentrated force under the influence of wild and romantic scenery . . . Now his soul was possessed by the majesty and beauty of Scotch scenery to a far greater extent than would be traceable from his pictures alone.' In a similar vein, James Manson, an early biographer of Landseer, wrote: 'For ever afterwards Landseer's heart was in the Highlands.'

The first major picture inspired by his Scottish visit was a history painting, 'The Hunting of Chevy Chase', for the Duke. It is steeped in the wild landscape and chivalric stories of the border between Scotland and England. Based on the ancient *Ballad of Chevy Chase* and permeated with the romantic imagery of Sir Walter Scott's writing, it records the battle between the leaders of two great border families, the English Earl of Northumberland and the Scottish Earl Douglas. The picture is of the hunt preceding the battle, but in the final fight both leaders and most of their men were killed. The Duke took a great interest in the picture and wrote in detail to Landseer about which species of deer should appear.

While the Duke's professional relationship with the artist was developing, the Duchess's friendship with Landseer was increasing in intensity. When their romance developed into a sexual relationship cannot be precisely pin-pointed but it seems likely to have been between 1823 and 1825. Certainly by 1824 the Duchess's attitude to Lord Grey had become cooler. Although she tried to reassure him nothing had changed between them, it seems the politician noticed a difference in her tone and the frequency of her letters. She wrote to him:

> I must however take the liberty of finding fault with your letter to me on containing observations I do not deserve, for I never did discard you as a correspondent, which if I had done would be a bad proof of my head and a still worse of my heart; No my dear Lord Grey, be just, and be certain that the greatest affection on my part exists for you and ever will do and that I can never be invincible to any thing that regards you, on the contrary, always anxious to please you and delighted to hear from you, therefore pray write.

It is also clear that by this time Georgina was back to her cheerful self, and although she still expressed concern about the Duke's health, she seems to have regained a sense of proportion about it. Her letter to Lord Holland in January 1825 reveals she was once again able to see the situation with a sense of humour:

> The Duke . . . has been to all appearances less comfortable than his usual state, his head has been troublesome, and altogether there has been more universal malaise. I have most freely and plainly stated to him the consequences to be feared from his indulging at dinner but my dear kind Lord Holly, we must not urge the point any further, for though one of the most gentle and amiable of human beings, he has his peculiarities. On Friday after some medicine, he ate nothing but the leg of a chicken and yesterday after having taken infinitely too much exercise, dined upon salad and vegetables . . . He is so perfectly aware of what he ought

to do that I think he is more likely to comply with our wishes, if now left to himself, for experience has taught me, that beyond a certain point, he does not like to be dictated to, and having once decided upon a measure it is useless to try to change his opinion, for I should not succeed, only worry him which is bad for his state of health and perhaps drive him to continue on vegetables, without wine which would be equally pernicious.

The added dimension injected into Landseer's art since meeting the Duchess was mirrored in the new vibrancy in Georgina's life. *Joie de vivre* exudes from all her letters at this time; she wrote to Lord Grey that her 'joy at being in London is not to be expressed'. The surviving bills from her shopping expeditions at this time illustrate what was on her mind and who was responsible for her ecstatic mood. On 8 March she visited R. Ackermann, a book and print-seller, to buy two volumes of *Buchanan on Painting*. The next day she bought sheet music from I. Willis and Co., music sellers, for some sentimental love songs, including 'Wake My Love', 'Such Tears are Bliss' and 'Remember Me'.

For once she was equally enthusiastic about Woburn. She even wrote in verse to Lord Auckland inviting him to stay:

> O come, and rich in intellectual worth,
> Blend thought with exercise, with knowledge health,
> Long, in this sheltered scene of lettered talk,
> With sober step repeat the pensive walk;
> Nor scorn, when graver triflings fail to please
> The cheap amusement of a mind at ease,
> There every care in sweet oblivion cast
> And many an idle hour – not idly passed.

I am thus inspired by the most energetic hail storm I ever witnessed, which

> I hope will not deter you from leaving
> The joyless glare, the maddening strife
> And all the dull impudences of life
> On Saturday next.

Her self-esteem and her beauty were restored. By the time of her forty-fourth birthday in 1825 she was blooming and her attraction for men was as strong as ever. Lord Holland wrote a poem to capture her new lustre in his usual pose as her courtly lover:

> How is't that since I last essayed
> To sing our sprightly Dutchess [*sic*]
> Time has on me such ravage made
> My muse is grown a weary fade
> And I crawl out on crutches,
> While she I sang in form in face
> Still charms each rash beholder.
> Birthdays succeed – no change I trace
> Or if 'tis change in faith her Grace
> Grows lovelier as she's older.
> Tis the plain truth – Folks lame and grey
> May speak their mind sincerely
> And so without offence I say
> I love her better every day
> And long have loved her dearly
> Nor wife Nor Duke shall blame my song
> How passionate so'er
> They know to her the arts belong
> The days to gladden and prolong
> Of those my heart holds dear.

One of the arts Georgina never lost was the art of surprise, and in the autumn of 1825 there was a shock for her family and friends. Four years after her last child was born, her longest ever period without having a child, she was pregnant again. Many people, including some contemporaries and, according to Campbell Lennie in his biography of Landseer, the present Duke of Bedford, believed her daughter Rachel, born 19 June 1826, to be Landseer's child. The dates fit this theory because Georgina was in Scotland from July to October 1825 without the Duke and Landseer was also in the Highlands during this time. He wrote to William Ross in September 1825 from Blair Atholl:

> I have no time at present to give you my adventures, only that I have been further north this season and am a little crazy with the beauties of the Highlands – and have been working very hard and painting deer and grouse shootings etc . . . My career is now nearly over . . . after the Marquess of Huntly [Georgina's brother] where I am going to revisit, my movements will be south.

The Duchess was in the same part of Scotland at this time; a letter from the Duke to his son written on 10 October said she had just been to see her father at Gordon Castle. It seems likely that Rachel was conceived in the Highlands at the end of September 1825. The idea that the Duke was not the father is also supported by the fact that letters from him at around this time show that he certainly did not expect the Duchess to become pregnant. Perhaps after his severe illness their physical relationship was limited. Assuming that Georgina was still exceptionally fertile, if their sex life had returned to its normal pattern it is likely she would have become pregnant before 1825. Admittedly, in December 1824 there were rumours that the Duchess was pregnant again but the Duke wrote to Lady Holland: 'The Duchess is very so-so looking pale, thin and drawn and deadly sick every day – Woolryche [their doctor] says – "perhaps there may be a cause you know" – but he is quite wrong.' Such an emphatic denial suggests it must have come as a surprise to the Duke when the Duchess did become pregnant a year later.

At the end of October, just as Georgina probably became aware that she was expecting a baby, she had to leave her lover behind and travel to France with the Duke. On 5 November they arrived in Paris, where they stayed in the Hotel de Bristol in the Place Vendôme, but Georgina enjoyed few of the pleasures of the capital city as she was very unwell and confined to her room. In January she wrote to Lord Grey:

> I have delayed till now answering your kind letter in hopes of being able to do so with my own hand, but I still suffer so much from exertion or sitting up that I am compelled to make Eliza [her niece, the daughter of the Duke's brother William, who had made her home with the Bedfords] write for me – my complaint is not a deadly one and in time wise ones say I shall regain my strength which at present would be quite unequal to a walk, even with you. I have not moved out of the house for these two months, therefore know very little of what is going on in Paris.

A month later Lady Granville, the British ambassador's wife, came to visit her and found her on good form: 'She is still on her couch, very entertaining and agreeable, and her "franc-parler" is a treasure here.' However, despite the Duchess's candid talk on many subjects, there was one topic she seems to have been particularly sensitive about – Landseer. Woolryche, the doctor who travelled with the Bedfords, wrote to him:

> I want to know if you received a letter I addressed to you six weeks or two months since – it was directed to E Landseer 1 Lisbon Grove, Regent's Park which the Duchess informs me is not right. We had an odd story in the newspapers of a business which occurred at a house which I thought yours – not that I thought you concerned in the affair, but that the reporters had given your number by mistake and that it furnished a fair subject for a joke. However I begin now to fear my joke has lost its way and has fallen in to hands that will not enjoy it.

Dr Woolryche's joke seems to have been about Landseer entertaining

The Art of Loving

kept women. In 1826 the artist moved his studio to 1 St John's Wood; at this time St John's Wood and Regent's Park were notorious for having several famous mistresses in the area. The Duchess was evidently not amused by the idea of Landseer seeing other women so Woolryche's joke certainly did not appeal to her sense of humour.

In fact, Georgina could not wait to leave France, and in April she returned to England without the Duke. Her journey was not advisable so late in a difficult pregnancy, but although she was feeling very unwell she was determined to go. Her doctors prescribed opium to lessen the pain. Despite the discomfort, she seems to have been very happy at this time; she loved all her children but perhaps the thought of bearing her talented young lover's baby gave her particular pleasure. Mrs Arbuthnot wrote: 'I hear she is "immense et tres glorieuse" about it.' Lady William, in a typically bitchy tone, wrote: 'I thought her looking ill and immensely large, but in violent spirits.' The Duchess was very open about her happiness; she wrote to Lord Holland: 'My heart is as light as a feather. I could almost fancy myself strong, which is not quite the case.'

On 19 June, Georgina's last child was born. Whatever her true parentage, the Duke always accepted her as his own; however, as she grew up Landseer seems to have taken a special interest in her. He painted her more frequently than any of the Duchess's other children and his pictures of Lady Rachel Russell cuddling a pet rabbit, in a dancing dress and as Little Red Riding Hood show particular affection, and he kept a beautiful sketch in sepia of her with a fawn. One of his most famous pictures, 'The Naughty Child', is thought by some critics to be modelled on her.

Although it suited the Duchess that Rachel was treated as her husband's child, because it gave her daughter the social status she would never have had as the illegitimate child of an artist, there is a hint in a cryptic poem among Landseer's papers that the artist was not happy with the situation. If the 'hound', 'sketch' and 'ewe lamb' in the poem are treated as metaphors for his child and the 'candidate' mentioned is for the position of father of the child, it suggests that Landseer felt cheated out of both his daughter and his lover:

In climbing up the hill of life
Mid envy, avarice and strife,
Good luck to him that's tall!
It is the province of the great
Their wishes to substantiate
And trample on the small.
The man whose veins contain a flood
Of antiquated, noble blood,
Much reverence inspires.
But he that's made of coarser stuff
Must be content with wages rough
And curbs to his desires . . .
I heard that some great man had been
And cheated me through thick and thin of what I thought my own.
However great the man may be
In stature fortune or degree
In this I claim my right
My twenty shillings in the pound
Was hoarded up to buy the hound
Before it met his sight.
Tho' acts of courtesy combined
With gifts appropriate and kind
My language may restrain
Yet having been of that beguiled
Which was more precious than a child
How can I but complain?
When I became a candidate
I asked if patron small or great
Had forestalled my design
And being told that no one had
I said I was extremely glad
And begged it might be mine . . .
The great man should forthwith be taught
That he has quite unfairly bought
The 'Ewe lamb' of a small

If after that, he still holds out
I should consider him a lout
And no great man at all.

Rachel is Hebrew for ewe lamb and readers of the poem were told to refer to the speech of Nathan in the case of David versus Uriah the Hittite in the Bible. The story is about a rich man with many sheep taking a ewe lamb from a poor man who had no other sheep and treated his lamb like a daughter.

Whatever Landseer may have wished, neither the Duke nor Duchess considered divorcing. Affairs were commonplace in Regency society but divorce was rare; there were on average two divorces each year. Aristocrats were willing to accept adultery as long as it was done discreetly; as Lady Airlie wrote in her book *In Whig Society*: 'Good breeding demanded that the outward conventions should not be violated, but asked few questions as to what went on beneath the surface. Scandals were glossed over by the decent acquiescence of the wife or the husband.' Outwardly nothing changed in the relationships between the Duke, the Duchess and Landseer; the Duke even continued as the artist's patron and wrote friendly letters to him. To modern minds it may seem odd that a cuckolded husband should be so benign, but it was not in the Duke's nature to take an aggressive stance. It is also clear that he did not want to lose Georgina because, whatever she did, he loved her very much, and he knew that his happiness depended on her. As a man fifteen years older than her, in bad health, perhaps he accepted that Landseer could give Georgina a totally different relationship from the one they shared. From the earliest days of his engagement to Georgina, the Duke wrote about a relationship based on friendship and sympathy, not passion. He was a loving but not a passionate man and so jealousy was not a natural emotion for him.

It is also worth noting that the Duchess was not the only one in their marriage to have close relationships with the opposite sex. The Duke had romantic friendships of his own with other women. He was particularly close to Lady Holland, Lady Elizabeth Vernon and Lady

Sandwich; nor did Georgina ever completely step out from the shadow cast by the Duke's first wife. Until his death, John kept a battered red leather wallet with him containing neatly folded love letters from Georgiana Byng telling him again and again how much she loved and adored him. It seems that emotional or even sexual exclusivity had never been an essential part of the Duke and Duchess's marriage. Whatever the shortcomings of her marriage, there is no evidence that Georgina ever considered leaving the Duke permanently. In fact, just after Rachel's birth she seems to have been trying particularly hard to ingratiate herself with her husband. For his birthday in July she made him 'a beautifully executed sort of Register of her children' that was richly illuminated and emblematically decorated, two sailors and a soldier representing the professions of their sons. Using the artistic skills she had honed with Landseer, the work was 'all admirably executed', but it was not finished because Georgina's confinement occurred before it was completed.

It appears that Georgina liked her position as the Duchess of Bedford and the wealth and lifestyle it gave her, and even if she had found a passion to match her own nature with Landseer, that did not mean she wanted to be his wife. No doubt she realised that if she followed her instinct too far she would become a social outcast like her sister Susan. She must also have realised the damage a scandal would have done to all her children's futures. However, it is unlikely Georgina's motives for staying with the Duke were purely mercenary. As her attitude during his illness had shown, she genuinely loved her husband and while remaining within her marriage Georgina was able to have the best of both worlds. She had the upperhand with both men, and enjoyed two very different relationships on her own terms. When she was with the Duke she played the conscientious wife, entertaining at Woburn and staying with him at Endsleigh (although there is evidence that Landseer came too – he painted a picture of a river view of Endsleigh called 'The Rabbit Warren' that Georgina later etched).

To appease Landseer, who had a far more jealous, possessive temperament than her husband, the Duchess made sure that she had time alone with her lover. In 1827 she spent four months away from the Duke at

Invereshie in the Highlands. Her father, the Duke of Gordon, had died that summer during a visit to London. Georgina had been with him during his final hours. The Duke wrote to Lady Holland on 17 June:

> The Duchess is just returned – the last struggle was over about an hour ago – my poor little wife never left his bedside from half past eleven last night till he breathed his last at 9 o clock this morning. This is too much for her – so I shall not go to town this morning as I had intended.

Although her mother had played a much more important role in Georgina's life, she had loved her father. In 1820 he had finally married his long-term mistress, Jean Christie, by whom he had already had a large family. Jean died four years later leaving the Duke a widower. Georgina visited her aging father at Gordon Castle whenever she was in Scotland. Now her brother George was the new Duke.

A holiday in the Highlands, with her lover and not far away from her brother and sister-in-law at Gordon Castle, was just what Georgina needed to raise her spirits. Despite her husband's eagerness to see her, she kept prolonging her stay. The Duke expected her to join him in Brighton in the first week of November, but the Duchess changed her plans and stayed in Scotland for an extra month. She justified her long absence to herself and others by claiming the Duke was happy on his own. She wrote to Lord Grey in October:

> I thought by this time I should have settled my time for leaving the North but I find the Duke so gay without me ... that I shall remain amongst my mountains till the snow drives me away. The Duke has been at Althorp for the first time in his life but was to be at home on Monday to receive Lady E Vernon and her charming husband. The Duke is I hear looking better than he has done for twenty years.

In another letter to Lord Grey a month later she continues to feel the need for self-justification:

My 'widowhood' is not the most agreeable part of my sejour here, but as the Duke promised to follow me in a fortnight and proposed moving about with the rapidity of a steam engine, here, there and everywhere, I have remained enjoying the wild country with my children, who are quite as fond of the Highlands as their Mother. I never feel and I believe I may add, never look as I do here (in England). I have not had one second of any thing but perfect health and I own that I shall be too happy if possible to pass the horrid gloomy month of November where fogs and damps do not prevail . . . My movements depend upon my brother's coming to see me and the Duke's going to Brighton, where I have no wish to dance attendance 'dans les pays Bas,' which does not suit my Highland blood.

Although she said to Lord Grey that she was alone with her children in the Highlands, evidence suggests that Landseer was with her for much of the time. On her way back to England in November she met Sir Walter Scott in Edinburgh and he recorded that Landseer was in her train. Edwin showed him many sketches done in the Highlands, which suggests he had been there for some time. Scott was a critical observer of the Duchess and he wrote in his journal:

NOV 28 1827 – Dined with the Duchess of Bedford at the Waterloo and renewed, as I may say, an old acquaintance, which began while her Grace was Lady Georgina. She has now a fine family, two young ladies silent just now, but they will find their tongues or they are not right Gordons, a very fine child Alister [sic], who shouted, sung and spoke Gaelic with much spirit. They are from a shooting place in the Highlands . . . which the Duke has taken to gratify the Duchess's passion for the heather.

NOV 29 – Dined at Lord C Commissioners to meet the Duchess and her party. She can be extremely agreeable but

I used to think her Grace 'journalière' [everyday]. She may have been cured of that fault, or I may have turned less jealous of my dignity. At all events let a pleasant hour go by unquestioned and do not let us break ordinary gems to pieces because they are not diamonds.

When Georgina did eventually return to the Duke it seems their marriage went through a difficult period. Unwisely, Georgina even complained to her stepson William about her husband. Lord William recorded in his diary:

> 28 FEB 1828 . . . Long and curious conversation with Mrs Grundy [the Duchess]; appears sore and out of humour, complains of her husband, declares she knows nothing of her future prospects or of her children's.

> 11 MARCH . . . Long and singular conversation with Mrs Grundy; accusations of falseness against Mrs Tavy [Lady Tavistock]. Protestations of sincerity, friendship; mi pare loca [she appears to be mad].

Although Lord William did not criticise the Duchess directly for having an affair, he attacked her indirectly by complaining that all she talked about was 'Rachel, Rachel' and that she was spending too little time with her other children. He implied that because of her lack of attention they were becoming unruly. He wrote to Lady William:

> My two brothers are here Henry and Cosmo. They are forward in classical learning, but in everything else they are little savages, with minds not elevated above the grooms. This disgusts me . . . besides you may remember the dirty tricks and language they taught little H [Lord and Lady William's son Hastings] at Brighton. As for their father and mother, they scarcely know them. Beyond all doubt the greatest blessing a child can have is an attentive mother, the

greatest misfortune is to have no mother, or a negligent, or foolish or vicious mother . . . They [the Russell children] bear an illustrious name, but a name that want of education to the young men or from the spurious blood, that a vile women has thrust into it may sink to insignificance, if not to something worse.

In April the Duke suffered a slight stroke, but this did not deter the Duchess from again spending several months away from him in Scotland. Intoxicated with her love affair, it seems Georgina felt no guilt about putting her lover's interests above her husband's needs. Under the brooding shadow of the Cairngorms, Landseer could find the inspiration for his art and Georgina could enjoy exploring the powerful landscape with her lover. In Scotland Landseer was seeing his mistress in her natural habitat; she could play to perfection the sophisticated society hostess but the real Georgina was a far more earthy, sensuous character who relished getting back to nature in one of the most remote parts of Britain. Landseer had a similar dual character, and although he could appear a dandy in the drawing room, the essence of him, his creative spirit, was freed by the raw Highland landscape.

Although the Duchess left her husband in England, she did not leave her children, and Landseer had to share Georgina with her family. It seems he was quite happy to find himself surrounded by children, particularly if the baby of the family was his own daughter. As the youngest of seven, Landseer was used to being pampered and adored by his mother and his siblings so no doubt there was a comforting familiarity in the equally affectionate environment created by the Duchess and her children. It seems that despite Landseer's success artistically and socially, he needed the security of a mother figure. With a typical Victorian interest in phrenology, one of his biographers, James Manson, wrote: 'His bump of what phrenologists call self-esteem was so slight that he was constrained constantly to lean on the opinion of others.'

The Duke was not altogether happy about the Duchess leaving him alone for many months for the second year running and at times he seemed lonely. He wrote to Lady Holland: 'I am "en garçon" without my Duchess . . . Charles and his wife I should be of course delighted to see them and at all times, but I fancy she had quite enough of my individual dullness this time last year.' He admitted to his friends that he hoped Georgina would come back earlier than last year. In another letter to Lady Holland he wrote:

> One thousand thanks for your long and amusing letter of yesterday – it is so much 'couleur de Rose' in every respect that it cheers me and gives me spirits, which I regain after bad nights . . . you are going to Brighton on the 25th – I shall follow you as soon as I can get a house and I trust the Duchess will be south in time to be there by the beginning of November.

In fact, Georgina did not return until the end of November. As usual, Scotland had done her good and she seemed 'merry and well'. The Duchess appeared to have just what she wanted, while both the Duke and Landseer had to compromise. But somehow, despite occasional tensions, the triangular relationship worked.

Although the three main protagonists had, to varying degrees, come to terms with the dynamics, not everyone accepted this strange *ménage à trois*. It seems Lord Grey, perhaps piqued by jealousy, became less friendly towards the Duchess. Typically, the Duke acted as mediator between his wife and her admirer, writing to him after Georgina's 1828 Highland holiday: 'She [the Duchess] thinks she has reason to complain of you, as you did not once write to her whilst she was in Scotland to propose her to go to Howick.'

Other people were more vehement in their criticisms. In 1829 the artist Benjamin Haydon was furious to see Landseer 'on a blood horse with a white hat, and all the airs of a Man of Fashion'. Haydon commented: 'I never gave in to the vices of Fashion, or degraded myself or disgraced my Patrons by becoming the pander to the appetites of their wives.' No doubt Haydon's outrage was not based on purely moral grounds; he was also jealous of his former pupil's success because while his career was in decline, Landseer's was flourishing. Edwin had been elected an associate of the Royal Academy at the age of twenty-four, the earliest age at which it was possible for an artist to receive this reward. Through the Bedfords, Landseer met many other members of the aristocracy and they were soon commissioning work from him.

Haydon was not the only critic of the situation and gossip about the Duke and Duchess living separate lives was spreading. In March 1829 Isabella, Marchioness of Bath, who was the sister of the Duke's first wife, wrote to her nephew Lord William criticising Georgina for her behaviour as both a wife and mother: 'The Duchess, whose object now seems to be to separate herself from the Duke, has been living in London whilst he was at Woburn, and when Georgy required a mother's care, she brought her up, only staying a day at Woburn.'

A poem by Laetitia Landon in a keepsake book accompanying Landseer's portrait of the Duchess also attacked Georgina's hypocritical lifestyle, although outwardly it is a homage to the Duchess's beauty:

> Lady, thy face is very beautiful,
> A calm and stately beauty; thy dark hair
> Hangs as the passing winds paid homage there,
> And gems, such gems as only princes cull
> From earth's rich veins are round they neck and arm;
> Ivory, with just one touch of colour warm,
> And thy white robe floats queenlike, suiting well
> A shape such as in ancient pictures dwell . . .

The poem does not continue in such a flattering tone. It states that in the conventions of chivalric art, a Duchess is said to represent 'sovereign beauty . . ./For which knights went to battle'; in contrast, in the present 'there is nought/About thee for the dreaming minstrel's thought'.

Discussion of the Duchess, her husband and her artist lover was not restricted to high society. Soon newspapers were publishing stories about the unconventional relationships. The Duke was willing to accept the Duchess's infidelity in private, but once it became public knowledge it was more humiliating. Lord Tavistock told his brother Lord William: 'The wicked world has been full of sad and scandalous reports, and so have the newspapers. It is very distressing.' As usual, the Duke's first priority was to protect Georgina, and in the autumn of 1829, although he was not feeling well, he considered going to join his wife in Scotland in an attempt to repair the damage done to her reputation. On his doctor's advice he did not go, but Lady Holland explained to Lord William: 'Indeed his only motive for going was a most kind, but unnecessary reason, there having been libellous paragraphs against the Duchess which he wanted to refute by joining her, but these matters are always best to be left to die a natural death.'

Despite the widespread gossip, Georgina and Landseer had no intention of giving up their relationship and the Duchess was taking steps to make their Highland trysts easier. In 1830 she leased the Doune from her childhood friends the Grants, who had financial problems. This simple but substantial Scottish house, built in the sixteenth century but extended in 1780, was the ideal place for Georgina to spend time with her lover. As part of the Rothiemurchus estate, the house was close to her mother's old farmhouse at Kinrara, which was owned by her brother. Surrounded by powerful natural beauty and steeped in Gaelic folklore, it was the perfect romantic setting for the Duchess and Edwin to share both art and love. They could walk or ride around Loch an Eilein, a beautiful loch with a centuries-old ruined castle on its island, or explore the ancient Caledonian forest of Rothiemurchus, where they would have found rare wildlife including ospreys. They could fish in the sparkling lochs or the River Spey, or ride into the heather-covered Cairngorms and experience the changeable moods and many shades of the mountains.

In this remote part of the Highlands, Georgina and Landseer could escape malicious tongues and prying eyes and enjoy complete privacy and peace. The Duchess cared more about her young lover than her reputation and as long as the Duke was willing to accept the situation it seems that as far as she was concerned people could say what they liked. Since her first romances almost thirty years before, she had faced criticism and spiteful attacks about her unconventional behaviour. Now her enemies had fresh ammunition, but it seems the intensity of her passion for Landseer made her impervious to their sniping fire. Her marriage to the Duke had been more to satisfy her mother's dynastic demands than her own romantic requirements, so perhaps now she wanted a partnership that satisfied her needs. More than twenty years of her life and energy had been devoted to being a wife and mother, pleasing others. Perhaps she felt it was time to have a relationship that was purely to please herself. As a mature woman in her forties, she knew just what she was looking for and having found that person she was not willing to sacrifice him just to conform to society's stultifying image of how a middle-aged Duchess should behave.

CHAPTER NINE

Family Affairs

*T*he 1830s were golden years for Landseer. During this fruitful period he became increasingly famous and created some of his finest and happiest works, including 'Harvest in the Highlands', 'Crossing the Bridge' and 'Highland Drovers' Departure'. Many of these pictures were inspired by his annual visits to Scotland.

After being elected a Royal Academician in 1831, his list of patrons became ever longer and grander as he was welcomed into not just Woburn but also Chatsworth, Badminton, Goodwood and Holland House. His prestige increased further when Queen Victoria came to the throne in 1837 because he soon became the royal family's favourite artist. His first contact with royalty was in 1836 when Victoria's mother, the Duchess of Kent, commissioned him to paint her daughter's dog, Dash, for a birthday present. Victoria was so impressed with Landseer, both as an artist and an attractive young man, that like Georgina before her, she asked him to teach her how to etch. When the Queen married, Edwin made friends with both Victoria and Albert; sometimes the royal couple would visit his studio while riding in the park or he would be invited as a guest to Buckingham Palace.

He was a charming character and became as much in demand socially as professionally. Constable described him at a dinner party as 'perfect – his shirt frills reaching from his chin to below his navel – his head was beautifully decorated with one thousand curls'. His personality was as attractive as his appearance; Lord Ossulston wrote: 'He was acknowledged to be the best company of his day ... His powers of description whether of people or scenery, were most graphic and amusing, and though simple in words, had very much of natural poetry in them.'

As well as socialising with his fellow artists, he became friends with the leading actors and writers of the time, including Charles Kean, W. C. Macready, Dickens and Thackeray. While men enjoyed his stimulating company, women found him very attractive and he was adept at flattering their egos and flirting with them. During the early 1830s it seems the Duchess had some rivals for his attention. He became friendly with the beautiful poetess Caroline Norton and the blue-stocking Kate Perry, but whatever the other attractions, Landseer always came back to Georgina, and it seems that her hold over him was as much to do with his social as his sexual needs.

Some critical contemporaries saw him as a social climber; certainly he had a penchant for the aristocracy and he was keen to be included in their world. Through his relationship with Georgina he became an insider in aristocratic circles. It is clear that her social position mattered to him. To the disgust of some of his acquaintances, he liked to boast of his closeness to dukes and duchesses. His eagerness to be accepted was one of his least attractive characteristics; having watched his behaviour, Harriet Martineau thought him vain and socially insecure:

> There was Landseer, a friendly and agreeable companion, but holding his cheerfulness at the mercy of great folks' graciousness to him. To see him enter a room, curled and cravatted, and glancing round in anxiety about his reception,

could not but make a woman wonder where among her own sex she could find a more palpable vanity.

As time went on, Landseer's role in the Bedford household developed and he became a friend of not just the Duchess but the whole family. Surprising as it may seem, the Duke and the artist established a genuine friendship. The age gap between them was more than thirty years, so perhaps it became almost a father and son relationship. Sometimes the two men would spend time together at Woburn without Georgina; the Duke enjoyed taking Landseer shooting. As they walked through the grounds, guns in hand, it was a good opportunity for the Duke to ask his friend's advice about painting. When in London the Duke often called into Landseer's studio, where he looked forward to having 'a little quiet artistical conversation', seeing his friend's latest pictures and meeting his 'brother artists'. Sometimes they were seen at exhibitions together, engrossed in conversation as the younger man pointed out the best paintings to his patron.

Landseer also became friendly with the Russell children, and in some ways this seemed quite natural as the eldest were about his age. Like their father, they valued his artistic expertise. Cosmo wrote to him about a visit to Dresden, describing the pictures he had seen there. Whether they all knew the true nature of their mother's relationship with the young artist is hard to tell; it is possible that they did. Some of the children stayed with Georgina and Landseer when they were alone together in Scotland. Perhaps, like their father, they just accepted the unconventional situation or turned a blind eye to it. However, Wriothesley, the Duchess's pious eldest son who had become a vicar, had some concerns about the turbulent spirit who had become part of their family. He sent Landseer some religious books and seemed to feel it was his duty to save Landseer's soul:

I hear that in your pictures you have surpassed yourself. But . . . human applause, fascinating as it is, cannot confer one moment's real happiness. God permit that you may soon know what that means in the fullest extent of the word –

that deep overflowing feeling of joy and peace 'Which the World cannot give' ... As you have now probably made some progress in the books I sent you, I wish that you would let me hear your opinion of them. Write me freely with confidence and be assured that no one can feel a deeper interest in your welfare ... I trust that the two read together may put you in possession of those spiritual gifts I so earnestly desire for you.

Whether or not they knew of the relationship, there is no evidence that Georgina's children interfered; by this time they were too busy building their own lives to meddle in their mother's affairs. In 1829 Wriothesley married his first cousin Eliza. His half-brother Lord John was delighted:

It is an excellent arrangement; indeed it seems so natural as to be almost inevitable. Wrio always was in love with her, and would have been very lonely in his parsonage, but now with a pretty wife and a good house that requires alteration, and a certain quantity of duties that are agreeable to perform to a man of kind heart, and a nice comfortable country about him, I think he could not fail to be happy.

Georgina, however, was less sanguine about the marriage because she was concerned about the match of such close relations. She wrote: 'Though it is an event I have long expected, it fills me with such a mixture of feelings that I am quite nervous.' Although the couple were to have a happy marriage, some of Georgina's concerns were justified as one of their three children was born mentally handicapped.

While the Duchess's children were starting their own families, her own prolific pregnancies continued, and in December 1830, when she was almost fifty, she discovered that she was pregnant yet again. It was an inconvenience and a threat to her health that she had not expected, and while visiting Scotland she became ill and had to stay in Edinburgh. She wrote to Lord Holland: 'I had felt very unwell for some time, but would not believe the worse, until Dr Hamilton confirmed my suspicions for I have been going on as ill as possible . . . I hope he will send me home when I am safe. If I go on I shall be confined in June.' In fact, to the Duke's relief, she miscarried the baby. He told Lady Holland: 'I rejoice at it for at her age the "perils of Child-birth" are no light matter.' This was to be Georgina's final pregnancy, and at last after almost thirty years of child-bearing, she was freed from her fertility.

Like her mother before her, Georgina's attentions now turned to finding the right husbands for her eldest daughters Louisa and Georgy, but unlike the Duchess of Gordon she encouraged her children to marry for love, not just social position. Unfortunately, the marriage prospects of one of her girls looked much less promising than the other's; Louisa was very beautiful while Georgy was plain. Not just her elegant sister but even her fifty-year-old mother outshone her, as the diarist Le Marchant wrote cruelly: 'The Duchess of Bedford passed the day with us – a bold, bad woman – with the remains of beauty. Her elder daughter Lady [Georgiana] a dull dowdy.'

The social rituals had hardly changed since Georgina's youth and so she presented her daughters at court and they stayed in London for the Queen's drawing rooms and the season. The Bedfords had moved from their town house in St James's Square to Belgrave Square but the Duchess also entertained at their Kensington house, Campden Hill, holding a 'déjeuner' every Thursday. Georgina applied her rigorous aesthetic values to her party planning as much as to her creation of houses, and everything was done to make her events a visual delight. The Duchess enjoyed gathering beautiful people together to complement the attractive setting. On one occasion, Lord Holland rode over to the party from Holland House on a pony that ate the Duchess's roses, but it was instantly forgiven because it 'gave great pleasure to the admirers of the picturesque'. On another occasion, Lord John and Lord William brought their friend Thomas Moore and he described the captivating scene: 'The assemblage of pretty women in these green flowery grounds very charming. Lady Cowper gave me her arm and we walked together to have strawberries and cream . . . Pretty as it all was, I soon got tired of it and returned to town.'

Typically, after enjoying her hospitality Lord William complained about the extravagance of the Duchess's parties. The Duke admitted to his son: 'I have what is vulgarly called run out in household expenditure and Stagg [his steward] says the cause of it is housekeeping going on at so many residences.' However, although he was willing to make petty economies – cutting back on a few staff at Endsleigh, for instance – he had no intention of interfering with Georgina's parties and perhaps undermining his daughters' marriage prospects at this crucial time in their lives. But whatever his stated intentions, it seems the Duke would never understand the true meaning of economising, as his letter to Lord William shows:

> Your sarcasm about the Duchess's 'splendid fête and the £1000,' [approximately £42,000] was misplaced as your sarcasms usually are. You saw about the Duchess's Thursday evenings here – some eatables supplied by my own maitre d'hotel, cook and confectioner, without the aid of any Gunters or Jarrods, and a few bottles of wine from my own cellar. This on the night of the fête, with the addition of £20 or £25 [approximately £840 or £1,050] for fireworks and a few lamps in the shrubs, with a band of music for the young folks to dance, was the whole of the additional expense. I hate grand dinners and never give them, so these fêtes (so called) cost about the same as ten or twelve dinners, for which you have hauled me over the coals.

Almost a decade after their first feud, Lord and Lady William still could not resist scrutinising every aspect of the Duke and Duchess's lifestyle. But when Lady William criticised the dowdiness of Georgy and Louisa's clothes, the Duke retaliated by writing to his son: 'If you think my girls are shabbily dressed, you should make Lady William send them some better dresses from Paris.' To his surprise, his daughter-in-law did what he suggested and sent two splendid ball dresses.

When the girls went with their parents to Scotland in autumn 1831, the parties continued in the Highlands. The Duchess took them to a Grand Ball at her cousin Mrs Balfour's in Fife. Shortly afterwards, Georgy became seriously ill, developing typhoid fever that nearly killed her. Although she survived she was 'shattered' by the illness and spent many weeks in bed. Perhaps reminded of the time when she was left alone to cope with Lady Jane's terminal illness in Naples, the Duchess was furious when the Duke returned to Woburn in late November, leaving her alone to care for their child. Whether it was due just to selfishness or an inability to deal with family crises, the Duchess was not amused by her husband's behaviour. She wrote to Lord Holland:

> Our good Duke is certainly a very odd composition. Nothing would induce him to remain here a few days longer, so he left his favourite child in bed where she had been confined for twenty one days with a fever and myself without a friend near me. He actually even took considerable risk at one stage, from the depth of the snow, being obliged to have men with spades to clear the snow and in some places on the road the snow was up to the body of the carriage but he preferred that to remaining here a few days longer . . . How would Lady Holland like to be in my place. Nursing the remains of a Typhus fever thirty miles from Dr Nicol . . . and no one to speak to – still my Dearest Holly, I am so grateful at Georgiana's life being spared, and neither of the others having been ill, that I try to look on these feelings and smother all regrets.

Gradually, Georgy recovered, but at first she was very weak and could hardly walk or see properly in sunlight. Unfortunately, her hearing was permanently impaired by the illness and although she was supposed to use an ear trumpet she often refused to do so because she did not like people to know about her disability.

When Georgy was strong enough, mother and daughter made the long journey home to Woburn, travelling through a country swept with a cholera epidemic. There were two global outbreaks of cholera in the first half of the nineteenth century, one beginning in 1816 and the other in 1829. It was a deadly and untreatable disease, spread through the water supply via inadequate sewerage systems. Death from cholera was particularly unpleasant, violent vomiting and diarrhoea becoming increasingly severe as the sufferer's intestinal tract disintegrated.

At first Georgina was sceptical about the extent of the epidemic, as the Duke related to Lady Holland:

> The Duchess brings an amusing account of the cholera from Newcastle. She stopped there and conversed with the Inn Keeper, who told her there was no cholera – that it was complete fudge and all a Job! That the board of health sent down two physicians who had no practice in London and were to have 10p a day as long as they remained at Newcastle, so their intent is to keep the cholera going there and every death and every illness that takes place is put down to cholera.

However, Georgina changed her opinion as the epidemic reached its height in 1832, claiming 7,000 lives in London alone and affecting some of the Bedfords' friends.

Georgina and Georgy returned safely to Woburn in time for Christmas 1831, and as usual it was a boisterous family celebration. Lord John joined his father and stepmother for the festivities but it was a stressful time for him as he was piloting the Reform Bill through the House of Commons.

This legislation was and remains one of the most important pieces of political reform in British history, as it removed many arcane voting procedures and opened the way for further reforms. Radicals like Jeremy Bentham had been advocating parliamentary reform for years as the existing system was riddled with anomalies such as the 'rotten' boroughs which had small populations but still had the right to elect MPs, while large industrial areas like Birmingham, Leeds and Manchester failed to be adequately represented. The Duke of Bedford and Lord John, together with many of their Whig colleagues, had also supported a change to the voting system for many years. One of the greatest catalysts for reform at this time was the fear of a revolution in Britain unless something was done. Revolutions had swept across Europe in 1830 and many people felt it was only a matter of time before one took place in Britain.

The death of George IV in June 1830 opened the door to reform. The King's death automatically forced an election and the Whigs, who supported reform, won. Lord Grey was now Prime Minister and he asked Lord John to prepare the legislation to change the voting system. In March 1831 the first bill was presented to the House of Commons, but was rejected. Grey resigned and fought the ensuing general election solely on the issue of parliamentary reform. The Whigs returned with a large majority that was seen as a mandate for reform. A revised version of the bill was introduced by Lord John and was passed by the Commons but was defeated in the Tory-dominated House of Lords in October. Nevertheless, the appetite for reform in the country was so great it could not be ignored. There were outbreaks of violence across the country, in Nottingham, Derby, Bristol and London, and the houses of several members of the Lords were attacked.

In December, Lord John introduced a third bill to Parliament. This time the terms were so new only he knew exactly what it contained; apparently he was still trying to dry the ink on the paper as he entered the Commons to present the proposal.

After all the political pressures of the past year, John came to Woburn to relax, knowing his stepmother would fill his stay with fun and games and prevent him from becoming preoccupied with his work. Georgina had always been enthusiastic about amateur dramatics and she involved all her friends and relations in her productions. Over the years, the theatricals had become increasingly elaborate, with Landseer painting the scenery and doing the make-up. Lord John was distracted from political problems by playing the part of a doctor in Georgina's play. The Duke described the scene to Lady Holland:

> John will have told you of all our Christmas gaieties and gambols – he was an excellent German Doctor on twelfth night, feeling pulses and urging with much earnestness the efficacy of his 'homopatique' system! I have been making an old fool of myself by acting with my children, but it amuses them 'et cela suffit.' John gave us a very sprightly epilogue.

The Duke was very proud of what his son was doing politically. His own lifelong political ideals were turned into reality by many of the reforms John helped to bring in. A few years earlier, John had been instrumental in the campaign for Catholic emancipation. After he had successfully passed legislation to allow Non-Confirmists to hold office in 1828, it became more difficult to avoid a similar concession for Roman Catholics. The issue was brought to a head in 1828 when Wellington appointed the Irish MP Vesey Fitzgerald as President of the Board of Trade. As this post carried a salary, Fitzgerald had to stand for re-election in his County Clare seat. In the County Clare election Daniel O'Connell, who was a Catholic, stood against Fitzgerald. The law as it stood was inconsistent: a Catholic could stand for election but if he won he could not take his seat.

O'Connell won with a massive majority, putting Wellington in a very difficult situation. He could either pass a Catholic emancipation act and let O'Connell take his seat or declare the election null and void. With emotions running so high, stopping O'Connell becoming an MP would have led to violence and possibly civil war. Wellington was determined to avoid bloodshed and realised emancipation was now inevitable. It would have been natural for him to resign, but he realised that only a Tory government could get the bill through the Lords and get the King's consent.

In spring 1829 the Catholic Emancipation Act was put through Parliament by Wellington's government, with the support of Lord John Russell and the Whigs. The act allowed Catholics to sit as MPs at Westminster and made them eligible for all public offices, except those of monarch, regent, Lord Chancellor and Lord Lieutenant of Ireland. This important reform prevented revolt in Ireland but it split the Tory party as the anti-Catholic, or ultra-Tories, believed their government had betrayed the constitution. This was a fascinating time in politics and, although the Duke claimed to be no longer involved, he was still capable of pulling strings behind the scenes and using his considerable influence when necessary. In 1830 he supported the Duke of Wellington's government. Wellington had become a friend and often stayed at Woburn and no doubt Bedford was delighted that Wellington's government had brought in Catholic emancipation – even if it was more due to political expediency than principle. However, when the Duke of Wellington lost the election later that year, Bedford returned to his traditional allegiances, backing his old friend Lord Grey's Whig administration. The new Prime Minister treated the Russells with respect; John was offered the post of Postmaster-General while his father received the blue ribbon of the Garter.

Wellington's friend Mrs Arbuthnot was sceptical about the Duke's capricious behaviour. She wrote:

> He has always affected to admire and support the Duke of Wellington, while all his House of Commons men voted against us; and he now accepts a favour from Lord Grey the very moment he gets the Government. I never thought the support of the Duke of Bedford worth one pin, nor did I ever think the Duke [of Wellington] wise for doing anything for him.

Although the Duke had discovered public life did not suit him, he knew his son had the potential to hold high office and so he used his political contacts to advance Lord John's career. Once Lord Grey became Prime Minister, he wrote to him lobbying for a place in the Cabinet for John. Lord Grey wrote back explaining that he had shown his support for John by putting the conduct of the Reform Bill into his hands and allowing him to attend meetings of the Cabinet when the issue was being discussed.

Since the 1820s, John had been the leader of the Whig campaign in the House of Commons for parliamentary reform. Over the years, he had tried unsuccessfully to get an investigation into parliamentary representation and to introduce a bill to reduce bribery at elections. Now he was in the final stages of the battle for reform his father did everything he could to help, and he continued to apply pressure on the Prime Minister. He wrote to Lord Grey in March:

> I have been urged by some of my friends, both in and out of Parliament to express to you their anxious hopes that you will not suffer the Reform Bill to go into the House of Lords without a positive security that it will pass through that house in all its stages, with its principle unimpaired entire with or without a new creation of peers . . . I dare not contemplate the consequences of the Bill being a second time rejected by the Lords.

The bill passed its second reading in the Commons in March. Although the Duke's friends and family were not sure it would be good for his health, he insisted on being in the House of Lords for the debate when the bill was sent to the Upper House at the end of the month. He wrote to Lady Holland:

> You all seem to think that like Lord Chatham I am going to die in the House of Lords, but I assure you that I feel strength of body and head, fully equal to sit out the debate even should it last till ten o'clock in the morning so you will not lose my vote.

On 14 April 1832 he wrote triumphantly: 'I could not bring myself to leave the debate – I sat thirteen hours in one place without moving an inch to the right or the left – I am going to Campden Hill to breathe a little fresh air – I consider the battle won now.'

In fact, there was still one more battle to go in the long war. On 7 May the bill was thrown out by the Lords in committee. Lord Grey demanded the creation of fifty peers but the King refused, so Grey resigned again and there were widespread riots throughout the country.

In this tense atmosphere, the Duke of Wellington was unable to form a government, Lord Grey returned to power and the King finally gave in. Knowing there was no alternative, Wellington and many of his colleagues agreed to abstain to let the bill through. On 4 June, the bill passed the Lords and three days later the King gave his assent by commission. Due to years of perseverance by many people, not least the Duke and his son, Parliament was at last to be reformed.

The Duke was jubilant about the result and enjoyed basking in his son's reflected glory. Shortly after the bill had passed, he went to Endsleigh to recover from all the excitement. While there he watched the celebrations with a deep sense of satisfaction. He wrote to Lady Holland on 13 July:

> The whole country is occupied by rejoicings on the triumph of the Reform Bill and the people really seem to think of nothing else – the pageant at Plymouth and Devonport was really one of the most beautiful and gratifying sights I ever witnessed and conducted in the most admirable manner, and with the most perfect good humour on all sides – not a single harsh or ill tempered expression any where – Not even constables to keep the Peace, amongst the thousands of people assembled, but the good humour and happiness of the people alone kept perfect order.
>
> Today Tavistockians . . . have processions, flags, music, dinner . . . fireworks . . . and our little village has also its day of rejoicing and the joy seems universal.

Another proud moment for the Duke and Duchess came later in the year when their daughter Louisa married the future Duke of Abercorn. As well as being an acknowledged beauty, Louisa was a very compassionate person, adored by her family and friends. Many years later, her son Lord Frederick Hamilton described her:

> My mother's character was a blend of extreme simplicity and great dignity, with a limitless gift of sympathy for others

. . . Throughout her life, she succeeded in winning the deep love of all those who were brought into contact with her. Very early in life she fell under the influence of the Evangelical movement, which was then stirring in England and she always remained faithful to its tenets. It could be said of her that, though in the world she was not of the world . . . The atmosphere of London, both physical and social, was distasteful to her.

The Marquis of Abercorn (as he was when they married) was an excellent match for Louisa, even by her late grandmother's standards. Not only was he exceptionally handsome, he was also from one of the wealthiest families in Ireland. They had known each other from an early age – Abercorn first proposed to Louisa when she was six and he was seven, at a children's party given by the Prince Regent. As soon as he came of age their romance developed, encouraged by the Bedfords, who invited him to house parties at Woburn. According to Lord Frederick, dinners were often hard-drinking affairs and so after the meal Georgina and her daughters retired to the serenity of the drawing room. The old family butler would later report to the Duchess what state the men were in and if he said 'The gentlemen have had a good deal tonight' she would send her daughters off to bed. Once banished, the girls liked to stand on the upper gallery of the staircase watching the shouting, riotous crowd come out of the dining room. It seems that as well as enjoying the live entertainment, the girls were assessing which of the young men would make the best husband. Frederick wrote: 'My father very rarely touched wine, and I believe that it was the fact that he, then an Oxford undergraduate, was the only sober young man amongst the rowdy troop of roisterers that first drew my mother to him.'

The courtship soon became public knowledge and the talk of the family. Lord and Lady William's teenaged son Hastings observed its progress with interest as he rode daily with his young aunts Louisa and Georgina. He wrote to his parents:

What's in the wind about Abercorn and L? I don't twig but
I know that she has ridden alone with him to Richmond
Park on his Arabian while I rode another way with Georgy.
We rode to Putney Bridge, Wimbledon Common and the
Park by Hammersmith . . . We met a quantity of chaps.
Abercorn of course.

At this stage, Georgina resorted to tactics worthy of her mother to get
the desired result, pressurising the young marquis into proposing.
Hastings wrote:

The Duchess went to Woburn with the Duke of Abercorn
and Louisa soli! To make him pop the question but he did
not though everybody in town believed he had, so when
they came back after three days everybody said I wish you
joy on your marriage some of them rather sourly.

As a protective mother Georgina was not pleased to see her daughter
compromised, and no doubt the situation brought back unhappy
memories of her own engagement débâcle thirty years before. Aware
he had inadvertently hurt Louisa and her mother, Abercorn apologised
to the Duchess for the embarrassing misunderstanding:

I am glad that the Duke understands the footing I am upon
and that you have explained to him that I am not shackled by
any other person, that tho I do not conceive it possible for a
man of my age to know his own mind thoroughly, I like Lady
L more than any other girl and that I consider myself bound
if I so feel a preference for any one else . . . It would have
given me great pain had any embarrassment or misunderstanding taken place which from the protracted and peculiar
nature of our conversation, I was fearful might have taken
place, on which account I write this as well for the Duke's eye
as your own, as you would naturally be anxious that he should
have no doubt whatever as to the nature of my feelings and

the tenure of the acquaintance which you were so good as to
say you were happy to continue.

The couple were soon engaged but the announcement was delayed
because Lord Abercorn's mother, Lady Aberdeen, was ill. Georgina
was delighted with the match, but hated the thought of being separated
from Louisa. She wrote to Lord Holland from Scotland: 'My Scotch
Doves are very happy and as long as they are with me, so am I, but I
dread the parting with my favourite child.' To delay the final separation
for as long as possible, she decided that she would go with the couple
to Ireland after their marriage for five or six weeks to settle Louisa in
her new home, Barons Court.

As this was a dynastic marriage as well as a love match, there were
hectic negotiations before a final date could be set for the wedding; a
detailed marriage contract had to be drawn up. The Duke gave £12,000
(approximately £500,000) as a marriage portion for his daughter; this
dowry was paid to Lord Abercorn but the Duke gave a personal
allowance or 'pin money' of £1,000 (approximately £42,000) each
year for Louisa's 'sole and separate use'. If her husband died, she would
get £5,000 (about £210,000) each year and a one-off payment of
£10,000 (approximately £420,000). The negotiations were delaying
the wedding so the Duchess seized the initiative and went with Lord
Abercorn to Edinburgh to try to accelerate the process. After the
meeting she described the scene to her husband, who turned it into a
humorous story to tell his friends.

> I have been a good deal amused by some of the details of
> our marriage settlement. Lord Abercorn having of necessity
> both his lawyers here, Scotch and Irish, the grave, sedate
> pose, businesslike manner of the one contrasted with the
> quickness and vivacity and volatile spirits of the other was
> highly diverting.

Once the settlement was finalised the wedding could go ahead. For both
the Duke and Duchess it was a very emotional time. They both adored

Louisa and although they were pleased with the match they knew they would miss her dreadfully. The night before Louisa's wedding her father wrote a touching letter expressing his feelings. It gives an insight into a loving man who did not always find it easy to express his emotions:

> The time approaches my dearest child . . . when I am giving her away to one who I hope and trust is in every part worthy of her and who I am sure will do everything in his power to grant her happiness . . . I give you away dearest child cheered by the enduring hope that you are about to be happy. I am a man of few words but strong feelings, and I take this mode of expressing them when you are on the eve of quitting the paternal roof, though without relinquishing (I think) the strong hold you will ever have on my affections. I am an old man with all the infirmities of age hanging heavy on me, among them, I must include an overweening fondness for those who are, and ought to be dear to me – you are one of the first of this set dearest Louisa, for I may truly say that you have never in the whole course of your life given me one moment's pain or uneasiness – your mother will laugh at me for writing this long letter to you before I go to bed, but it is the only way I have of expressing what I feel, and I am sure you will read it with patience. I wish I had the talent of expressing myself with more brevity, but I have not – good night dearest child, may every blessing be showered on your head in the new sphere in which you are about to move, in the duties you are about to undertake, is the anxious prayer of your very affectionate Father.

On 25 October 1832, Louisa's wedding was held at Georgina's childhood home, Gordon Castle. It was held in the Highlands instead of London because Lady Aberdeen was not well enough to travel. The wedding was a grand event and a detailed description appeared in the *Aberdeen Journal* under the headline 'Splendid Nuptial Festivities'. The article continued in the same flowery, sycophantic tone:

> The banks of the Spey have recently presented an aspect of unwonted gaiety and animation . . . the young Marquis of Abercorn led to the hymeneal altar the beautiful and accomplished Lady Louisa Russell, second daughter to the Duke of Bedford. Gordon Castle, the princely residence of the bride's maternal uncle was the chosen scene of the nuptial festivities which were conducted on a scale of superb and costly magnificence worthy of the noble host and the illustrious occasion . . . by the condescending kindness of the Duke and Duchess of Gordon, a few neighbours were invited to attend, and all the domestics of the castle wearing white favours, and suitably attired, were also privileged to witness the ceremony.

The wedding service took place in the castle's chapel. Georgina had made sure everything was planned to perfection with no expense spared. As the bride and bridesmaids entered, dressed in simple white satin dresses, ethereal music came from a choir singing above the congregation in the gallery. Holding her father's arm, Louisa walked towards her bridegroom, who was standing in front of the altar, which was draped in purple velvet embroidered with gold. The *Journal* continued in matching purple prose:

> Where all was unique and imposing, the blooming bride was of course the most interesting object of attention; veiled in virgin modesty, and apparelled in the richest and most magnificent attire, although independent of the aid of foreign ornament, she indeed was 'loveliness itself!'

> Grace was in all her steps, Heaven in her eye;
> In every gesture love and dignity.

> She was conducted to the altar amid the smiles and blessings of her juvenile attendants, and was given away by her noble sire, with a patrician dignity and tenderness of manner which forced a tear into the eye of some of the beholders,

most deeply interested in the alliance of the day, although well assured that they witnessed nothing which did not authorise the fondest anticipations of prospective felicity.

As soon as the young couple had exchanged their vows, a flag was flown from Gordon Castle. When they saw this signal, the crowd outside burst into cheers and applause and a band accompanied by a piper began to play Scottish airs. The wedding party moved to the drawing room of the castle where there was a wedding cake fit for a queen let alone a marchioness. The *Journal* described it as

> . . . a pyramid of huge concentric circles, of seven feet full in circumference at the base supported on the top the mimic form of an elegant cathedral Gothic church, where, amid the thousand figures which adorned the triumph of confectionary art, might be seen the effigies of two devoted lovers and their nuptial attendants assembled at the altar, along with the Lilliputian image of the officiating clergyman, in the act of pronouncing over them the matrimonial benediction.

Once the monumental cake was cut and distributed, the young couple left for their honeymoon, but the party continued in the evening with a banquet for the Duke of Gordon's staff and tenants. The aristocratic guests joined them to drink the Lord and Lady Abercorn's health and to watch a brilliant display of fireworks that ended the celebrations.

A month after the wedding, Georgina travelled with her three daughters and new son-in-law to Ireland. It was a rough crossing; the wind was so violent they had to return and stay all night at anchor off shore, and when they did finally set sail they all suffered sea-sickness. Once in Ireland, the Duchess was enchanted with the Abercorn estate, which was situated among lakes and mountains. The foundations for the elegant neo-classical house had been laid in 1776 but it took six more years to complete. In 1791 Sir John Soane was involved in improving the house but five years later it was damaged by fire. As a relatively new house, Louisa was able to put her own stamp on Barons Court and some of her interior design ideas echoed her family home. The style she chose for the gallery, for instance, is reminiscent of Henry Holland's library at Woburn. The Abercorns employed Sir Richard and William Morrison to update the house and they mixed Soane's original designs with their own sophisticated spatial effects. The shallow dome in the white library was inspired by Soane's design for the Bank of England while the superb rotunda was originally Soane's top-lit billiard room.

Although Georgina was delighted with her daughter's new home, early in the new year her visit was ruined by an accident. She fell from a carriage on to her back and although she did not break any ribs, she developed a chest infection. At first the Duke was not concerned, thinking his wife was being a hypochondriac. He wrote to Lady Holland on 7 January 1833:

> My hospital report this morning is as favourable as possible, the Duchess is wonderfully well and Parker told me yesterday that he had no idea she would have recovered from her very serious illness in so short a time, but she is (entre nous) something like you, and not willing to acknowledge herself better when she is so essentially.

But the Duke's report was too optimistic and he soon had to revise his opinion. The Duchess was in great pain and started spitting blood. As reports of her health deteriorated, he became so anxious that he travelled to Ireland to be with her. At this time the magazine *The Satirist* alluded to her relationship with Landseer, writing: 'The Duchess of Bedford has been suddenly taken ill in Ireland. Strong draughts were resorted to which relieved the patient. Edwin Landseer is her Grace's draughtsman!' In fact, it was her husband, not her lover, whom Georgina wanted when she thought that she was dying. Her reaction reveals that, *in extremis*, it was the Duke from whom she drew strength and that her marriage, not her affair, was the bedrock relationship in her life. The Duchess wrote to Lord Holland:

> I cannot describe the agony I have suffered nor the wretchedness I felt during many hours when I was aware I was dying, at the idea of never again seeing the Duke, a fly would have turned the balance against me . . . when I looked up and saw these three young creatures, Georgy, Louisa and Abercorn round me I thought what a cruel sight it was for them and sent them away, without expressing my feelings tho' I thought all would soon be over – the Duke's arrival was such a moment to me that I dare not trust myself upon the subject.

It seems the Duke was slightly surprised and very moved when he realised how much his wife needed him, but while he was reassured by his wife's enduring love, he was shocked at the change he saw in her:

> You may imagine to what a state of debility she is reduced. Her poor legs which used to be so round and elastick [*sic*] are now two complete drumsticks. Any little inconvenience I might have been put to by the journey is more than compensated by the real pleasure she seemed to experience by my arrival.

The Duchess took a long time to get better and the only treatment available was primitive. The doctors applied 'ten dozen and a half leeches' and bled her, and as she was in great pain they gave her opium to make her sleep. At first, she was so weak that she got up for a few hours only each evening to have her bed made. Although her husband and children tried to amuse her, she became very depressed and was desperate to get back to London to see her own doctors.

In early February, the Duke and Duchess returned to England, although Georgina was still not fully recovered. Even her stepchildren were concerned about her health. The Duchess had always seemed so robust; suddenly everyone was reminded that she was not indestructible. Lord John Russell wrote to Lady William at the end of February: 'The Duchess is rather better, but her lungs are certainly affected, and it will take her a long time to recover. It is as you say, she would now be a loss to her children, and I must say I should be very sorry to see her illness take a bad turn.'

In the spring the Duke and Duchess went to Endsleigh to recuperate. They were joined by many of their children, who were worried about their mother's health and wanted to share this relaxed, family time together. By the end of April, Georgina was able to walk 'or rather crawl' for a mile but she was still not her usual healthy, exuberant self. Lord Holland knew the Duchess was still suffering from low spirits, so he wrote her one of his flirtatious poems to make her feel better about herself and to let her know how loved she was:

> Dearest, Dearest, Dearest Duchess
> Whether on my legs or crutches
> And whether late or early
> Although from distance, age, respect,
> I may from doing more be checked
> I still can love you dearly –
> And so I do – 'tis not your form
> Though that's so tempting it might warm
> To amorous thoughts a hermit
> Nor yet your wit and sense that move
> Though they are made to kindle love
> And kindled to confirm it,
> But tis a something lovelier yet
> Than features, figure, grace or wit
> A charm I can't explain
> Persuades me, had not fortune frowned
> I might in you a heart have found
> That loved, had loved again –
> If this be seen, it is a truth
> And would to God in happier youth

I'd had the sense to own it
But now when scandal can't ensue
I claim a blush from you to show me that you've known it
Grant but a smile to warm it too
And shew me you have known it.

Georgina was delighted with the verse and took it in just the light-hearted, affectionate way it was meant. It seems that both the Duchess and Lord Holland knew the limits of their flirtation and valued it for what it was, a charming expression of courtly love, without needing to take it further. Although fulsome in praise, such declarations did not threaten their marriages and they were an accepted part of the dynamics of the foursome. Lord Holland's poems, like the Duke's intimate letters to Lady Holland, were written with the knowledge that they would be shared with their partners, not hidden from them. Georgina wrote back:

> Now dearest Holly, one word about Self, you do all you
> can to make me in love with myself, for your approbation
> and affection is dearer to me than any one else's on whom
> I have no claim. You have from the first day of our
> acquaintance always been most kind to me, forgetting my
> faults and magnifying what ever of good you can find in
> me. Mon Coeur est bon and warm and if once I become
> attached I do not forget those I love, therefore you and
> Lady Holland are sure of a large share of my affections –
> The Duke is delighted with your verses and I am very
> grateful for what they express.

In the summer, partly because of Georgina's illness and partly because of the expense, the Duke and Duchess did not entertain lavishly in London. The Duke told Lord William:

> Your satire about the Campden Hill breakfasts is misapplied
> in the present instance, as not a single strawberry or cup of

tea has been given them this year. Economy and retrenchment have been as much the order of the day with us, as with Joseph Hume, and the House of Commons . . . You are aware that very little port wine is consumed in my house since I discontinued it in the Steward's room – not more than a pipe in two years.

However, by August the Duchess was well enough to entertain Landseer and his friends with her usual vivacity and style. They were planning their autumn trip to the Highlands and Georgina let her lover treat her home as his own, even encouraging him to invite his friends whenever he liked. Landseer wrote to his friend Charles Matthews:

Could you send your fiddle to No. 6 Belgrave Square, during tomorrow? As the Duchess gives us a supper after the play, when we shall most likely have a lark. This is all my arrangement, and I hope you will not send your guitar to sup without the poor player as I wish my good friends to become better acquainted with you as they will most likely be bored by us for a month in the Highlands.

While Georgina went to Scotland with Landseer, the Duke stayed in England, but unlike on previous occasions he seems to have been genuinely happy about the situation. While the Duchess was away he saw Lady Sandwich frequently and perhaps she reminded him a little of his fiery wife because he told Lady Holland she was a woman with 'a warm and irascible temper'. During his wife's absence he also spent time alone at Woburn in what the Duchess called 'solitary grandeur'.

Georgina's Scottish party was youthful and lively, with more guests from her children's generation than her own, including the Abercorns and Landseer's friends Charles Matthews and Lord Ossulston. At the Doune, Landseer was able to relax and paint in his favourite environment. G.D. Leslie described how he liked to work 'in an old home spun shooting jacket; calico sleeves were tied on his arms like those that butchers wear. He wore generally an old straw hat, the brim of which was lined with green, had his palette and brushes in his hand and looked extremely picturesque reminding me strongly of the figures in Rembrandt's etchings.'

Georgina joined in the fun with the younger generation, her energy and enthusiasm having returned after her illness. The party travelled a few miles from the Doune to Glenfeshie to stay in a hamlet of bothies in a romantic glen. Here, as at Endsleigh, the Duchess had capitalised on the natural beauty of the area to create her own escapist world. With more than a hint of nostalgia, Georgina recreated for her friends and lover the simple life she had enjoyed so much with her mother and sisters in her childhood. It was a remote place to get to. The men rode on ponies, Georgina, Lady Rachel and the maids came in a tilt cart, and Georgy and her cousin Miss Balfour walked. The Duchess was determined to give her young companions a real Highland adventure, even making them all dress the part. The gentlemen wore kilts while the ladies wore 'dress of the country shape and material' – blue or grey short petticoats, scarlet, grey or blue stockings, aprons and mittens and snoods of red or blue through their hair. No bonnets were allowed; instead coloured handkerchiefs were worn to protect their heads from the wind and rain.

The hamlet was 'like an Indian settlement' with one low building made up of three or four bedrooms and a kitchen, and two smaller buildings of one room each; one was used as a dining room, drawing room and hall while the other contained two beds for female guests. All the buildings looked like peasant cottages with walls made of turf and overgrown with foxgloves and the roof made of untrimmed spars of birch. The bedrooms were so small they were only just large enough to turn around in and the furniture was basic, with no curtains, chairs or mirrors, just mattresses and pillows stuffed with heather. The women slept in the huts, and the men camped out in a cave above the loch in tents furnished with two small heather couches, one small table and a washstand and footbath. The carpet was turf on which was laid the occasional piece of wood to act as a wardrobe.

There are many pictorial records of this visit that portray an idyllic time. Landseer did a sketch of one of the Duchess's huts showing the turf walls and an entrance guarded by a stag's head. A degree of sophistication is suggested amid the simplicity; inside the hut can be seen silver candlesticks and a glass decanter on a chest of drawers. He also sketched the Duchess and her party enjoying a picnic and riding on ponies. Charles Matthews sketched the inside of Georgina's bothie, capturing the comfort and homeliness of the room. A large armchair stands by an open fire next to a simply laid table. Matthews told of the atmosphere of the party in words as well as pictures, writing a detailed account for his mother:

> Everything here is wild; the country is wild, the animals are wild, the weather is wild; the two young ladies who are here are wild as March hares and I verily believe that if I stay another week here I shall be wild myself . . . The party is much too full of fun to allow anything like study to go on.

During the day the men hunted and fished, bringing their catch back to the camp to be cooked by the ladies over open fires of peat and clear-burning fir. They dined on venison, grouse, hares, partridges, blackcock, ptarmigan, plovers, salmon, pike and trout. Evenings were spent around a campfire dancing reels or singing duets and Highland ballads, accompanied on the guitar or a small portable piano. Georgina believed she had created 'a little paradise' at Glenfeshie and her guests seemed to agree with her. It was a magical time for everyone in the party, as Matthews wrote:

> It is without any exception the most delightful sort of life I have ever seen or experienced . . . Lord Ossulston and Miss Balfour both sing beautifully, and we get up songs, duets and trios without end. A more charming spot for midnight serenading cannot be imagined.

Providing their own entertainment was part of the fun and one evening they put on a play called *My Wife's Mother*. Always willing to tell a

Maternal to her core, Georgina was to have twelve babies (two died shortly after birth). Here the young Duchess is holding one of the first of her many offspring.

Henry Richard Fox, third Baron Holland, painted by François Xavier Fabre. Lord Holland and his wife Elizabeth were life-long friends of the Bedfords. Georgina enjoyed flirting with Lord Holland, while the Duke found a good listener in Lady Holland.

Dominant and beautiful, Elizabeth, Lady Holland, met Georgina as an equal. They were both Queen bees who enjoyed holding court and, although this led to the two women occasionally clashing, over the years they developed a friendship.

Landseer's first portrait of Georgina. After the Duke's serious illness in the early 1820s the Duchess felt isolated and vulnerable. The young artist has perfectly captured her mood.

Evocative and tender, Landseer's
sensitive studies of Georgina
reveal the growing intimacy of
their relationship. In this sketch
(*left*) the young artist observes
his voluptuous mistress sewing,
and (*below*) happily lying back
to reveal her breast.

A precious moment between mother and daughter captured by Landseer. This drawing shows Georgina with her youngest daughter, Lady Rachel Russell, who is thought by many to be the artist's child.

Landseer drew Lady Rachel more than any of the other Russell children. Here she is sketched wearing a dancing dress.

Landseer's sketches were like a modern photo album, capturing the everyday life of three generations of the Russell family. This series of sketched 'snapshots' show Georgina was a very involved grandmother who took great pleasure in her grandchildren. Lady Harriet Hamilton, eldest daughter of the Abercorns, was a particular favourite of Georgina's. Here she is sketched (*above left*) taking her first steps helped by her grandmother; being cuddled by the Duchess (*above right*); and riding on a dog (*below right*). Georgina's grandson is shown (*below left*) brushing her hair.

As time went on, Landseer and the Duke of Bedford became friends not rivals; they went shooting together and enjoyed discussing art. This sketch by Landseer shows the Duke with his dog in the Highlands.

By the mid 1830s the *ménage à trois* was at its most harmonious. In this sketch Landseer captures the tenderness Georgina felt towards her ailing husband.

Enchanted places. After the Duke's death Georgina was exiled from her beloved Endsleigh. In this picture the house is sketched from the Swiss Cottage, by Landseer.

'It is without exception the most delightful sort of life.' Georgina enjoyed creating the 'simple life' in the Highlands for her family and friends. This drawing of the dining bothie at Glenfeshie by Charles Matthews was drawn during one of the Duchess's Scottish holidays.

story against herself, as a practical joke the Duchess wrote a spoof letter to Charles Matthews' mother, pretending to be Charles, describing his experiences:

> Nothing can be more disagreeable than my séjour here. Lady Georgiana hates music, therefore my talents are not appreciated. Miss Balfour thinks she sings well; quite a mistake. Her grace is the very personification of 'My Wife's Mother.' If she were on the boards she would have no trouble in learning her part. I am prevented by obstacles being always put in my way from sketching, the only thing that could compensate for all the various torments I have to endure. Imagine the cruelty of making me sleep in a tempestuous night under a stone! I am threatened with being banished into a tent. Oh for the joys of home, sweet home!

During the visit the Duchess gave a Highland ball for all the young people in the neighbourhood. Two fiddlers and a piper played from eight in the evening until six in the morning and although the girls were half her age, Georgina out-danced them all. Matthews wrote: 'The Duchess, notwithstanding a slight failing – from a previous accident – in her knee, danced as well as any of the party and in the reels decidedly beat all.' The Duchess also enjoyed meeting her new neighbour, Edward 'Bear' Ellice, who was leasing part of the Glenfeshie estate. (His nickname alluded to his connection with the fur trade of North America where he had business interests.) He was a Scottish Whig MP and became the Whip in Lord Grey's government during the Reform Bill. He had been married to Lord Grey's youngest sister, Hannah Althaea, but she had died in 1832. Ellice had recently bought the estate next to Georgina's and her party was invited to dinner. Matthews described the evening:

> At seven o clock . . . in the midst of a hurricane we set off. The tilt-cart held six, and the rest were accommodated on

ponies ... The cart, not particularly easy in itself, falling from stone to stone, and threatening an upset any moment; the water tearing down with the greatest rapidity, and filling the bottom of the cart; and the wind, with the most frightful gusts, positively rocking it to and fro. On the other side we were met by the piper, who walked before us to the house, and half-a-dozen gillies walked in procession on each side of the cart, the horsemen followed. On reaching the Wooden House ... a tremendous fire of wood and peat blazed upon the hearth and a long well-secured table stood in the middle of the room, well covered with candles of wax stuck in turnip candlesticks of the most elegant workmanship; on the timbers of the roof other similar candlesticks were fixed, so that the illumination was splendid. The banquet was profuse and the dressing exquisite. Venison in every shape and disguise; wild game and fish of every sort and description; ending with cranberry and blueberry tarts, and all sorts of clotted cream, custards, apple puddings and turnip pies. Lots of champagne, claret, moselle, ices etc were disposed of ... The feast was exceedingly gay, the piper playing all the time outside and an enormous bonfire of birch and fir trees kept constantly alive, in spite of the most tremendous unceasing hurricane which raged outside.

A friendship developed between Georgina and Edward Ellice that was to last for the rest of their lives. It seems she had found a new courtier to add to her coterie because she described him as 'a most agreeable man, a delightful person to live with, few people have ever pleased me so much and if he is as honest, kind and sincere as he appears to be, his friendship will be quite a treasure to me'. A month later she wrote with equal enthusiasm: 'I rejoice that the Bear is so fond of me, as it is mutual.'

Georgina was always susceptible to charming men and although there were new admirers in her life, she did not forget the old ones. A letter to Lord Holland at this time reveals she still thought nostalgically about Eugene Beauharnais, and rumours that Princess Victoria might marry Beauharnais' son made her reminisce about her early romance. 'If Eugene's son is as captivating as his father was – in spite of his teeth – I am sorry the little Queen does not marry him for agreeable humour and a cheerful disposition are good foundations for a happy ménage.'

After such an enjoyable stay in the Highlands, the Duchess returned to the Duke 'more than usually gay, cheerful and agreeable'. However, her good mood was soon shattered when she developed jaundice. She turned the colour of an orange and could not eat. As her skin became increasingly lurid, her spirits sank. She told Lord Holland: 'No old Nabob after twenty years baking in India could look more shocking than I do, I am completely jaundiced and the deepest bronze colour you ever saw. The lassitude and general malaise almost subdue me.' As well as being physically unwell, Georgina was in a bad mood with her husband. Although she had been happily ensconced in the Highlands with Landseer, it seems she was annoyed by the amount of time the Duke had been spending with Lady Sandwich. When she visited her husband in London she felt that she was not wanted and left promptly for Woburn. She wrote with a hint of jealousy:

> Certainly as far as relates to self [I should have done] much more comfortably had I remained in London, but you know the Duke has his little habits and tho' I am no use here [Woburn], but to order the rooms, still he thinks I am just as well here as in Belgrave Square. Had I remained in town perhaps there would have been an order sent to put me out of the way with other brood mares.

Despite feeling ill and miserable the Duchess did not want to be 'a wet blanket', so she made sure the Christmas and New Year celebrations continued as normal. She rallied remarkably when her old admirer Lord Grey visited Woburn, and he described the effort she made on his behalf to Princess Lieven:

You can conceive nothing like her colour. I do not exaggerate when I say that it is not exceeded by the brightest orange. She came, however, into the library for an hour or more each morning that I was there, and was still cheerful, notwithstanding the depressing nature of her complaint.

Gradually, Georgina's jaundice faded from orange to a delicate lemon, then back to her normal colour. In January she was cheered by the thought of another wedding; her son Charles was marrying Isabella Davies who the family had known for seven years. Unlike her mother, Georgina was not a materialistic matchmaker and she did not mind that the bride was poor; she liked Isabella and was willing to welcome her into the family and treat her as another daughter. She wrote:

I do not think if Charles had tried all the world over he could have found anyone else so perfectly calculated in every respect to become his wife, nor anyone I should have liked so much for a daughter ... Her charming simplicity and cheerful temper will make my coming old age quite happy.

CHAPTER TEN

The Duchess's
Indian Summer

G eorgina's next role in life was as a grandmother. Throughout the 1830s she regularly attended the births of her grandchildren. She was particularly involved during Lady Abercorn's pregnancies (Louisa was even more fecund than her mother; she had fourteen children) and she nursed her favourite daughter through seven births and a miscarriage. When the Abercorn children were small, Georgina helped her daughter look after them, and the close bond that developed between the Duchess and her granddaughter Lady Harriet is captured in some charming sketches by Landseer. Like a modern snapshot, Georgina is caught cuddling Harriet and reading to her; there is even a sketch of the Duchess helping the little girl take her first steps.

Georgina was also very supportive of her daughters-in-law, drawing on her own extensive experience to help them through childbirth and motherhood. She enjoyed being 'Good old Granny with her specs upon her nose, working when she is not nursing the babies', but it did not really fit her self-image. She wrote to Lord Holland: 'Think of my having four grandchildren, I really am so well that I forget J'ai passé la premiere jeunesse.' In a similar vein, she commented to Lord William: 'What an altered picture, the once lovely, charming etc etc Georgy Gordon to become a darling old soul.'

Georgina had always been a very involved mother and this did not change once her children were grown up. She loved having her children and grandchildren around her, but her stepsons saw this as favouritism and they were jealous of the treatment their father's second family received. Lord Tavistock complained that the Duchess had given the Abercorns their own suite, including a sitting room, at Woburn:

> The great object now seems to be to make everything as agreeable as possible to Abercorn, who between ourselves told Russell the other day that he found Woburn very dull! A strange speech for a man just married, and for whom every thing has been done.

The Duke's eldest sons resented the close relationship Georgina's children had with their father. Tavistock complained that Charles was allowed to manage the shooting, stables and invitations at Woburn and he added, 'it is curious to see how completely he rules my Father.' He described another of Georgina's sons, Frank, as 'strange' and intellectually challenged, while he wrote in hyperbolic terms about his youngest stepbrothers as if he was dealing with young demons. 'I cannot describe to you how uncomfortable I feel about Alexander and even Cosmo,' he told his brother William. 'If they turn out well it will be a miracle. The former is at present the most wicked, cruel, spoilt child I ever saw, and has complete power over my Father, to a degree that would be hardly credible without witnessing it.'

Both the Duke and Georgina had always involved their children in their social life, and this continued once they were adults. House parties at Woburn included the ever-extending family as well as many friends, old and new. Lord Melbourne, the new Prime Minister, joined elder statesmen such as Lord Grey and Mr Ellice among the guests, but despite the new blood, some visitors felt life at Woburn was in dull decline. The Duchesse de Dino wrote of her visit in 1834:

> The party at present at Woburn are almost the same as I met on my first visit. There are Lord and Lady Grey with their daughter Lady Georgina, Lord and Lady Sefton, Mr Ellice, Lord Ossulston, the Duke and Duchess, three of their sons, one of their daughters, Monsieur de Talleyrand and I. All these people are clever, well educated and well mannered, but, as I observed before, English reserve is pushed further at Woburn than anywhere else, and this in spite of the almost audacious freedom of speech affected by the Duchess of Bedford, who is in striking contrast to the silence and shyness of the Duke and the rest of the family. Moreover, in the splendour and magnificence, and the size of the house, there is something which makes the company cold and stiff.

Lord William was also critical of the parties, although for different reasons:

> There is something very unsatisfactory in the English country house life; it is gossip and nothing but gossip. Ask yourself on going to bed how you have passed the day – the answer is most pleasantly – but how? – in gossiping. Ask yourself the same question the next day, same answer.

Lord and Lady William were frequent visitors at this time but as usual there was tension between the older and younger couple. While Lord William had been a diplomat in Portugal, Lady William had been accused in the newspapers of interfering in Portuguese affairs. The root of Portugal's troubles lay in the Napoleonic period. When the French invaded Portugal in 1807, their king, John VI, went into exile in Brazil. On his return to his own country after fourteen years, he brought his son Dom Miguel with him while his eldest son Dom

Pedro was left as Regent of Brazil. The Queen, who was the sister of the King of Spain, encouraged Dom Miguel to put himself forward as pretender to the throne. Mother and son tried to overturn the democratic government in Portugal. Eventually King John banished Miguel first to Paris and then Vienna.

When John VI died in 1826 Dom Pedro chose to remain in Brazil and gave up his rights to the Portuguese throne in favour of his daughter, Donna Maria. At the time she was only a child, so her aunt, Donna Isabella, was made regent. But Dom Pedro tried to conciliate his brother Dom Miguel by offering him Donna Maria's hand in marriage once she was of age. This was too long-term a plan for Miguel's supporters and soon they started to cause trouble. Backed by the Spanish, Miguel's supporters tried to take over Portugal.

Donna Isabella appealed to England for help. Britain's official policy was not to interfere in the internal affairs of other countries, but British troops were sent to provide moral support. The invading troops supporting Miguel were then trounced by the Portuguese army. When two years later Donna Isabella became seriously ill, Dom Pedro, now the Emperor of Brazil, agreed to Miguel becoming regent. This time Miguel promised to uphold the constitution, but his supporters wanted him to make himself absolute king. Unable to resist, Miguel accepted the crown offered him by the Cortes.

The country was divided. In the north the people of Oporto supported Dom Pedro so Miguel sent troops to fight these supporters of the constitution. In Britain opinion was also split. The Tories wanted to recognise Miguel as king but in 1830 the Tory government lost power. The Whigs, as supporters of the constitution, were unwilling to back Miguel.

When Dom Pedro was driven from Brazil by a revolution, he began to rally forces to fight for his daughter's rights. Aware that Portuguese affairs were in chaos, but keen to maintain their policy of non-intervention, the English government decided to send Lord William Russell, as British Minister, to Lisbon.

In 1832, Dom Pedro landed near Oporto and took the town, making Miguel's forces withdraw towards Lisbon. The war continued into the following year. Back in Britain the Tories encouraged the Whigs to recognise Miguel as ruler, but they still refused. At this time the Russells were criticised for being too close to the Spanish Minister, General Cordova. He was an entertaining but devious man. As an ardent supporter of Miguel he encouraged Lord and Lady William to back his candidate for King, suggesting Miguel's government could be liberalised. Letters between Lady William and the Spanish Minister suggested she was infatuated with him. These letters fell into unsympathetic hands and were used against the Russells in England.

The Whigs, including the Duke of Bedford, who supported Dom Pedro, were not pleased. When Dom Pedro won the war and his daughter Donna Maria was placed on the throne, William was moved from Portugal. On their return home to England the controversy about the letters continued. The Duke was more concerned about the political than the amorous implications of his daughter-in-law's behaviour. Lady William told Lord Holland:

> The Duke of Bedford has written me enigmatical innuendos and the Duchess informed me at Endsleigh that he had been very much annoyed as he was told by — that a political correspondence of mine to Cordova was in the hands of Ministers. Notwithstanding the absurdity of the fact, I am compelled to take notice of it and mean to ask everybody likely to have been mixed up in the transaction until I have achieved the Herculean labour of coming to the bottom of it.

Apparently, Lady William blamed Lady Holland for spreading gossip about her but the Duke defended his old friend and wrote to his daughter-in-law:

> You asked me last night whether I was angry with you for what you said about Lady Holland. We had just sat down to our whist party, and I could not enter into a discussion on such a subject, at such a time, but I will freely confess that I

was much hurt at what you said, and my feelings entirely corresponded with those of the Duchess who expressed them with warmth. Lady Holland has unquestionably her faults like all other people, for who is without them? But she has been uniformly kind to me and to all my family. She certainly has been so to you, and I could not but regret to hear you speak of her as you did, and especially before a stranger like Miss Eden.

Lady William soon had a more serious personal problem to face and a betrayal on a different scale. In 1835, while Lord William was a diplomat in Germany, he fell in love with a thirty-nine-year-old widow known as Rebecca, whose real name is thought to have been Henriette de Haber, the daughter of a Jewish banker. When Lord William met her, the attraction between them was instant and they soon started an affair.

At first Lady William hoped it was just a brief fling, little more than a flirtation. She wrote to Princess Lieven: 'The family believe that it is a minor adventure (very disagreeable for the partner) but will end like the love affairs of his father with Lady Elizabeth Vernon and Lady Sandwich!! And not with a serious and very dangerous scandal.' However, the affair was serious and Lord and Lady William started leading separate lives. The Duke and Duchess supported William, welcoming him home to Woburn, and without his wife's disruptive influence his attitude to the Duchess changed completely. Instead of criticising Georgina's extravagance he attended her balls at Campden Hill and praised her hospitality at Woburn, writing in his diary: 'What splendid luxury, what refinement, what comfort.' Freed from his possessive wife, his stepmother once again became his confidante. In January 1836 he wrote in his diary: 'The Duchess spoke to me on the subject of marriage kindly and sensibly; kindness and sense always make an impression on me.' The following month he stayed with the Duke and Duchess in Dover. He recorded: 'The Duchess talked to me very frankly and kindly about Frankfurt and Rebecca.' Their relationship became so close that William showed his

stepmother intimate letters, knowing Georgina would not be judge-
mental and that she understood just how complex relationships could
be. Her letters to William at this time are particularly interesting as
they reveal her philosophy on affairs. Like many Regency aristocrats,
she believed extra-marital affairs were acceptable as long as you kept
up appearances and showed some discretion:

> According to your desire I return the letters. Had I followed
> my own inclinations, I should have put them into the fire.
> My giving you advice would be ridiculous, as you know
> perfectly well what is right. The only use I can be is to be your
> physician and to prescribe for your disease which I hope is
> not incurable, though I fear it will be a work of time before
> you get rid of its effects, without great care it might become
> fatal. You must strictly avoid everything that tends to weaken
> your determination to avoid everything that can let other
> people into your unfortunate state, keep that to yourself and
> remember that your private conduct no one has a right to
> enquire into, but your official situation has placed you in a
> responsible and exalted state, and you must not allow yourself
> or others to tarnish the bright name of Russell.

Lady William was furious to hear about Georgina's reconciliation
with her husband and in retaliation she tried to smear the Duchess
with malicious gossip, old or new. She wrote to Princess Lieven that
the Duchess's 'actual lover is no longer the painter but I have heard it
is now a Swiss valet . . . she is like her sister the Duchess of Manchester
who left her husband for a game-keeper, it is in the blood and
apparently irresistible.'

In fact, Georgina had more on her mind than love affairs; in 1836
her brother, the Duke of Gordon, became seriously ill. The Duchess
was close to him and his devout wife, and she became so anxious
about his condition that in May she travelled to Gordon Castle to be
with him. When he died a few weeks later she was distraught. Since
their childhood, brother and sister had been close. Georgina always

visited her brother when she was in Scotland and he was fond of her children, even hosting Louisa's wedding at Gordon Castle. As the Duke and his wife Elizabeth had no children and his brother, Alexander, had died unmarried in 1808, George was the last Duke of Gordon. The title passed to his eldest sister Charlotte's family so her descendants became Dukes of Richmond and Gordon. The Duke of Bedford wrote to Lady Holland about Georgina's grief:

> I have delayed writing to you from day to day in hopes that I might be able to send you a better account of the Duchess, but alas! She does not rally in the slightest degree – both you and Holland would grieve to see her complete prostration of spirits – I am really apprehensive that her health may be seriously injured by her very deep affliction.

The loss of Georgina's brother made her very aware of mortality and the Duke's failing health was a constant concern. The feelings of isolation she had felt when he first suffered a stroke returned and she wrote to Lord Holland: 'I cannot conceal from myself that he does not rally as he used to do – and that I am a being without a companion to love, cheer and protect me when in sickness and to laugh with me when in health and spirits.' To try to extend the Duke's life, Georgina appointed a new young Scottish doctor, Allen Thomson, to attend the Duke wherever he went. Intelligent and conscientious, Dr Thomson became a part of the family, often dining with the Duke and Duchess; his detailed letters to his parents give an insider's view of the Bedford household:

> The family consists of two daughters as well as the Duke and Dutchess [*sic*]. The oldest Lady Georgina is rather a retired person but very good and with considerable talent and humour. The youngest is a lively girl of ten, Lady Rachel, who is a little spoilt, remarkably clever and the pet of the rest.

His analysis of character was perceptive; Lady Rachel was a precocious child whose every achievement was lauded. She had a gift for writing and enjoyed inventing stories for her young nieces and nephews. There was nothing unusual in that, but the fact that when she was twelve her parents paid to have the stories published in a book, *Memoirs of a Dormouse and Memoirs of a Doll*, was unusually indulgent. Perhaps her creativity was inherited. Rachel certainly had a vivid imagination and, like Landseer, she readily anthropomorphised animals, writing at the end of her *Memoirs of a Dormouse*: 'NB The Dormice above mentioned were all in the possession of the writer for some time; when, in cleaning Cracknut's cage, the memoir was discovered hidden in the bran, and was thought worthy of being printed.'

As well as capturing the personalities, Dr Thomson's letters give an insight into the daily routine at Woburn. The doctor breakfasted with Lady Rachel and her governess at nine and then at half past ten he usually saw the Duke to monitor his health. After a few hours to himself, he lunched with the whole family at two o'clock, but the main meal of the day was dinner at half past seven. Thomson noted that even when the Duke felt ill he always ate a good dinner and drank half a bottle of claret. After the meal, the party stayed in the drawing room until the Duke went to bed at half past ten.

Part of the young doctor's duty was to travel with his patient to Scotland. Unlike many visitors he found the routine at the Doune dull and he described the accommodation as 'not of the best'. He wrote: 'We jog on here in our usual trot and considering the monotony of the employments it is inspiring to me how quickly time flies.' He observed that the Duke was happy to see the Duchess enjoying herself, but Dr Thomson had doubts about Georgina's true happiness:

> The Duchess is not I suspect the same person she used to be
> at least if I can judge from what I hear some people
> whispering. There is a certain want of restraint, which at

her age I should fear would increase. Her anxieties too become greater and one can always read in the expression of her opinions the varying state of her own spirits.

From Scotland the Duke and Duchess travelled with Dr Thomson to Ireland to visit the Abercorns at Barons Court. Concerned about his old friend, Lord Holland opposed the trip as he thought it might damage the Duke's health, and as usual he expressed his feelings in verse to the Duchess:

I said Dear Duchess and twas true
When I could write, I'd write to you
And swift as racehorse to the goal
Pure as the needle to the Pole
Eager as school-boys broken loose
Seek playground, fruit or parent's house
My constant muse, at length let out
From her close prison of the gout
Had long an overflowing rushes
To bear his tribute to the Dutchess
And to pour out in tides of ink
What I have never ceased to think
Tho' absence doomed me to be dumb
And pain, made envious, spiked my thumb

But if I do persist in saying what I have thought in verse, my letter will never finish and so I cut short my doggerel and in plain form I therefore prevail to tell you that I was at first quite unhappy at your wild Irish excursion. Bah.

However, the Duke showed what Georgina called 'Russell firmness' in his determination to see his daughter, and at the end of November the party sailed to Ireland, braving strong winds and rough seas. As Dr Thomson noted, the Duke's sea-sickness was not helped by his typically luxurious diet: 'When I returned from Glasgow I found that they had all been exceeding in lobsters and oysters and the Duke had the stomach somewhat deranged.'

Once at Barons Court, the young physician's observant eye assessed the scene. He described Lord Abercorn as

> . . . one of the handsomest men I ever saw, a great dandy and tho' agreeable enough in external manners very selfish . . . The Marchioness is very beautiful and one of the most amiable and agreeable persons I ever saw. She is neither quite like the Gordons nor the Russells but a happy medium between both. She is not remarkably clever but has a good deal of quiet fun and sets every body quite at their ease and makes them pleased with themselves and her.

Overall he was no more impressed with Barons Court than he had been with the Doune. The large estate, covering thirty-seven miles by fourteen miles, was situated on one side of a string of lakes and he complained about the wet weather and damp atmosphere in the house:

> Everything here is of course Tory and Protestant. The standard John Bull, Morning Post, Frasers Journal etc on the table. The house is a large one but exceedingly ill laid out. There is one very fine room in it near one hundred feet long but the others are neither well looking nor comfortable. . . . The Marchioness's boudoir, a small drawing room, has a number of pretty things in it among others, the complete Toilette (that is dressing table, mirror, gold basins) which belonged to Josephine Bonaparte.

The Duke was equally critical of his son-in-law's home, telling Landseer that 'there is nothing in the "beautiful and sublime" or even the picturesque in this part of Ireland.' In a similar tone, he wrote to Lady Holland:

There is nothing remarkable in this place, except that it is surrounded by bogs, which is not remarkable in Ireland – altho' it is called Barons Court there is nothing in it to remind you of the Baronial Court of a long line of ancestry – everything is modern – a modern house tumbling down for want of repairs, and modern plantations which in two or three hundred years will be fine woods – Abercorn is not disposed to lay out much money upon it – beyond making the house comfortable and habitable which he will do.

It seems there was a tense atmosphere between the Duke and his son-in-law; not only was the older man rude about the younger man's estate he also disagreed with him on politics because Abercorn was a Tory. The Duke wrote: 'In this remote corner we hear little of politicks and what we do hear, does not much accord with mine; but I hold my tongue and say nothing.'

Despite his many criticisms, the Duke enjoyed his stay and was in excellent health and spirits. The Duchess was on less good form and although she was with her favourite daughter and her three grandchildren, she was in a bad mood. She had a cold and complained of a pain shooting through her chest from her ribs, but Dr Thomson thought she was a hypochondriac and her main problem was lack of occupation. He wrote: 'She has an idea that she is becoming dropsical at present and says she is breathless which I think proceeds chiefly from the unwieldiness of her body.' He wanted her to lose weight so he put her on a strict diet: 'She is very stout, and not a bit reduced by my plan of starving her, for tho' she says a great deal about it she takes her food and wine as usual. She has been stooping a good deal of late and I think that is the cause of the pain being worse at present.' Dr Thomson was fighting a losing battle with Georgina; she had her own ideas about dieting and over the years she had developed her own idiosyncratic beauty regime. There were shades of Cleopatra, as her household bills show that large quantities of asses' milk were regularly bought for the Duchess; the idea of her bathing in the milk, like an Egyptian Queen, certainly fits her image. After her bath she would douse herself in her favourite scent, Esprit de Rose, bought at great expense from Bourgeois and Huguenin, Perfumers to the Royal Family. Although she denied being vain, she certainly cared about her appearance. She explained her attitude to beauty to Lord Holland:

> I thought you knew your informer's style of writing too well, not to make some allowances for a letter written on a bad day, for excellent exercise, read steady exercise and substitute less fat for thin . . . I hope to be tolerable till my last day. I therefore should not try to grow thin, which shows wrinkles and destroys colour, consequently admiration, which we all like. And tho I fancy I care less about it in a general way than most of my sex, I make no doubt you think I am mistaken — the truth is, that we have been quite alone and that to amuse the family I have quizzed myself by talking of my obesity, which I told them Parker [a doctor] called the corpulence of age and that I intended to walk it off. Make your mind easy about me, rest assured that with all my good spirits and gay humour, there is a more solid foundation than many give me credit for.

*

Although the Duchess was now a matronly figure, her relationship with Landseer was as strong as ever. He stayed with her at Endsleigh and built a hut of his own next to her settlement at Glenfeshie so that every autumn he could paint and be near her. His friendship with the Duke had also developed over the years and by the mid-1830s it was often the Duke, not the Duchess, who invited him to stay at Woburn and in the Highlands. Lord William described coming to Woburn and finding Landseer and the Duke 'tete a tete', while in Scotland the two men visited the Duchess of Sutherland at Dunrobin Castle together, leaving Georgina at the Doune. Landseer returned with a sketch of the house and both men assured the Duchess that she would 'delight in it as it is very close to the sea'. At this time, the *ménage à trois* seems to have been perfectly harmonious. The Duchess wrote, 'we have all enjoyed our delicious summer', and a sketch by Landseer captures the balance of the relationships. The sketch suggests that the artist had come to terms with the situation and accepted that the Duchess could love two men at once but in very different ways. It shows a frail, elderly Duke sitting hunched in a chair reading a paper while the Duchess is standing behind him with her hands tenderly resting on her husband's shoulders. This image leaves no doubt that Georgina cared deeply about her husband but did not exclude her lover, who sensitively observed the scene.

Although the trio's personal life had developed its own equilibrium, occasionally professional matters could upset Landseer's relationship with the Duke. Shortly after the Scottish holiday there was a temporary rift in their friendship. Two years earlier the Duke had commissioned a painting called 'The Departure of the Highland Drovers' from Landseer for £500 (approximately £21,000), but when it was finished the Duke claimed that he could not afford it. Landseer was furious. His friend the Count D'Orsay told him to ignore the Duke's behaviour, and in a comment perhaps more applicable to the Duchess than her husband he added: 'You ought not to be losing your precious time running after old breeches which you cannot obtain.'

By April 1837 the rift was obviously repaired because Landseer was back at Woburn. At one house party he sketched John Allen, the Hollands' companion, and later in the year he brought his fellow artists Calcott, Wilkie and Leslie to visit the Abbey. The Bedfords had become like a second family to Landseer, so in July when he suffered a bad head injury after falling from his carriage, he turned to the Duke and Duchess for help. He came to stay with them at Campden Hill and was nursed by Georgina and Dr Thomson. Although he seemed to recover well, it was later thought that this injury contributed to the mental illness that was to last for the rest of his life.

Later that year, the Duke and Duchess planned a trip to the Continent, hoping a winter abroad would improve the Duke's health. Now aged seventy-one, he was sceptical that it would help, explaining that he felt his 'old shattered frame is so completely worn out that botching and patching can be but of little service', but he went to please the Duchess. Knowing they needed a doctor close at hand, Georgina used all her powers of manipulation to persuade Dr Thomson to come with them. He had intended to leave their employment to marry his fiancée and take up a teaching post in Scotland but Georgina thought her needs should take precedence over his plans. Dr Thomson told his mother:

> The Duchess the other day speaking of going abroad next winter came again over the subject of my staying and said: 'Oh! You know you promised me two years.' You do not seem to be quite aware that she has not a very perfect recollection of what she or another person says and is apt to model her reminiscences according to her views. I said nothing more than respecting my engagement at Edinburgh. It is quite impossible with her to make any confidences. I could not unless I saw you explain the points of her character which give rise to this impossibility but I believe I know her very well.

Having tried a direct approach, Georgina decided an indirect one might be more successful. She knew flattery was the way to a man's heart, even her young doctor's, so she now turned the full force of her charm on him. She wrote:

> Let me add in the Duke's name and my own how much comfort and pleasure, we have derived from your society, and how grateful I feel for your kind attention to Rachel, and how sensible the Duke and I are of your constant, unremitting and cheerful attendance.

Her charm offensive worked and Dr Thomson agreed to delay his plans for a year and to accompany them on their journey. His critical attitude towards the Duchess changed and it seems they reached a new level of understanding. Although he sometimes found her interference in his medical treatments irritating, he began to appreciate her sense of humour. Shortly before they set off for France he wrote to his mother:

> Her great joke against me just now is my objection to calomel [a medicine] which she brings out upon all occasions, particularly at the dinner table. 'There's a dish Doctor I would recommend to your attention, it always requires to be followed by eight gros of calomel.' Then imitating my voice in the midst of the dinner party she bawls out: 'Your grace must excuse me I am determined to give no calomel.' She has completely regained her spirits and is a most astonishing woman, extremely clever, with information on all subjects, a great mimic and always ready for a joke, scrupulously attentive to the most minute arrangements of house affairs, kind and affable to everyone but rigidly tenacious of dignity and rank as expressed in the formalities of manner and conversation, but forgetting it entirely in most other circumstances. She is extremely kind to me and on the whole, tho' she contradicts my practice has considerable confidence in my judgement.

At the end of November, the Duke and Duchess and their entourage set off for Paris. The Duke did not enjoy his stay in the capital, writing: 'Paris is indeed a desert to me – I had a few friends here, who are all gone – acquaintances very few indeed.' While in Paris the Bedfords heard that their son Henry had had an accident and was seriously ill. The young sailor had been severely injured when a block fell on his head while he was helping to fit out the ship *Melville* before it sailed to the Cape. The Duchess rushed back to England to be with her son, who had been taken to Haslar Hospital, until he was out of danger. At the end of February Henry was fit enough to leave hospital, but the accident meant he had to give up his position with *Melville*; in the long term it left him with epileptic fits which were to lead to his premature death in the 1840s.

Once Henry was better, the Duke became as concerned about his wife's mental health as his son's physical well-being: 'All my anxiety is now about the Duchess, I fear much for the wear and tear of her nerves, and great bodily fatigue – when she can obtain calm and repose of mind and body, I am I fear weak from a state of reaction – but I will not anticipate evils.'

The Duke's mood improved when Lady Sandwich arrived in Paris with news of her travels, but there is a hint in a letter to Lord Holland that when Georgina returned from England she was not happy to find her rival ensconced. The Duchess realised there was someone very willing to fill her place in the Duke's life every time she went away, and although her husband was now a frail septuagenarian she still felt jealous if he paid too much attention to any other woman. She wrote:

> I did not suffer by my rapid journey. I left Dover at nine o'clock on Thursday and was with the Duke at six o'clock on Friday. All he said was: 'Oh you are arrived.' I think he is more occupied with the beauty or beauties of Paris than is quite good for his health and I believe change of air and new amusements will be better for him, tho' I fear less attractive.

Spurred on by the unwelcome competition, the Duchess was keen to leave Paris as soon as possible and travel to their destination of Nice. In fact, the Duke also wanted to leave, but the Duchess, still irritated by Lady Sandwich's presence, had convinced herself that he wanted to stay close to his sweetheart. It seems Georgina was willing to brave arctic conditions to remove her husband from her adversary's delicate clutches. In early January the Bedford party travelled in extremely cold weather down to the South of France. At times the temperature was six degrees below freezing, the roads were snowed up and there were blocks of ice on the Rhone. The Duke described it as 'more like advancing towards Siberia than le beau midi de la France, the cold and frost and snow have been intense – I have never experienced anything like it before.' When they stopped at one inn, the cold was so severe that although there was a large fire in the room, the water brought in for washing froze in about five minutes. Georgina recounted a story to Lady Holland, illustrating the Duke's selfishness:

> I fear the Duke's galanterie will not be thought much of by travellers, for some English coming to Nice had at one of the Inns ordered tea, they had not dined and looked with impatience to the happy moment when the kettle boiled. Allen, the Duke's valet, rushed into the room and ran off with it for his Grace's foot water but said, 'I gave them back the kettle when empty.'

On the whole, it was a tedious journey, although Georgina did her best to inject some fun. She wrote to Lord Holland:

> I assure you it required all my warmth to keep my party alive (in mind). Dr Thomson is a capital assistant, never was a better being, he is like a good Scot, true to the bone. We are all well and I believe all happy, but that point is difficult to be ascertained when a party of Russells get together. We want Lord Brougham to tie us up and hurl anything at their heads that would produce a sound. I chatter when I can catch a victim, but they are fewer here.

For the Duke, it was 'a sentimental journey'; he had last visited the South of France with his first wife more than half a century before. The Duchess was well aware of this evocative connection and wrote with the same degree of empathy for his feelings that she had shown when they were first engaged:

> I perfectly understand his wishing to revisit places where fifty two years ago he was with her he loved, here his first born came into the world dead and is buried in a garden where he lived. The 'long ago' has charm for him, the days of youth to the memory of age, which memory is very

surprising. He recollects every circumstance as if they had occurred yesterday.

Despite the effort made to enhance the Duke's health and happiness, he was at times morose and the rest of the Russell family were also uncommunicative. Only the Duchess seemed to be making any attempt to be amusing and Dr Thomson was impressed with her tolerance of her family's behaviour:

> Perhaps after all the trouble we have had to bring him [the Duke] here he is disappointed. Perhaps the circumstances in which he returns to Nice are so different from those of his former visit as to affect him . . . The excellent Duchess needs some rest also after the journey. I think that making allowances for her little peculiarities, I never saw a person placed in the same trying circumstances acquit herself more admirably. Her principal fault is over anxiety and consequently her want of 'laisser aller les choses,' or patience to let things take their natural course.

The atmosphere improved when the Bedfords got settled into a villa called la Maison Guilia in the English quarter of Nice, about half a mile west of the town. The Abercorns joined them, renting the house next door called la Maison Avigdon. Georgina liked Nice partly because the landscape reminded her of Scotland. She wrote:

> The place is delightful and as my idea of happiness, like a true savage, lead my thoughts to the Highlands I shut out the hundreds of white houses and look at the high hills, very like my own mountains, particularly since last night when the snow fell so fast they were as white as the Cairngorms ever was.

Soon the weather improved and the Duke and Duchess were able to enjoy basking in the sun in the garden of their villa. It was an idyllic spot. Their two acres of garden ran down to the seashore; on one side it was bordered by a row of cypress trees and on the other by oranges, lemons, vines and figs. Although they had guests to stay, including Lord William and the Duke of Manchester, and there was an international set of French, Russians and English, Georgina missed her social life in England. She wrote to Lord Holland: 'The evenings are somewhat long, not very lively, "mais que voulez vous", I do the best I can, think of the happiness of seeing many I love in England and a few who have an attachment to me.' Most of all she missed seeing Landseer and wanted to share the beauty of the place with him: 'A friend or two would be very agreeable and none to me would be more so than Mr Landseer, to whom I hope you are very kind, as the loss of Woburn is a great one to him – what sketches he would make – the peasants, male and female are picturesque.'

The Duchess tried to stimulate the social life of Nice but some of her parties were too controversial for what the Duke described as 'this little bigoted town'. She cultivated the reputation of being a seductive temptress when she broke the solemnity of Lent by give a 'soiree dansante'. But although some people complained, it did not stop them attending and making the most of her lavish hospitality. The Duke wrote:

> All came and all heartily partook of the supper – She [the Duchess] jokes with the Governor and laughs at son Excellencie with his bigotry and rigid observance of the Careme [Lent], but she does it in so good humoured and at the same time dignified a tone, that he is quite charmed with her, and actually remained in the Ballroom to sanctify the waltzes and reels – the little man said to her 'dans la quieté de son coeur, si on peut pas résister à la tentation, il y a un autre moyen – c'est d'y succombre.' [In the stillness of your heart, if you can't resist temptation, there is another way – to give in.]

Once Lent was over she could give free rein to her party organising talents. On Easter Monday she performed the part of Lady Mayoress of Nice and gave a ball that went on until late into the night. But Georgina's activities were curtailed when several members of her party became ill. The Duke's footman, Rachel's maid and then Lady Rachel developed bilious fevers and were confined to bed for several weeks with the Duchess nursing them. As usual when members of the family were ill, the Duke left Georgina to cope alone while he went with Dr Thomson and the Abercorns to Genoa. The Duchess had resigned herself to her husband's vanishing acts in times of crisis but it made her miss her home and lover even more. She wrote to Lord Holland:

> You must expect a very dull letter for it is very hard to be left, a trio after having had such a large family party. The weather is a consolation, the last fortnight has been perfect, a bright and very warm sun and all the country beginning to be very green and very gay with the different blossoms, still I should have liked to have someone to make those observations to and there is no one person here I have any desire to talk to.

When Rachel was fit enough, Georgina took her to Cannes for a few days for a change of air. Cannes was just becoming fashionable and attracting English residents. The former Chancellor Lord Brougham was building a villa there but Georgina was not impressed with his architectural style, writing that his house showed

> . . . the total absence of judgement and taste which he has displayed in other matters – Cannes is a charming place at the moment but it is going to be improved, spoilt, for those who wish to find a quiet and beautiful spot on the Mediterranean shores.

The Bedfords left Nice in April to travel slowly back through France to England. Once they arrived in London they found everyone was preparing for Queen Victoria's coronation. As one of the leading duchesses, Georgina was invited to dine at the Palace with the Queen. She described the young Queen as 'charming and [she] gains very much by being seen in private, so cheerful and amiable and decidedly much more than very pretty, because she has good features, and great play of Countenance'. In June, the Duchess attended the coronation. The Duke did not feel well enough to attend so she rehearsed before him in her coronation robes and 'paraphernalia'. He enjoyed the preview, telling Lady Holland: 'I must confess she looked handsome in her old age, as she always says when she talks of herself.' The Duke no longer visited London often. Tired and fragile, he was happiest at Woburn so while Georgina visited friends and went to the theatre he stayed at home.

Shortly after the Bedfords' return from France the Duchess and Lady Holland had one of their periodic disagreements. Like a rival queen defending her territory, Lady Holland had built a 'formidable barricade' on top of the park palings that separated Holland House from Campden Hill to prevent Georgina from enjoying the view of her neighbours' beautiful grounds from her garden. To add insult to injury, Lady Holland also put a padlock on her gate to prevent the Duke and Duchess from entering her estate. It was not clear to the Bedfords exactly what the Duchess had done to offend Lady Holland but the Duke had his suspicions. He wrote to Lady Holland: 'Our former friend Brougham is exerting his best endeavours to foment discord between you and me, but as far as I am concerned he will fail.'

As usual there was soon a rapprochement between the two couples because the Duke and Duchess had more serious matters to worry about than petty squabbles. In November 1838 Lord John's wife Adelaide died from a fever a few days after giving birth to their second child. Adelaide had been the young widow of Lord Ribbesdale and the mother of four children when she met John. They married in 1835 and had three and a half happy years together before her death. Georgina was with Adelaide throughout her final illness and her nerves were severely shaken by her stepdaughter-in-law's death. The Duke also found her loss particularly poignant because she died at the same time of year as his first wife. He was very sympathetic to his son, perhaps seeing himself many years before in his grief. He wrote to Lord Holland:

> I sincerely wish he would [go to Holland House]. I am sure it would be far better for him than staying so much alone – he must not abstract himself too much – it is not good for him – his mind should be constantly occupied as possible with useful matters – if he once suffers his mind to become inert for too acute feelings, he will become miserable – you should encourage him to see as much of his colleagues as possible – I mean those he loves and values . . . Excuse all I have said I have no motive but an anxious and warm affection for John.

Unlike their friends Lord and Lady Holland, the Duke and Duchess had a religious belief and both turned to their faith in times of crisis. The Duchess wrote to Mr Ellice: 'It is indeed a severe visitation and one that requires all the duty we owe to God to bear, with resignation.'

The Duchess sensed she would soon have an even closer death to resign herself to as she realised time with her husband was running out. She knew he no longer had the strength to protect her and this left her feeling exposed and vulnerable, as she explained to Lady Holland:

> When the Duke was well all my grievances were hushed on his indulgent bosom, and all irritation occasioned by calumny and unkindness soothed by his unbounded affection and partiality, now the case is sadly changed. I have to fear alone, my tears to fall unheeded and never to hear the voice of kindness. I have much to bear, but not from him, his never tired patience, gentleness and love for me, only makes the contemplation of his impending fate a more agonising thought.

In the early summer of 1839 the Duke and Duchess had an idyllic stay at Endsleigh. The Duchess later recalled their visit in a letter to Lord John:

> In May we arrived at Endsleigh, I think I passed the happiest of weeks I ever enjoyed with your dear Father, he had not one days illness, the weather was lovely, we had both endless employment out of doors and no annoyances within – how little did I then know what a sad change a few months was to produce.

In August, the Bedfords went on their annual trip to the Highlands, where they were joined by many of their children. The younger members of the family came by the new railway that linked England to Scotland. They were impressed by this new mode of travelling and found 'nothing but pleasure, comfort and convenience'. The Duke and Duchess came by carriage and their journey took six days. They avoided the railway as they thought it might be dangerous to come via Preston, where the Chartists were protesting.

Although the 1832 Reform Act had improved the voting system, it had not gone far enough to create a truly democratic country. The wealthy middle classes were enfranchised but the working classes were left without a vote. The Chartist movement, which was most active between 1838 and 1848, aimed to gain political rights for the working classes. They got their name from the six-point charter of changes they wanted to see implemented. Although the Chartists claimed they did not support violence, there was concern that they were stirring up riots in the country.

Once in the Highlands the Bedfords experienced an Indian summer, with almost nine weeks of uninterrupted fine weather. Although the Duke could no longer shoot, he enjoyed the Highland air and spending time with his children. Georgina was particularly pleased that Lord William was there and that he was now on good terms with both her and his father. The Duchess readily forgot his past unkindness and wrote: '. . . never was there a more warm hearted, generous being than William'.

To make the gathering complete for Georgina, Landseer joined the party and Edward Ellice was a frequent visitor. It was a special time for the whole family; they realised the Duke was dying, but instead of being miserable they made the most of every moment. Georgina wrote:

> Nothing can go off better than our party, there is something to me so irresistible in unfeigned kindness, that it is impossible not to be for the time happy, when you see so many people full of anxiety and expressing interest about what is most dear to me, my husband and children. Everybody appears alive to his situation and in admiration of his amiable and patient suffering.

By September the Duke was not well; he was suffering from pressure in his head and sleeping badly. As time went on he missed Woburn and he wrote to Lady Holland: 'I would willingly be there at this moment as I am always fond of home; be it never so homely.' In fact, he was never to see Woburn again. He died of a stroke on 20 October 1839 at the age of seventy-three. Landseer was with the Duke and Duchess and he described the scene to his friend Frederick Lewis:

> I had not been away more than three weeks during which time the melancholy event occurred . . . I was with the Duke and Duchess at the moment when his face was attacked and remained till all was over – My holidays have been sad in the extreme.

CHAPTER ELEVEN

Widowhood

---

*A*fter the Duke's death there was a distressing delay of a month before his funeral was held. The weather made it difficult to take his body by steamer from Inverness to Woolwich, where it was to be met by a hearse and taken on to Chenies for the burial. Those weeks at the Doune were bleak for the Duchess. She was devastated by her husband's death, and at first she would not leave her room. Her daughters watched over her and dealt with all the correspondence and arrangements.

When she felt strong enough to write, Georgina told Lord Holland: 'My spirits are so broken and my heart so wounded that I can barely recollect anything and find at this moment the greatest difficulty in expressing myself.' In another letter she wrote:

> My loneliness is dreadful and I cannot yet at times help believing I have left him in England and that I shall see him

again and when the dark truth does appear my feelings are past expression. I have not yet left my room, tho' the good sense with which kindness has been shown here has done me good, still I cannot bear much and have no right or will to make others happy.

At first the Duchess had intended to travel on the steamer with her husband's body, but as the weeks went by she could not face the morbid journey, so instead decided to travel back to England by land. The Duke had requested a 'quiet unostentatious' funeral with 'no pomp, no parade of following carriages', and his family were determined to follow his wishes. Although in this era women often did not attend funerals, to begin with Georgina had wanted to be present. However, her stepsons did not approve, and suggested that if she insisted on coming she should remain in the church rather than be a mourner in the procession. Eventually, she accepted their advice, perhaps fearing that she would be overcome with emotion as she saw her husband of almost forty years interred in the family vault.

These were difficult days for Georgina. Although she had not been faithful to the Duke, she had always loved him. He was her security and she had known that while he was alive he would always support her. The world seemed a very hostile place without him. When the Duke died, she lost not only her husband but also her status; no longer the Duchess of Bedford, she became a dowager duchess with limited influence. Her position was worse than many widows because her stepson Francis, not one of her own children, inherited the title and most of the Bedford estates. The new Duke had never had a strong relationship with Georgina, and when his father died the situation deteriorated, partly due to financial arrangements but also because of deep-rooted resentments.

Georgina claimed she had never had a conversation with the Duke about her future, but trusted to his good judgement to provide for her. Unfortunately, the Duke had not made his intentions completely clear and this was to cause controversy. Shortly after his death there was a dispute between Georgina and Francis about exactly what his father had intended in the distribution of his estate. As the Dowager Duchess, Georgina was left Campden Hill in Kensington, but stepmother and stepson disagreed about what possessions she was entitled to take from Endsleigh. Although this house had been the Duke and Duchess's special home, with every element of its design carefully chosen by Georgina, at first the new Duke claimed she had no right to even the household items that had her initials embossed on them. He justified his harsh decision by stating that his father had left her Campden Hill and all its contents as a substitute. In fact, although the detail of the late Duke's instructions was ambiguous, the spirit of his intentions had been made plain in a letter to his son written in 1835:

> Campden Hill and Endsleigh, belonging to the Duchess, and on which she sets a store which I need not enumerate, as I feel sure that she will point them out to you, and that you feel a pleasure in anticipating her wishes. [He added, with more idealism than realism, that he was] confident that there will be that harmony and good will, right understanding, and affection between you, the anxious desire of which has at all times and under all circumstances invariably been uppermost in my heart.

Not willing to sit back and allow her stepson to take her precious personal belongings which had so many memories attached to them, Georgina took legal advice. Eventually, to avoid an embarrassing legal battle, Francis was forced to allow Georgina to take the plate and whatever other items she wanted from Endsleigh. It became a business-like deal which depended on Georgina's legal rights, not her stepson's goodwill, which could not be trusted.

As well as losing half her homes, Georgina's income was also greatly reduced. On the Duke's death she had £649 (approximately £27,000) in her Child's bank account. Francis gave her £10,000 (about £420,000), £5,500 which her husband had borrowed from her when he got into debt, and £4,500 as a present. In addition, she received

£600 (about £25,000) a year for Lady Rachel's board, staff and clothes, but this arrangement still meant she had to make economies. She had only one pair of horses for her carriage and she could no longer afford a town house.

Georgina was not the only one having to economise; Francis discovered his father had been so extravagant that he had left debts of half a million pounds; this meant Woburn had to be shut up until the Bedford finances improved. Understandably, Francis was resentful and he wrote of his father to his brother William: 'He had not the power or resolution to hold his hand whenever money was within his reach . . . It led him (thoughtlessly) to do things, that nothing but his high character and confidence and affection could have enabled us to pass over.' Francis wondered how the family fortunes had diminished to such a degree. His great-grandfather John, fourth Duke of Bedford, was considered the richest man of his day and he died without debt. The decline started with his uncle Francis, the fifth Duke, who sold the family estates in Surrey and Hampshire and died leaving a debt of £200,000 (about £6 million). Georgina and the Duke more than doubled this figure. The new Duke was not pleased to have inherited such a large debt and no doubt he blamed his extravagant stepmother for leading his father astray. Perhaps this accounts for his mean-spirited approach to Georgina immediately after his father's death; he sent his chief agent to collect from his stepmother all the cash the Duke had left in the house. This amounted to £310 (about £13,000), half of which Georgina had used to pay bills and travelling expenses. She asked her stepson if she could keep the rest but he insisted that she handed over every penny, justifying his action as necessary for accounting purposes.

The late Duke's mishandling of the family fortunes was not the only shock for his heir after his death. The new Duke also received a series of letters from a woman who claimed to have had a relationship with his father, demanding money to prevent her making her embarrassing allegations public. From a letter Francis wrote to his brother, it seems Lord William met her to find out if her claims were valid:

[She] promises if I will send that sum, never to apply to me or to any of the family again. She says 'I am confident your brother really felt for my situation, and had no vestige of doubt upon his mind.' Again 'Your Grace knows well the extreme delicacy and fastidiousness of him whose memory is ever to be cherished. I could relate volumes of circumstances to you which I am proud and happy to say I have never divulged. Alas! I see too well the ill effect of reposing implicit confidence' – meaning the loss she had sustained by giving up the letters. It is a strange mysterious affair and must rest where it does.

Francis discussed with his brothers how to handle this 'Mrs B' or 'The Lady' as they called her and it seems eventually they agreed to pay her some money. Francis wrote to Lord William:

Mrs B dwelt so much on your opinion that she had claims upon me, that I thought it best to tell her, at once, that she must have misunderstood you, and that you consider I have done enough – you will see her answer which you may burn – I have reason now to believe in the truth of her story, and that the Duchess knew it.

It is quite possible that Georgina did know about this woman and accepted the situation because it gave her the freedom to continue her affair with Landseer. Although there is no further evidence to show who this woman was, her demands for money suggest that she was not one of the aristocratic ladies with whom the Duke had enjoyed sentimental flirtations. As a woman from a lower class, she would not have been a real rival to Georgina's social position, just a useful distraction to prevent the Duke becoming lonely while the Duchess was away with her lover.

The financial and sexual legacies from his father's era did nothing to endear Georgina to Francis and he wrote to his brother: 'With respect to the Dss. D. [Duchess Dowager] the D. of Wellington once said that she would be "like her sister the Duchess of R – Never without a grievance." I fear we must expect this, but I look to Wrio and John to keep her in order.'

With the new head of the family unsympathetic, Georgina relied on her own children to look after her. The Duke and Duchess of Abercorn were particularly supportive, and two months after the Duke's death Georgina went to stay with them at Barons Court. Gradually she began to come to terms with her loss by going for a walk every day around their beautiful estate and contemplating her situation. Her Christian faith gave her comfort, and as she believed in an after-life she trusted that she would see her husband again.

As time went on, she began to look to the future and to plan her return to England. She took practical steps to make her lifestyle as comfortable as possible; for instance, as her Kensington house was to be her main residence, she asked Lord Holland to allow her to graze a cow on Holland House land so that she could have fresh milk. Her youngest stepson, Lord John, was sympathetic towards her, and she invited him to stay with her at Campden Hill and to spend the summer with her in Scotland. It seems John's kindness reminded her of her husband, and after spending time with him she wrote:

> I have enjoyed being with you, I hope that my constant wish of seeing you this summer in Scotland may have some influence with you, any year, your society would be valuable to me, but this summer, beyond what I can express . . . how very much your presence will help to fill up the sad blank your dear Father's loss has made.

Although beneath the surface Georgina was still grieving, she made an effort to be cheerful. By March her old sense of humour had returned and she joked about her sister Charlotte, the Dowager Duchess of Richmond's visit to the Doune. Charlotte had a habit of calling everyone 'Me deer', so Georgina wrote from the Highlands:

Sister Richmond Me dear, has been with more feathers on her head and gold chains and bracelets and rings than were ever seen in this house before. I came 'Me deer' by the horrid rail road and instead of going to Lancaster as I intended 'Me deer' I found myself at Manchester. My own carriage and servants all gone on, too dreadful to stand all night in a Fly to catch them at Lancaster – the poor old lady was asleep and forgot to change trains.

However, just as Georgina was regaining her equilibrium another emotional crisis was to destabilise her. Landseer had also been greatly affected by the Duke's death. He wrote to his aunt: 'My head is considerably addled. I can think of nothing correctly but the melancholy time I passed at the Doune and the sad termination of our anxious watching.' The Duke's death changed the dynamics of his relationship with the Duchess because Georgina was now available. The pressures on the sensitive artist increased when, a few months after the Duke's death, his mother Jane died on 19 January 1840. As Landseer's world became increasingly insecure, he tried to create a new stability in his life. According to contemporary gossip, it seems that in the spring of 1840 he proposed to Georgina, but she turned him down.

Why Georgina refused is debatable. As a handsome man of thirty-eight, Landseer was an eligible bachelor and thus a considerable catch for a corpulent fifty-eight-year-old widow. Although he was not an aristocrat, his genius placed him outside class divisions and he had become a fêted member of Victorian high society. The aristocracy courted him both as an artist and as a guest, and he was firmly established as Queen Victoria's favourite painter. The timing of his proposal, however, was insensitive because Georgina was still genuinely mourning her husband. Perhaps she felt Landseer was suitable as a lover but not as a husband because of his temperament. Erratic and unreliable, he was hypersensitive to criticism and often fell out with even old friends. There was a very dark side to his character. He was deeply interested in the occult, showing a fascination with ghost stories and spiritualism and a morbid obsession with murder cases and criminals. The Duke had been her rock; Landseer would have been shifting sands.

Whatever the reasons for Georgina's refusal, its effect was drastic. In the early summer of 1840, Landseer had a nervous breakdown, becoming full of 'terror and horror' and unable to stand light. A letter to his friend the Count D'Orsay suggests that his instability was linked to his tangled relationship with the Duke and Duchess:

> You may be quite sure I should not have left London without seeing you had I not been in great haste, by the advice of my physician who ordered me off immediately. Since I have received fishing, farming and regular pilling, my nervous system has in part regained its strength. The only thing against me is self-torture. My unfinished works haunt me – visions of noble Dukes in armour give me nightly scowls and pokings . . . I cannot get well till my fancy is turned – my imagination is full of children in the shape of good pictorial subjects. Until I am safely delivered, fits of agitation will continue their attacks – being all undone, without the permission to indulge one's wishes or schemes in any thing but tranquillity . . . There is an old friend of yours here in the shape of a widow! – <u>Tears and Crape always touch one's heart</u> . . . I am full of blue pills and very wretched – in consequence of that same flaw in heart.

It was decided that his mental health might be improved by a trip abroad with his friend and business manager Jacob Bell. Before he went, Georgina was so concerned that she sent her doctor Sir Stephen Hammick, who had been Surgeon Extraordinary to George IV and William IV, to see him. It seems Georgina was very upset by what she heard, as she wrote to Lady Holland:

> I have been very unwell, yesterday morning fainting. I am better today but not capable of going out – there is no end to shocks, when I returned from the Priory [Lord and Lady

Abercorn's home in England] I heard of Mr Landseer's health. He is in a very precarious way. Stephen Hammick who attends him will tell you all about him, he was I gather more composed yesterday evening tho' obliged to keep a Medical Man to sit up with him.

Georgina did not think it was just a temporary problem; she knew her lover well enough to be very aware of his fragile mental health. She told Lord Holland: 'The accounts of poor Mr Landseer have given me great anxiety and great pain. I heard he is in another country and I hope the change may restore his health and mind to their natural state, but I own I have great fears about him.'

In August, Jacob Bell took Landseer through Belgium and up the Rhine to Switzerland. He watched over his friend with great care, allowing him to sketch now and then to 'keep his hand in'. In Geneva, Bell was taken ill with an attack of quinsy [an inflammation of the throat], leaving his charge to his own devices. After six weeks they returned to England via Paris. Landseer was not cured but he was better.

The emotional strain of Landseer's illness, so soon after the Duke's death, was almost too much for Georgina to bear and she admitted to Lord John that, as a result, she sometimes released all her pent-up anger on the wrong people. 'When the body is weakened the mind shares the same fate,' she wrote. 'And I really do feel so desolate and unable to occupy myself, that unintentionally, I fear I torment you, your brother and everyone.'

Without her husband or her lover to support her, and without the finances and homes she was used to, Georgina had to build a new life for herself. On rare occasions she visited Woburn but now she was no longer the mistress, only a tolerated guest. When Queen Victoria and Prince Albert visited the estate, she was invited by the new Duke and Duchess to meet them. Still appreciative of a handsome man, Georgina particularly enjoyed meeting Prince Albert. She wrote:

> Nothing can have been more fortunate in every respect, than the Queen's visit here – the weather has been charming,

the reception without doors enthusiastic by thousands, and within doors as magnificent as possible – The Queen most gracious to every one, and particularly kind to me. The first day she came up and kissed me – Prince Albert has the most bewitching countenance I ever saw and appears a charming person.

Woburn had always been more like 'a mausoleum' than a home to Georgina and it seems she did not regret giving it up. The place she really missed was Endsleigh and she often thought about the happy times she spent there with her husband. After hearing that Lord John had visited her old home she wrote to him with nostalgia: 'Your father and I created it together, every walk, every plant and most of the trees, for years and years we watched their growth – and such another place I do not believe is to be found – I shall often follow you in thought along my favourite haunts.'

But Georgina was never a woman to wallow in self-pity for long; instead, she tried to be positive. With the old routine closed to her, she developed a new one, dividing her time between London and the Doune. In her Highland home she was respected and admired by all sections of the community, partly because as a Gordon she was a true Scotswoman, but also because she treated everyone with compassion. Since 1830 she had been an exceptional tenant to the Grants at the Doune, improving their house without altering its intrinsic character. She had even had all their family portraits framed, and she redecorated the house when carpets and paintwork began to look worn out. She had also, with their consent, capitalised on the beautiful views at Loch an Eilein by clearing trees to build a road around the loch.

When she took over the Doune from the Grants, she also took on many of their staff. One old widow called Christy had lost her only son, Allan, opening some sluice gates and after his tragic death she never recovered her reason. She was 'harmless and half simple', and she spoke very little English, just enough to say 'my jewel' or 'my dear' as children passed. When Georgina became mistress of the Doune, she took charge of Christy, making her head of the scullery, and made sure that this vulnerable old woman was always looked after. She also used her influence with other landlords to get help for local people; for instance, she persuaded Mr MacKintosh to settle £5 each year on a poor man who was the tenant on a farm near Glenfeshie. When he died, she asked MacKintosh to provide protection for his widow, who used to work in Georgina's kitchen, and their nine children. Now Georgina was the person in need, her fellow Highlanders provided the sympathy, support and peace she required to recover. In Scotland she was particularly glad to be near her old friend and neighbour Edward Ellice, who was able to raise her spirits and was 'the only person who stirred up our peaceful thoughts and led them "over the hills and far away" '.

However, just when the Duchess needed the security of her home in the Highlands, she was in danger of losing the Doune. The Grants intended to return from India and, understandably, wanted to move back into their house. The Duchess used all her considerable powers of persuasion to discourage them, even offering them money if they would move to a house nearby at Inverdruie instead. Eventually, a compromise was reached; the Grants divided their time between Inverdruie and the Doune, thus allowing the Duchess to use the Doune for several months each year. The arrangement was not altogether harmonious; for instance, one year the Duchess complained that Mr Grant and his family had left the three bedrooms they used so dirty that she was obliged to paint and paper them. She said she had also papered the drawing room and two other bedrooms but had not received any reimbursements, so she intended to deduct the cost from the rent as it was not a tenant's business to keep a house in good repair.

Although familiar places were in some ways comforting, at times they only highlighted the loss of her husband. In all her homes there were many memories of the Duke. She wrote to Lord Holland: 'Campden Hill would be sad and dull all winter alone, everything now appears changed, my happy fireside is cheerless and what I used to delight in no longer pleases me.' In London she relied heavily on the Hollands, who still included her in their social life. Lady Holland described a pleasant, quiet dinner with her old friend in June 1840:

She bears up with great moral courage the sad change in her condition besides very many vexations and even mortifications. Her looks and whole 'maintien' are strikingly handsome. The melancholy badge of widowhood on her head, so frightful in general does not disfigure her.

Just a few months later, Lady Holland joined Georgina in widowhood. Lord Holland's death in October was another great loss to Georgina, depriving her of yet another close, supportive friend. She wrote to John Allen: 'To write all I feel would be impossible, the few that I loved or that loved me are dropping off, tell Lady Holland if you think such a message can afford her the slightest comfort, that I will go to her instantly if such a step could in anyway be useful to her.' But although she sympathised with Lady Holland, she expected her friend to follow her example of putting on a brave face and adopting a stoical attitude to the situation. She wrote to her: 'I wish you could cheer a little and reconcile yourself to uncontrollable circumstances, you have many devoted friends and none more sincerely than GB.'

After a year of so many losses, Georgina needed to get away from the sad memories of England. In 1841 she travelled through France and Italy with her daughters Lady Georgiana and Lady Rachel. Although Georgina loved her daughters, the three women were not always in tune, as she described to Lord John:

> Every hour I live, I feel the desolation of being alone, no one with whom I can exchange a thought or a word, for most unfortunately for me, Georgiana never does speak to me, nor does she show, tho' I am sure she feels it, the slightest interest about myself, my plans or any thing connected with me, this makes my home most melancholy . . . I feel how few are left to love me, and how very few understand me.

No doubt Georgy had her own concerns; at the age of thirty-two, she was in serious danger of becoming an old maid. Fortunately, an old friend, Charles Romilly, came to the rescue and proposed to her. The couple married in Naples in January 1842. The Duchess was delighted: 'They are very happy and I hope will always remain so – This happy termination of their long acquaintance delights me for Mr R has always been a great favourite of mine.'

The wedding day was poignant for Georgina, emphasising the absence of the Duke, and although her old friend Edward Ellice was there to give her daughter away, she felt the loss of her husband acutely. She wrote: 'Everyone must know how different everything would have been had her excellent father been alive.'

Georgy's wedding led to another clash with her stepsons because they sent no letters of congratulations. She also believed the new Duke had been mean because when she wrote asking him to provide some money for his half-sister's trousseau, the Duke sent £200 and Georgina felt this was not enough. She believed all the Russells were being snobbish about Mr Romilly because he was not well connected:

> Not one Russell has written to him or taken any notice of the marriage to him and they are all wrong, for he is all Man quite worthy of being taken by the Hand, not only from his private character, but from his talents, had he been a grand partie, the letters of congratulations would have been numerous.

The Duke heard of her criticisms and wrote to his brother William:

> The Duchess I know exists and flourishes upon grievances. She had them in the full career of her prosperity, and so we can't expect her to be without them now . . . I have tried excess of kindness to the Duchess and her sons, but have now got to the end of my tether in that direction. If I had not done so I might have had reason to reproach myself or have furnished them with ground for doing so. Now I have given them no weapon but that of ingratitude.

It was clear that he did not have much affection for his half-brothers and sisters, and that he blamed Georgina for their shortcomings. He went on:

> As for gratitude or thanks, I never expect them. I know the Duchess's children except for one or two, have no affection for any of us, and that they are glad to take the advantages of Woburn, for the sake of their own conveniences and not from any feeling they have towards us . . . Recollect how the Duchess's children have been brought up, self, self, self, nothing else and no good feelings.

Although the uneasy relationship with the new Duke was an irritation, Georgina was more concerned about being estranged from Landseer than her stepson. As a woman who preferred male to female company, and one who thrived on admiration, she missed seeing her lover and wrote to Lady Holland in 1842: 'I wish you had mentioned Mr Landseer as we hear nothing of him and fear he will paint "a day too long".' Eventually, Landseer and the Duchess re-established their relationship because it was an essential part of both their lives. After returning to England, Landseer seemed to recover from his nervous breakdown and his work was as popular as ever. His famous painting of Queen Victoria and Prince Albert as Queen Philippa and Edward III at a fancy-dress ball was done at this time, and he was lauded as being an equal to the great masters of the past. Mrs Jameson wrote in her *Companion to the Most Celebrated Galleries of Art in London*: 'Edwin Landseer, the painter of life in every form, [is] as dextrous and accomplished in the use of his materials as Rubens himself.'

In the autumn of 1842, Landseer visited Lord and Lady Abercorn on their Scottish estate at Ardverikie on the southern shore of Loch Laggan. While there, he used charcoal from the hearth to sketch the first drafts of his most famous picture 'The Monarch of the Glen'. It was during this year that Queen Victoria paid her first visit to Scotland; she fell in love with the landscape and a few years later leased Balmoral. The Scottish link yet again served Landseer well; his work perfectly captured the Queen's romantic view of the Highlands, and she commissioned several new pictures from her favourite artist. A few years later she rewarded Landseer with a knighthood for his work.

Although Georgina and Landseer never formalised their relationship, it continued for the rest of the Duchess's life. He would visit her in London and stay with her at the Doune, and they became such an established couple that Landseer felt free to invite his friends to her parties. Not everyone found this informal, avant-garde behaviour acceptable. Landseer's friend Count D'Orsay took it as a slight when instead of receiving a formal invitation from the Dowager Duchess, the artist invited him to Campden Hill. Such a criticism from D'Orsay seems particularly hypocritical as he had been living with Lady Blessington for many years, but nonetheless Landseer had to apologise, writing:

> I fully enter into the merits of your delicacy – don't be startled
> if I say in this instance your skin is thin in the wrong place.
> The inference I draw from your note just received is that I
> have presumed on my intimacy with both parties to give an
> invitation that should have been prevented by tact, formality
> and nice feeling. You have put your foot on your old friend
> . . . I have only to regret that you have not trusted me in this
> affair as I would, and have trusted you.

It seems that although Landseer was a difficult man for most people to deal with, he was dominated by the Duchess and did whatever she wanted. Even in her sixties, Georgina was still a mistress of manipulation and she expected him to cancel any other engagements if she needed him. On one occasion he told D'Orsay: 'I have just had a second note from Campden Hill to say neither of the Duchess's sons are in London and that I _must_ go.' On another occasion, he wrote to D'Orsay: 'I am _obliged_ to go to Campden Hill before I appear at Gore House but hope to be with you by six.' In return for his loyalty, Georgina gave Landseer the stability and structure that was so essential to his finely balanced life. With his mother now dead, her role as a mother figure became even more important to him, and he relied upon her to care for his mental and physical needs. In 1844, on his way to visit the Duchess at Campden Hill, he had a bad fall from his horse and suffered a severe blow to his forehead; without hesitation the Duchess delayed going abroad to nurse him.

Dealing with Landseer's physical illness was much easier than trying to keep his mind on an even keel, and Georgina confided to Lord John what a strain his mental illness was for her. After one recurrence of his psychosis she wrote:

> Poor Landseer is very far from well, he has put himself under Dr P, who gives the same opinion that others have done, that he is sadly shattered and that he must not attempt to do anything that would fatigue mind or body, at present he has got a bowel complaint – he is the most difficult Person to Manage I ever met with, for when the attacks of nervousness come on, which are simply apprehension that he is going to be ill, nothing can be done, for he cannot, by any soothing, assuring, or reasoning, be diverted from his imaginary complaints – I nurse him, as I would do my brother, I feel, that it is a duty now when he is sick, and unable to amuse others, as he has done for so many years – still I own the task is a very hard one.

Although it was not an easy relationship, Georgina and Landseer seemed to be inextricably bound together. Despite the frightening bouts of mental illness, in the later years of their relationship, as in the earlier ones, there were still times of heightened perception between them when one partner would enhance the other's creativity. While in Scotland, Landseer painted a series of frescos on the walls of Georgina's Glenfeshie huts, including a particularly fine picture of a stag on the rough plaster above the dining-room fireplace. In return, she advised him on the decorations for his house in St John's Wood. It seems the Duchess's taste was as extravagant as ever because she suggested her lover should have the latest gas lighting and white as opposed to black marble. Prone to paranoia, Landseer became obsessive about protecting his privacy, so high walls and trees were planted around his property to exclude any prying eyes.

In the autumn of 1844, while the house was being remodelled, Landseer went to the Doune to be with Georgina, leaving Jacob Bell in charge of the building works. The weather in Scotland was severe and during October there was thick snow and floods that washed houses and bridges away. But the Duchess and Edwin found plenty to entertain them whatever the weather, simply enjoying a domestic routine and being together. On one occasion when they were kept indoors by torrential rain, the couple, aided by the chef and lady's maid, experimented in the kitchen and invented pommes duchesse.

The following year, Georgina and Landseer shared the loss of a great friend when Lady Holland died. In death, as in life, Lady Holland was a formidable woman: 'She evinced during her illness a very philosophical calmness and resolution, and a perfect good humour, aware that she was dying and not afraid of death.' Her death marked the end of an era not just for Georgina but for a whole generation. Charles Greville wrote:

> She will be regretted by a great many people, some from kindly, more from selfish motives, and all who have been accustomed to live at Holland House . . . will lament over the fall of the curtain on that long drama, and the final extinction of the flickering remnant of a social light which illuminated and adorned England and even Europe for half a century. The world never has seen and never will see again anything like Holland House.

Her will caused controversy; instead of leaving her property to her children, she left it to Lord John Russell, who had been like a son to her. She had not liked her daughter-in-law, who wrote of her: 'I think no one could find such a woman as Lady Holland, my mother in law. She surpasses everything that could be imagined in the way of rapacity and selfishness, and in a novel her character would be thought exaggerated and impossible.'

As she grew older, Georgina's own health deteriorated. She frequently suffered from chest infections, and began to winter abroad, taking a villa in Nice. The town was becoming very fashionable with European aristocrats but it kept much of its old character. One of the most colourful events was 'The Battle of Confetti' which took place before Ash Wednesday. On the day, everybody gathered on the promenade to throw handfuls of confetti or bunches of violets and roses, while sailors danced to a military band. There was a carnival and in the morning the streets were filled with people wearing masks, but in the evening they removed their masks and dressed as penitents. At the same moment, processions of people carrying candles would appear from every church and the bells would ring. The priest, carrying the holy sacrament, came out last to join the parade and wherever the procession went, people would fall on their knees in prayer. The evening would end with a masked ball.

Although the visiting aristocrats were entertained by the local customs, they were often not sympathetic to the local people. The Duchesse de Dino wrote:

> The churches here are most displeasing. It is very difficult to sit down and one is surrounded by dirty and unpleasant people who spit and are verminous. The architecture is also spoilt by wretched rags of gilt and silken material . . . The singing of penitents is by no means melodious . . . In the streets you are attacked by the most hideous beggars; all the staircases are crowded with them and are so filthy that one's skirts are only fit to throw away when one gets home.

Brought up to relish flamboyance, Georgina loved the colourful environment and Mediterranean climate of Nice. Every day she enjoyed going for a drive in an open carriage and seeing gardens full of orange trees and flowers. Even in the winter it was sometimes so hot that the blinds of her house had to be pulled down to keep the sun out. However, she found the social life, mixing with the other international aristocrats, boring and although there were dances and plays put on, she was often not fit enough to take part. She wrote: 'The sun, the ever shining sun, what we all come here for, is the chief, I might almost say only charm of the Place. No rain for months and months.'

Ironically, now the Duke was dead Georgina became friendly with her old romantic rival Lady Sandwich, who also spent the winter in Nice. Lady Sandwich's parties were among the few events she enjoyed; perhaps now both women saw the other as a welcome link with the past instead of competition. Her old acquaintance Lord Brougham also entertained her and she spent one Christmas Day at his villa in Cannes. Never known for her consistency, the house Georgina had once criticised as vulgar was now praised by her as 'charming and hospitable'.

During their winters in Nice, Lady Rachel, by now in her twenties, was a great comfort to her mother. Georgina wrote: 'Rachel is quite well and most amiable, her Happy state of sunshine is delightful to live with and tho' she has no real amusement here she is constantly cheerful.' Rachel had grown into an attractive young woman, 'praised for her figure and graceful maintien', and was considered to be extremely clever, modest and agreeable. Although Louisa was the daughter who looked most like Georgina, Rachel had inherited her mother's acting ability and when Georgina and her youngest daughter spent one Christmas at Woburn they both enjoyed acting charades.

Although Georgina did not get on with the new Duke, their disagreements never developed into a complete rift. However, the only stepson who continued to be genuinely supportive to Georgina was Lord John. He became her confidant, and she treated him and his second wife Fanny with the same affection she showed her own children. When Fanny needed to rest during a pregnancy, Georgina offered to have her to stay at Campden Hill so that she could benefit from 'the country air'. When Lord John became Prime Minister in 1846 his stepmother was extremely proud of him – in fact, no natural mother could have been more loyal and protective. She told him:

> I assure you my affection for you can only be equalled by
> my admiration of you, for the noble manner you sustain
> your battles in the House, the calm dignity you preserve
> towards those I should like to attack, and with whom I have

no patience, but against whom I feel the greatest indignation, it surprises my irascible temper – and makes me feel very humble, when every day trifles produce more irritation in me, than the affairs of the whole world do upon you – How proud your dear Father was of you and often has he observed to me, that he could not understand where you had acquired all your knowledge, nor how you found Time to do all you did, he used to say 'poor John is the willing Horse and they all work him' – too true.

A few years later, Georgina was delighted when John came with Fanny and their children to stay with her at the Doune. Enchanted by the Highlands, Fanny described their visit:

> John had a very pretty reception here. A number of people ranged along both banks of the Spey at a ferry by which we crossed to this place, who hurrahed with all their might, while bagpipes played. An address was presented. We crossed, stepped out on a Gordon plaid, and were received by the Duchess and her sons and daughters in a most cordial way.

As an accepted member of the family, Landseer was there during their stay and sketched Lord John's two children, Lord Amberley and Lady Victoria Villiers. Although Georgina and Landseer's unconventional partnership was anathema to the new, priggish Victorian values that were beginning to take hold, in the Russell family their relationship was treated as normal. Even Fanny, as a new member of the clan, described the artist as 'very intimately acquainted with the Duchess'.

As friends of her own generation died, Georgina sometimes felt isolated, but fortunately her connection with the younger generation had always been strong. For many years Landseer and her children became her main concern. She wrote to Lord John from the Doune in 1852:

> I cannot command the cheerful feelings I have always (with one sad exception) felt here. Every mark of affection from

those I love and value does my heart good; you can understand returning here, with the absence of so many kind faces, some I love in danger, and a compleat [*sic*] set of new Scotch servants must have been a trial . . . Undoubtedly when my children were young they were my joy and now are my comforts, tho' not without anxiety.

She was worried about her son Cosmo's health. He suffered from fits that sometimes left him 'insensible for some time'. She was also concerned about her youngest son Alexander, who was serving in the army in India. In times of trouble she turned to her faith, going to church regularly and praying every day. As she approached the age of seventy, Georgina seems to have become aware that her own life was drawing to a close. In the same letter to Lord John she wrote: 'I must pray, and hope that the Almighty, will allow us all to meet here next year.' During the summer of 1852, Georgina's pious sister-in-law, the Dowager Duchess of Gordon, came to stay with her in England. She later recalled that they had many serious conversations and that Georgina was thinking a great deal about her soul. The Dowager Duchess of Gordon believed that at the end of her life, by putting her faith in Christ, Georgina had reached a state of grace.

Perhaps Landseer also realised time was running out because he often put aside other attractive offers to spend time with his elderly mistress. Although she was now an old woman, her hold over him was still greater than any other woman could exert, no matter how young or beautiful. He wrote to a female friend at this time:

Since we met I have been drawing and drawing consequently am not sufficiently brave to exhibit anything yet I really believe the best scheme would be to start for a holiday and return with new eyes – not that I have any positive plans for fun – I suppose, inspite of beautiful ladies who ask me to go to foreign lands my amusement will take place in the old form (drawing the Highlands and stags).

Georgina's instincts were right and the autumn of 1852 was to be her last visit to her beloved Highlands. The following February, while she was staying in Nice, she developed influenza; as her condition deteriorated, her daughters were with her. Landseer was in England but his friend, the artist C.R. Leslie, kept him informed of her health. He wrote to Landseer on 22 February 1853:

> My dear Lanny –
>
> I regret very much that I have at any time to write to you anything disagreeable but especially on the present occasion as it concerns one whom we both highly esteem. The Duchess of Bedford has been confined to her bed with influenza and I expect today it has fallen on her chest and she is now dangerously ill.
>
> I fear much from her age and from a predisposition to disease of the chest – it may be very serious and we must hope the best in the meantime. I will write to you again tomorrow as this night is a great crisis. The change takes place for better or worse this night.
>
> I confess myself – I have my fears but hope they may not be realised. She has two doctors with her, suffers no pain and is perfectly composed and resigned to anything that may await her health or death.

The following day Leslie wrote again:

> Since I wrote yesterday a decided change for the worse took place and with deep regret I must be the person who has to announce to you that this day at 2pm the Duchess resigned her spirit to Him who made it. She died composed and calm with her children that are here with her. Lady Rachel suffers most acutely. Lady Abercorn also.

Georgina chose to be buried in the cemetery of the English church in Nice rather than in the traditional Bedford burial place at Chenies.

In death, as in life, she was her own woman, not just another Duchess of Bedford. Her heart had always been in the Highlands, and in Scotland she was more than a duchess, she was 'the Queen of the Highlands'. Her death was genuinely mourned by her fellow countrymen and on the Rothiemurchus estate, a Gaelic verse was composed in her honour. It captured the spirit of a woman who could be grand and gracious but who was also such a fun-loving, life-enhancing person that she never lost the common touch:

> The blue waves that roll from the shores of Italia
> Have borne to the north a black-coloured tale –
> The good and the noble, the Queen of the Highlands,
> In a far distant clime lies breathless and pale.

> The breezes that play through the woods at Kinrara,
> The scenes of her youth, seem her death to bewail,
> Where repose kindred ashes, in oblivion's slumber,
> That once was the hope and the pride of the Gael.

> The Doune desolated, looks sadly and cheerless,
> Every object around long her pleasure and care
> Will never again wear the gala appearance
> They were wont to assume when her presence was there.

> Nor feigned are the tears which dim the eyes of the aged,
> Sincere the lament of the helpless the poor . . .

> The lamp that for ages did beam with refulgence
> Is now quite extinguished in the loss we deplore;
> For thus when we moun [sic] o'er the race of the Gordons
> We deeply regret that the last is no more!

$\mathcal{P}$ostscript

Georgina left a posthumous bombshell for her children that adds to the speculation about whether Lady Rachel was Landseer's daughter. Shortly after Georgina's death, there was an anxious exchange of letters between her solicitor, William Nicholson, and the executors of her will, Edward Ellice Junior and her son Wriothesley.

In a letter littered with crossings out, as though he was under great pressure and not sure how to phrase what he had to say, Edward Ellice wrote: 'I will not dwell upon the painful secret which leads thus to our correspondence, but I think it right to let you know that issue goes back many years.' Although neither executor stated exactly what the 'secret' was, it is clear that it concerned Rachel's position. Mr Ellice suggested Wriothesley should consult the head of the Russell family, the Duke of Bedford, 'as to the proper course to be pursued'.

If Rachel was not a legitimate child of the sixth Duke, it would affect her status and possibly even her name. At first, Rachel knew nothing about what was going on. Wriothesley wrote to Mr Ellice: 'Poor Rachel is much to be pitied. Perhaps when we have ascertained fully how matters stand you would be so kind as to write and explain fully her position – from me it might seem unkind and a mere dry letter of business is grating especially to a girl – yet her eyes must be opened.'

Apparently, Rachel was 'shocked' when she heard the secret, but no change was made to her position in the family. She later married Sir James Butler and became a novelist, writing romantic fiction set in the Highlands.

In death, Georgina acknowledged Landseer's importance in her life; he was one of the few people outside her immediate family to be left a bequest in her will. Appropriately, she left him a white marble clock with a weeping figure carved on it from her sitting room at Campden Hill. Landseer was concerned about what was to happen to the sketches he had done of the Duchess: they charted their courtship and had great sentimental value for them both. The Duchess had kept them in special albums, but when she died Wriothesley cut them out of the books, intending to sell them at a public auction and divide the money between all Georgina's children. When Landseer heard of this plan, he wrote 'a furious and unreasonable letter' saying that he was the author and had a right to be heard. Wriothesley invited him to look at the drawings and allowed him to withdraw several sketches. Landseer told Wriothesley that the sale of the sketches would be 'a professional injury to him – others ought not to be parted with on other accounts'. In the end a compromise was reached and most of Georgina's drawings and pictures by Landseer were kept in the family and shared between her children. They all realised that these were no ordinary works of art. Mr Ellice wrote: 'The natural feeling is against parting with pictures and sketches to which so many personal recollections are attached.'

There seems to be little doubt that Georgina was the love of Landseer's life. He never married and in the years after Georgina's death he gradually went mad. In March 1853, he complained of a 'nervous addled head' and over the following years suffered from depression and a whole range of phobias and complexes. Although he kept in touch with some of Georgina's children, often staying at Barons Court with the Duke and Duchess of Abercorn, he became a lonely figure. As his sanity became increasingly elusive, he turned to drink to block out his mental torment. He died on 1 October 1873, and as one of the most famous artists of the era, he was buried in St Paul's Cathedral. After his death, many pictures of Georgina and her children, particularly Lady Rachel, were found in his private collection.

$\mathcal{S}ources$

Dates have been given where available

Abbreviations
WP – Woburn Papers
HHP – Holland House Papers, The British Library ADD MS 51661–51676, 51681
ELP – Edwin Landseer Papers, The Victoria and Albert Museum Library
FCPF – Forbes of Callendar Papers, Falkirk Museums GD171/263
BP – Bradford Papers, Staffordshire Public Records Office D1287/18/12
PRO Kew – Lord John Russell Papers, Public Records Office, Kew
GP – Lord Grey Papers, Durham University Library GRE/B6/17
WSRO – Goodwood Papers, West Sussex Record Office
AP – Abercorn Papers, Public Records Office of Northern Ireland
LP – Lynedoch Papers, National Library of Scotland
AUCP – Auckland Papers, The British Library
PLP – Princess Lieven Papers, The British Library
TP – Allen Thomson Papers, National Library of Scotland
EP – Ellice Papers, National Library of Scotland
FLP – Frederick Lewis Papers, The British Library
OP – Landseer Letters to Count D'Orsay, Huntington Library, Harvard MS Eng 1272
PRP – Private Russell Papers
BLARS – Bedfordshire and Luton Archives and Records Service OR 2071/369B

Sources

CHAPTER ONE

'The shape of her face was'	Constance Russell, *Three Generations of Fascinating Women*
'above middle size, very finely'	Ibid
'a brilliancy and radiance about'	Pryse Gordon, *Personal Memoirs*
'unquestionably the most beautiful'	Ibid
'The Duchess was just a flower girl'	Ibid
'The Duke, though more inclined'	Margaret Forbes, *Beattie and his Friends*
'The Duchess of Drinkwater appeared'	T.S. Surr, *A Winter in London*
'far inferior to the Duchess of Devonshire'	*Memoirs of Sir N. Wraxall*
'with the lungs of a boatswain'	T.S. Surr, *A Winter in London*
'Confiding in her rank, her sex,'	*Memoirs of Sir N. Wraxall*
'The Scottish Duchess reserved'	Ibid
'There is an elegance in his taste'	Constance Russell, *Three Generations of Fascinating Women*
'Pray Sir, have you'	*The Journal of the Hon. Henry Fox*
'The Duchesses never met without'	T. S. Surr, *A Winter in London*
'Her conversation bore a very'	*Memoirs of Sir N. Wraxall*
'a great riot at the Opera'	Lord Bessborough, *Georgiana, Duchess of Devonshire*
'The Duchess of Gordon uses fifteen'	Horace Walpole, *Letters*
'From morning to night Georgiana's'	Duchess of Gordon to Dr Beattie, June 1783, WSRO Goodwood MS 1171 f87
'reconciled to the intrusion of this little'	Duchess of Gordon to Dr Beattie, 14 December 1785, WSRO Goodwood MS1171 f79
'one of the noblest palaces in Britain'	Rev. James Gordon, *Parish of Bellie*
'When I look at the thatch roof'	Duchess of Gordon to Dr Beattie, June 1783, WSRO Goodwood MS1171 f87
'For years I have given premiums for all'	Alexander Fergusson, *Henry Erskine and his Kinsfolk*
'I think I write more to you than'	Duchess of Gordon to Dr Beattie, 9 January 1780, WSRO Goodwood MS1171 f51
'her Grace's present ruling passion'	Constance Russell, *Three Generations of Fascinating Women*
'The town is all agog'	Mrs Alison Cockburn to a friend
'Wildly here, without control'	Robert Burns, 'Gordon Castle'
'The duke makes me happier'	Robert Burns, *Journal*
'I never composed a line on'	Robert Burns to the *Star*, 13 April 1787

'She [Georgina] always insists'	Duchess of Gordon to Dr Beattie, 14 December 1785, WSRO Goodwood MS1171 f79
'I have been acquainted with'	Maltby; *Recollections of the Table Talk of Samuel Rogers*
'Deed no, my Lady Duchess'	Elizabeth Grant, *Memoirs of a Highland Lady*
'You cannot think how delightful'	Duchess of Gordon to Forbes of Callendar, FCPF
'I came there from Edinburgh and'	Duchess of Gordon to Dr Beattie, 12 August 1784, WSRO Goodwood MS1171 f77
'a pretty little dairy maid'	Duchess of Gordon to Forbes of Callendar, FCPF
'running up and down the hills'	*Autobiography of Arthur Young*
'I am afraid you rather indulge the'	Duchess of Gordon to Dr Beattie, 9 January 1780, WSRO Goodwood MS1171 f51
'It was a sort of backwoods'	Elizabeth Grant, *Memoirs of a Highland Lady*
'A few candles lighted up'	Ibid
'a kind providence who ever'	Duchess of Gordon to Dr Beattie, WSRO Goodwood MS
'two of her daughters'	Pryse Gordon, *Personal Memoirs*
'I wish I had been present'	Constance Russell, *Three Generations of Fascinating Women*
'facetious and lively'	Pryse Gordon, *Personal Memoirs*
'living on the fat'	Ibid
'Her conjugal duties pressed on her'	*Memoirs of Sir N. Wraxall*
'Though you have not done your game'	Constance Russell, *Three Generations of Fascinating Women*
'behaved with courage'	Alice Robbins, *A Book of Duchesses*
'It will give you pleasure'	Duchess of Gordon to Charles Gordon, WSRO Goodwood MS1176 letter 652
'the most beautiful statue'	Elizabeth Grant, *Memoirs of a Highland Lady*
'Then why are you'	*Private Correspondence of Lord Granville Leveson Gower 1781–1821*
'His Grace of Manchester before'	Ibid
'to so enterprising a genius'	Ibid
'I know your reason'	Maltby, *Recollections of the Table Talk of Samuel Rogers*

'From what I have had the pleasure'	Marquis Cornwallis to the Duke of Gordon, 17 April 1797, WSRO Goodwood MS1172 f25
'young, gay and handsome'	Elizabeth Grant, *Memoirs of a Highland Lady*
'the best bred amongst them'	Ibid
'much liked; kind hearted . . . then'	Ibid

CHAPTER TWO

'Fair and lovely as the rest'	12 February 1799, *The Times*
'fascinating form, grace'	Ibid
'Mirth and plenty reigned around'	Ibid
'a tall, gawky, fair girl'	*Lady Jerningham's Letters*, 7 July 1800
'The probability is that'	*Journal of Elizabeth, Lady Holland*
'The town must be carried'	T.S. Surr, *A Winter in London*
'Deficient in wit'	Lord Holland, *Memoirs of the Whig Party*
'I look upon him to be'	*Journal of Elizabeth, Lady Holland*
'The Duke of Bedford eclipsed'	*The Letters of Horace Walpole*
'a certain person's behaviour'	James Hare
'The Duke of Manchester and'	Mabell, Countess of Airlie, *In Whig Society*
'His heart was affectionate'	Lord Holland, *Memoirs of the Whig Party*
'frolic and fun'	T.S. Surr, *A Winter in London*
'laugh and be merry'	Ibid
'I suppose it must be so'	Mabell, Countess of Airlie, *In Whig Society*
'entered with his usual calmness'	Lord Holland, *Memoirs of the Whig Party*
'I but ill bore this cruel scene'	John, Duke of Bedford, *Diary*, WP
'. . . although it is impossible for'	5 March 1802, *The Times*
'in the agonies of pain'	Lord Holland, *Memoirs of the Whig Party*
'The tide of life was ebbing'	John, Duke of Bedford, *Diary*, WP
'My head has been sadly confused'	John, Duke of Bedford to Lady Bradford, 11 March 1802, BP
'There seemed every reason to believe'	3 March 1802, *The Times*
'This Duke . . . set an example'	*Autobiography of Arthur Young*
'the most respectful way of claiming'	Duchess of Gordon to Duke of Bedford, 26 July 1802, WP
'I thought the moment would come'	Ibid
'She [Georgina] had every consolation'	Ibid
'. . . it was to gain her a friend'	Ibid

'She is so afraid of'	Ibid
'[The subject] has been'	Duke of Bedford to Duchess of Gordon, WP
'What he communicated to me'	Ibid
'They may carry me to new'	Georgina to Duke of Bedford, 12 August 1802, WP
'Nothing can be more extraordinary'	*Private Correspondence of Lord Granville Leveson Gower 1781–1821*
'Lady G Gordon is consoling'	Ibid
'Lady Georgiana Gordon appeared'	Mabell, Countess of Airlie, *In Whig Society*
'You will hardly believe'	Ibid
'Point du tout, jamais'	*Private Correspondence of Lord Granville Leveson Gower 1781–1821*
'obsequious court'	Lord Bessborough, *Georgiana, Duchess of Devonshire*
'breakfast in Ireland, dine'	Dictionary of National Biography
'I have thought that though'	Lady Stafford, *Letters*
'His personality displayed an elegance'	Albert Pullitzer, *The Romance of Prince Eugene*
'Your son is marching with rapid'	Ibid
'He seems gentlemanlike'	Mabell, Countess of Airlie, *In Whig Society*
'My Caroline made her debut'	*Private Correspondence of Lord Granville Leveson Gower 1781–1821*
'bled and blistered her'	Duke of Bedford to Lady Bradford, BP
'I have seen the Duchess'	Ibid
'I have more reasons than one'	Duke of Bedford to Lady Bradford, 20 May 1803, BP
'Your letters are ever precious'	*Letters of Lady John Russell to her Husband 1798–1801*
'Your goodness to me has been'	Ibid
'Alas! My dear friend'	Duke of Bedford to Lady Bradford, 23 November 1802, BP
'angel of truth and virtue'	Ibid
'. . . not a reproach or even'	Ibid
'I am constantly apprehensive'	Ibid
'lost angel'	Georgina to Duke of Bedford, WP
'The mention of her too'	Ibid
'I feel for your virtues'	Ibid
'I trust . . . That you will not'	Duke of Bedford to Lady Bradford, 20 May 1803, BP

Sources

'I take the earliest opportunity' Duke of Bedford to Duke of Gordon, May 1803, WSRO Goodwood MS1173 f20

'I feel highly flattered that' Duke of Gordon to Duke of Bedford, 21 May 1803, WSRO Goodwood MS1173 f21

'I feel that the world will be' Duke of Bedford to Lady Bradford, 20 May 1803, BP

'You know me, and in this' Georgina to Duke of Bedford, WP

'In the midst of my joy I remember' Alice Robbins, *A Book of Duchesses*

CHAPTER THREE

'Lady Georgiana Gordon looked' 24 June 1803, *Morning Post*

'The ball-room was most' 29 June 1803, *The Times*

'fitted out in the most magnificent' Ibid

'the excessive delight and rejoicing' Ibid

'The moving scene of' Charlotte Orlebar to Mrs Cuthbert BLARS, 21 September 1803

'a most brilliant one' Ibid

'a sort of Muslin Gause' Ibid

'. . . the improvements I have had' Humphry Repton, *Fragments on the Theory and Practice of Landscape Gardening*

'This poor Duke of Bedford' *Autobiography of Arthur Young*

'I am tired of the whole' Ibid

'I cannot forget my sorrows' Duke of Bedford to Lady Bradford, 8 August 1803, BP

'Why my own Johnny' Georgina to the Duke of Bedford, 4 October 1806, WP

'It is not in my power to express' *Letters of Lady John Russell to her Husband 1798–1801*

'I was very fond of her' Spencer Walpole, *The Life of Lord John Russell*

'I shall here attempt not' Lord John Russell, PRO Kew 30/22/1A

'I have great pleasure in' Duke of Bedford to Duke of Gordon, 21 May 1804, WSRO Goodwood MS1173

'Remember my own Johnny' Georgina to the Duke of Bedford, October 1806, f23

'The Duchess of Manchester' Elizabeth Grant, *Memoirs of a Highland Lady*

'[Susan has] a sweetness of temper' *Autobiography of Arthur Young*

'The Duchess of Gordon is returned' — Constance Russell, *Three Generations of Fascinating Women*

'Now my family are settled' — *An Autobiographical Sketch of Jane Maxwell, Duchess of Gordon*

'I am Duchess of Gordon' — Ibid

'By God Ma'am you are' — Ibid

'These scenes upon nerves' — Duchess of Gordon to Charles Gordon, WSRO Goodwood MS1176, letter 554

'very handsome and in every' — *Papers concerning Legal Separation Duke and Duchess of Gordon*, WSRO

'Wishing to avoid further' — *An Autobiographical Sketch of Jane Maxwell, Duchess of Gordon*

'Poor Lord Melville' — Ibid

'I came to this country' — Duke of Bedford to Lord Howick (Grey), 29 September 1806, GP

'How it warms my heart' — Georgina to the Duke of Bedford, 19 October 1806, WP

'The acclamations of the people' — April 1806, *Walker's Hibernian Magazine*

'The old women assembled' — Duke of Bedford to Lord Holland, 25 November 1833, HHP

'numerously and splendidly attended' — 12 April 1806, *Dublin Evening Post*

'the most polite acknowledgement' — 25 April 1806, *Dublin Evening Post*

'In all public places the company' — Edward Wakefield, *An Account of Ireland – Statistical and Political*

'went through the different wards' — 16 September 1806, *Dublin Evening Post*

'All the avenues to the Lodge' — 14 August 1806, *Dublin Evening Post*

'It must be confessed the charming' — 10 July 1806, *Dublin Evening Post*

'We were happy to observe a' — 15 April 1806, *Dublin Evening Post*

'a new zest to the enjoyment' — 27 March 1807, *Dublin Evening Post*

'The Caledonian muse with' — May 1806, *Walker's Hibernian Magazine*

'Conciliation and kindness' — Duke of Bedford to Lord Holland, 13 November 1806, HHP

'My aim is to steer' — Duke of Bedford to Lord Holland, 16 January 1807, HHP

'The vice-regal box and dress-circle' — William John Fitzpatrick, *Lady Morgan – Her Career – Literary and Personal*

'Never was anything' — Georgina to the Duke of Bedford, 9 October 1806, WP

'What a happy day'	Georgina to the Duke of Bedford, 4 October 1806, WP
'her Grace being at present far'	3 February 1807, *Dublin Evening Post*
'the amiable and accomplished'	12 February 1807, *Dublin Evening Post*
'crowded by the attendance'	16 April 1807, *Dublin Evening Post*
'It was through streets thronged'	23 April 1807, *Dublin Evening Post*
'They had proceeded but'	Ibid
'evil consequence'	Duke of Bedford to Lord Holland, 18 March 1807, HHP
'so manifest a breach'	Ibid
'When I consented'	Duke of Bedford to Lord Holland, March 1807, HHP

CHAPTER FOUR

'There is a fixed principle'	Duke of Bedford's *Reflections*, 12 August 1807, WP
'I entirely agree in'	Ibid
'Men are too apt to'	Ibid
'Of all women existing'	Ibid
'warm and ardent nature'	Ibid
'Her imagination full of'	Ibid
'She is beloved by all'	Ibid
'I think nobody can now'	The Earl of Ilchester, *The Home of the Hollands*
'luminous, animated and flowing'	Lord Brougham, *Historical Sketches of Statesmen of the Reign of King George III*
'When will you come'	Georgina to Lord Holland, February 1812, HHP
'It was in his private'	Lord Brougham, *Historical Sketches of Statesmen of the Reign of King George III*
'Your offer is so'	Duke of Bedford to Lord Holland, 7 October 1808, HHP
'a plan in every respect so beneficial'	Georgina to Lord Holland, October 1808, HHP
'I have sent his maid'	Georgina to Lady Holland, 12 May 1811, HHP
'She was certainly clever'	*The Greville Memoirs 1837–1852*
'Her love and habit'	Ibid
'the resort not only of the'	Lord Brougham, *Historical Sketches of Statesmen of the Reign of King George III*

'The tableau of the house'	*The Greville Memoirs 1837–1852*
'certain irritability of temper'	Lord Brougham, *Historical Sketches of Statesmen of the Reign of King George III*
'Lord Holland treated him'	*The Greville Memoirs 1837–1852*
'In all Europe I found nothing like'	A. Stirling, *Coke of Norfolk and his Friends*
'I have seldom seen'	Grierson (ed.), *Sir Walter Scott's Letters*, Vol I
'Upon the whole it is'	*Journal of Elizabeth, Lady Holland*
'It is essential that the'	Duke of Bedford to Lord Grey, 1808, GP
'Do me the justice'	Duke of Bedford to Lord Grey, 1809, GP
'rows, festivities and masquerades'	*The Creevey Papers*
'Laureats for one poor butt'	Poem by Caroline Fox, July 1811, HHP
'in the languour created by'	*Diary of Frances, Lady Shelley*
'We were very late'	Ibid
'Alas! It was chaos still!'	Ibid
'. . . disgusting familiarity of'	Ibid
'His disposition is really'	Georgina to Duke of Bedford, WP
'The Duchess is now quite well and'	Duke of Bedford to Lady Holland, 24 June 1810, HHP
'She has been far from well'	Duke of Bedford to Lady Holland, December 1810, HHP
'I never saw Woburn in such beauty'	Georgina to Lady Holland, 15 May 1811, HHP
'With respect to the manner'	Humphry Repton, *Fragments on the Theory and Practice of Landscape Gardening*
'It is one of the enjoyments'	J. C. Loudon, *Magazine of Gardening*
'The first question that'	Humphry Repton, *Fragments on the Theory and Practice of Landscape Gardening*
'The woodbine, the ivy and honeysuckle'	Neale's *Views of Seats*
'The furniture corresponds in all'	Ibid
'. . . that the most picturesque site'	Humphry Repton, *Fragments on the Theory and Practice of Landscape Gardening*
'Having provided against the'	Ibid
'grotto-like receptacle for specimens'	Ibid
'The singular beauties of this'	Stockdale, *History of Devon*
'The beauties, ENDSLEIGH'	Neale's *Views of Seats*

CHAPTER FIVE

'One evening when paying'	Lord William Pitt Lennox, *Reminiscences*
'now in the decline of his'	Elizabeth Grant, *Memoirs of a Highland Lady*
'Beautiful as the morning sun'	Lord William to Lord John Russell, PRP
'under the greatest distress'	Duke of Bedford to Lady Holland, May 1813, HHP
'This is a most delightful'	Georgina to Lady Holland, 3 September, 1813
'I rejoice for the Duchess'	Duke of Bedford to Lady Holland, 7 October 1813, HHP
'too much for her anxious'	Ibid
'The Duchess is going on'	Duke of Bedford to Lady Holland, October 1813, HHP
'never ceasing attention to us'	Georgina to Lady Holland, December 1813, HHP
'the country is very ugly'	Ibid
'It is the most abominable, dull'	Georgina to Lady Holland, 13 April 1814, HHP
'Although she [Jane] appears occasionally'	Duke of Bedford to Lady Holland, 20 January 1814, HHP
'with the necessary approbation'	Duke of Bedford to Lady Holland, 24 March 1814, HHP
'a most agreeable, amicable'	Georgina to Lady Holland, 13 April 1814, HHP
'there is a nonchalance and'	Duke of Bedford to Lady Holland, 24 March 1814, HHP
'I confess I depart from this country'	Georgina to Lady Holland, 13 April 1814, HHP
'Her's is a disheartening and'	Ibid
'Georgy is really as beautiful'	Ibid
'so proud, ignorant, inhospitable'	Georgina to Lord Grey, 29 October 1814, GP
'on the whole weak'	Duke of Bedford's *Diary 1813–15*, WP
'I the more regret it'	Duke of Bedford to Lady Holland, April 1814, HHP
'highly gratified by the'	Ibid
'a beautiful and highly'	Ibid
'were much pleased by'	Ibid
'I would rather have crossed'	Quoted in *History Today* Vol 44 1994
'his manner seems'	Ibid

'He inquired if I had'	Ibid
'everything I hear of this most'	Duke of Bedford to Lady Holland, 20 December 1814, HHP
'By William's last letter'	Duke of Bedford to Lady Holland, December 1814, HHP
'Since Mr Faz left Portugal'	Georgina to Lady Holland, 5 December 1814, HHP
'a good, comfortable, clean'	Duke of Bedford to Lady Holland, December 1814, HHP
'all the necessaries of life'	Ibid
'I am afraid you will find'	Ibid
'I've seen some balls and revels'	Lord Byron, 'Beppo'
'The extraordinary political events'	Duke of Bedford's *Diary 1813–15*, WP
'I envy you having seen my old'	Georgina to Lady Holland, 29 June 1815, HHP
'common kindness and attention'	Duke of Bedford to Lady Holland, 17 September 1815, HHP
'great anxiety still to preserve'	Duke of Bedford's Naples Minutes, WP
'not in the range of shot and shell'	Ibid
'frank and good humoured'	Ibid
'with more firmness and resolution'	Ibid
'she could not help feeling'	Ibid
'that she might render the'	Ibid
'full of gratitude but declining'	Ibid
'under much apprehension'	Ibid
'at least treated her with'	Ibid
'She then took an affectionate'	Ibid
'the patience, good humour'	Ibid
'I hope he will accept'	Duke of Bedford to Lady Holland, 14 January 1817, HHP
'unquestionably the finest'	Duke of Bedford's *Diary 1813–15*, WP
'She is suffering every possible'	Duke of Bedford to Lady Holland, 20 September 1815, HHP
'I have a letter from Captain'	Duke of Bedford to Lady Holland, 18 September 1815, HHP
'reduced and enfeebled almost'	Ibid
'It is so dreadfully melancholy'	Georgina to Lady Holland, 30 May 1814, HHP
'Altho' I was fully prepared'	Duke of Bedford to Lady Holland, 3 October 1815, HHP

'My poor Wife who loved' Duke of Bedford's *Diary 1813–15*, WP

'not only to rest herself' Duke of Bedford to Lady Holland, 10 October 1815, HHP

CHAPTER SIX

'The Duke of Bedford is a complete' *The Greville Memoirs 1837–1852*

'Considered as a whole, Woburn' *Life, Letters and Journal of George Ticknor*

'It was a day of no common import' Ibid

'The Honest God of wine' Lord Holland, poem, April 1822, HHP

'He is a good-natured, plausible man' *The Greville Memoirs 1837–1852*

'she expressed a wish that' *Memoirs, Journals and Correspondence of Thomas Moore*

'We have been on the point of acting' *Miss Eden's Letters*

'altho' the Duke of York is' Duke of Bedford to Lady Holland, 10 November 1816, HHP

'As Holland is so fond' Duke of Bedford to Lady Holland, 11 February 1817, HHP

'The Duchess . . . was very sorry' Duke of Bedford to Lord Grey, 19 January 1817, GP

'It was clever of me to expect' *Miss Eden's Letters*

'The Duchess appeared' *Countess Harriet Granville Letters 1810–1845*

'a beautiful creature with' *Life, Letters and Journal of George Ticknor*

'Lady Jersey is too absorbed' *Countess Harriet Granville Letters 1810–1845*

'The contempt she has for the understandings' *The Greville Memoirs 1837–1852*

'As soon as the Duchess found' Duke of Bedford to Lord Holland, 1818, HHP

'Gladden his days prolong' Lord Holland, poem, HHP

'Her Youth, is in a warm' Duke of Bedford, poem, HHP

'Your description of the sleeping' Duke of Bedford to Lady Holland, 30 March 1819, HHP

'I never do well' Duke of Bedford to Lord Holland, 11 August 1820, HHP

'a little disappointed' Duke of Bedford to Lord Holland, HHP

'the prettiest thing I ever saw' *Journal of Mrs Arbuthnot*

'Endsleigh is anything but' Duke of Bedford to Lady Holland, 20 March 1819, HHP

'Tho' there is much humour'	Duke of Bedford to Lady Holland, April 1819, HHP
'I tell Lord Holland with my love'	Georgina to Lady Holland, 15 May 1820, HHP
'a gay deceiver'	*Countess Harriet Granville Letters 1810–1845*
'Lord William looks quiet and pleased'	Ibid
'Avoid all unnecessary expense'	Duke of Bedford to Lord William, 22 May 1817, WP
'I am decidedly of the opinion'	Ibid
'exposing with the utmost'	Duke of Bedford to Lady Holland, 25 March 1818, HHP
'horrible and the roads'	Duke of Bedford to Lady Holland, 2 April 1818, HHP
'in a vortex of pleasure'	Lord William Russell to Lady Holland, 25 June 1818, HHP
'The Duc de B was most'	Georgina to Lady Holland, 4 May 1818, HHP
'Le peuple said a great many'	Lord William Russell to Lady Holland, 25 June 1818, HHP
'The Duchess commends him'	Duke of Bedford to Lady Holland, 13 April 1818, HHP
'What you say of the Duchess'	Duke of Bedford to Lady Holland, May 1818, HHP
'be a good child, always obedient'	Duke of Bedford to Lady Louisa Russell, 8 July 1818, AP D/623/A/251/4
'How do you do Mistress Pussy Cat?'	Duchess of Bedford to Lady Louisa Russell, 8 July 1818, AP D/623/A/257/2
'I am anxious to avoid'	Georgina to Lady Holland, 1818, HHP
'[I] rejoice more than I can'	Georgina to Lord William, 9 November 1819, PRP
'Kept like a frightened schoolboy'	Lady Elizabeth Russell to Lord Lynedoch, 24 November 1824, LP MS 3617 f217
'The Duchess of Bedford is'	24 December 1820, *John Bull*
'forced to go by'	14 January 1821, *John Bull*
'The Duchess did visit'	Ibid
'It is notorious that'	22 January 1821, *John Bull*
'He invited the Duchess of Bedford'	*Journal of Mrs Arbuthnot*
'I went to a ball at'	Ibid

'Dear Duke – for Cabinet'	*Countess Harriet Granville Letters 1810–1845*
'I said I thought it a great'	*Journal of Mrs Arbuthnot*
'bestowed opprobrious epithets'	Ibid
'very much flurried'	*The Journal of the Hon. Henry Edward Fox 1818–1830*

CHAPTER SEVEN

'as complete attack in its'	Sir Henry Halford, 22 August 1822, HHP
'I feel sanguine in my hopes'	Ibid
'It would make your'	Georgina to Lady Holland, August 1822, HHP
'There is always a little'	Ibid
'will not see how ill his father'	Georgina to Lord Grey, 16 March 1823, GP
'Unhappily the Duchess has'	Lord William Russell to Lady Holland, 27 June 1822, HHP
'Notwithstanding the anxious'	Lord William Russell to Lady Holland, 24 August 1822, HHP
'a melancholy and heart-breaking'	Georgina to Lord Grey, 22 August 1822, GP
'I found my father in a melancholy'	Lord William's *Diary*, August 1822, WP
'I am come in search of'	Duke of Bedford to Lady William, 21 November 1822, PRP
'I cannot help wishing that'	Duke of Bedford to Lady William, 19 December 1822, PRP
'The concluding sentence in'	Duke of Bedford to Lord William, 1823, WP
'Constant watching and miserable'	Georgina to Lord Grey, 16 March 1823, GP
'like a thermometer, and they'	Georgina to Lord Grey, April 1823, GP
'As long as I do not hear music'	Georgina to Lord Grey, 26 November 1822, GP
'write to me now and then'	Georgina to Lord Grey, 22 August 1822, GP
'To you I would say'	Georgina to Lord Grey, 9 October 1823, GP
'You are very kind my dear'	Georgina to Lord Grey, 16 May 1823, GP
'to laugh at your jokes'	Duke of Bedford to Lord Holland, 21 August 1822, HHP

'You are very kind towards'	Georgina to Lady Holland, HHP
'There is a passage in your letter'	Duke of Bedford to Lady Holland, 10 April 1823, HHP
'You must forgive the Duchess'	Duke of Bedford to Lady Holland, 13 April 1823, HHP
'The Duchess received me with'	Lord William Russell to Lady William, 27 April 1823, WP
'Notwithstanding all you have'	Georgina to Lord William Russell, 1823, WP
'I have accepted the stretched out'	Lord William Russell to Lady William, 1 May 1823, WP
'. . . remember dear love your'	Lord William Russell to Lady William, 1823, WP
'was cold and distant to me'	Lord William Russell to Lady William, 1823, WP
'neither is, nor can be, in'	Lord Holland to Lord William Russell, 9 June 1823, WP
'Mon beau pere etait grand'	Lady William Russell to her daughter-in-law, PRP
'I have just heard a most excellent'	Georgina to Lord William Russell, 1823, PRP
'I hope Bessy will take care of'	Ibid
'striding over the rivers, gun in hand'	Duke of Bedford to Lord Holland, 23 August 1823, HHP
'The return of his face to'	Georgina to Lord Grey, 9 October 1823, GP
'to be near you really and sincerely'	Georgina to Lady Holland, 30 September 1823, HHP
'Our intercourse will I trust be'	Duke of Bedford to Lady Holland, 8 October 1823, HHP
'Absence from those we love'	Georgina to Lady Holland, 2 October 1823, HHP
'very triste. Many houses built'	Ibid
'the shoals of City Dandies'	Duke of Bedford to Lady Holland, 8 October 1823, HHP
'it is a relief to me to be without'	Georgina to Lady Holland, 1823, HHP
'You are a very pretty little girl'	Lord Frederick Hamilton, *The Days Before Yesterday*
'As to the Duke I have nothing'	Georgina to Lord Grey, 29 December 1823, GP
'The Duchess looks miserably thin'	Duke of Bedford to Lady Holland, January 1824, HHP
'I confess I cannot comprehend'	Ibid

'The Duchess and I have'	Duke of Bedford to Lord William Russell, 2 May 1824, WP
'decorum and respect was due'	Ibid
'I own I think it a great pity'	Lord John Russell to Lady William, 20 August 1824, WP
'It is very bad policy to quarrel'	Lord John Russell to Lord William, 1824, WP
'haughty, proud, unbending'	Lord William Russell to Lady William, 1 May 1823, WP
'contributed so large a portion'	Duke of Bedford to Lady Holland, 8 November 1824, HHP
'I wish she could be persuaded'	Duke of Bedford to Lady Holland, August 1824, HHP
'. . . that being the case I cannot'	Lord William Russell to Lady Holland, 30 October 1824, HHP
'Little Johnnikins always repeats'	Lady William to old Lord William Russell, 1 August 1825, WP
'Whilst I regret that we should'	Duke of Bedford to Lord William Russell, 8 September 1825, WP

CHAPTER EIGHT

'My curly headed dog boy'	James A. Manson, *Sir Edwin Landseer RA*
'His eyes sparkled when he'	Lady Leslie, *Memories*
'become a cheerless blank'	Georgina to Lord Holland, HHP
'You must excuse me for saying'	Duke of Bedford to Edwin Landseer, 31 September 1827, ELP
'It was a bright fresh autumnal'	C. R. Leslie, *Autobiographical Recollections*
'Your little friend Cosmo'	Duke of Bedford to Lady Holland, 1824, HHP
'I am sure he will make'	C. R. Leslie, *Autobiographical Recollections*
'a new impulse to his work'	W. Cosmo Monkhouse, *The Studies of Sir Edwin Landseer with a History of his Art Life*
'For ever afterwards Landseer's'	James A. Manson, *Sir Edwin Landseer RA*
'I must however take the liberty'	Georgina to Lord Grey, 20 September 1824, GP
'The Duke . . . has been to all'	Georgina to Lord Holland, January 1825, HHP
'joy at being in London'	Georgina to Lord Grey, July 1825, GP

'O come, and rich in intellectual' Georgina to Lord Auckland, 1825, AUCP

'How is't that since I last' Lord Holland, poem, 18 July 1825, HHP

'I have no time at present' Landseer to William Ross, September 1825

'The Duchess is very so-so' Duke of Bedford to Lady Holland, 18 December 1824, HHP

'I have delayed till now' Georgina to Lord Grey, January 1826, GP

'She is still on her couch' *Countess Harriet Granville Letters 1810–1845*

'I want to know if you received' Dr Woolryche to Edwin Landseer, 3 March 1826, ELP

'I hear she is "immense et" ' *Journal of Mrs Arbuthnot*

'I thought her looking ill' Lady William Russell to Lady Holland, 1826, HHP

'My heart is as light as a feather' Georgina to Lord Holland, 1826, HHP

'In climbing up the hill of life' Poem in Landseer Papers, ELP

'Good breeding demanded that' Mabell, Countess of Airlie, *In Whig Society*

'a beautifully executed sort of Register' *Elizabeth, Lady Holland, to her Son 1821–1845*

'The Duchess is just' Duke of Bedford to Lady Holland, 17 June 1827, HHP

'I thought by this time I should' Georgina to Lord Grey, 16 October 1827, GP

'My "widowhood" is not the most agreeable' Georgina to Lord Grey, November 1827, GP

'NOV 28 1827 – Dined with' Sir Walter Scott, *Journal*

'28 FEB 1828 . . . Long and curious' Lord William Russell's *Diary*, WP

'My two brothers are here' Lord William Russell to Lady William, 7 April 1828, PRP

'His bump of what phrenologists' James A. Manson, *Sir Edwin Landseer RA*

'I am "en garcon" without my' Duke of Bedford to Lady Holland, 5 October 1828, HHP

'One thousand thanks for your' Duke of Bedford to Lady Holland, 15 October 1828, HHP

'She thinks she has reason to complain' Duke of Bedford to Lord Grey, 8 January 1829, GP

'on a blood horse with a white hat' *The Diary of Benjamin Robert Haydon*, 7 August 1829

'The Duchess, whose object'   Isabella, Marchioness of Bath to Lord
                 William Russell, 5 March 1829, WP

'Lady, thy face is very beautiful'   Laetitia Landon, *The Keepsake*, 1829
'The wicked world has been'   Lord Tavistock to Lord William
                 Russell, 1829, WP

'Indeed his only motive'   Lady Holland to Lord William
                 Russell, 22 September 1829, WP

CHAPTER NINE

'perfect – his frills reaching'   *Times Literary Supplement*, 19
                 February 1982

'He was acknowledged to be'   Lord Ossulston, *The Chillingham
                 Wild Cattle*

'There was Landseer, a friendly'   Harriet Martineau, *Autobiography*
'a little quiet artistical conversation' Duke of Bedford to Edwin Landseer,
                 ELP

'I hear that in your pictures'   Lord Wriothesley Russell to Edwin
                 Landseer, 3 February 1830, ELP

'It is an excellent arrangement'   Lord John Russell to Lady William,
                 8 May 1829, PRP

'Though it is an event I have'   Georgina to Lord William Russell,
                 1829, WP

'I had felt very unwell for some' Georgina to Lord Holland, 22
                 December 1830, HHP

'I rejoice at it for at her age'   Duke of Bedford to Lady Holland,
                 December 1830, HHP

'The Duchess of Bedford passed' Le Marchant, *Three Early Nineteenth
                 Century Diaries*

'gave great pleasure to the admirers' Duke of Bedford to Lord Holland,
                 HHP

'The assemblage of pretty women' *Memoirs, Journals and Correspondence
                 of Thomas Moore*

'I have what is vulgarly called' Duke of Bedford to Lord William
                 Russell, 15 July 1831, WP

'Your sarcasm about the Duchess's' Duke of Bedford to Lord William
                 Russell, 27 July 1831, WP

'If you think my girls are'   Duke of Bedford to Lord William
                 Russell, 11 May 1831, WP

'Our good Duke is certainly'   Georgina to Lord Holland, 28
                 November 1831, HHP

'The Duchess brings an amusing' Duke of Bedford to Lady Holland,
                 27 December 1831, HHP

'John will have told you of all'   Duke of Bedford to Lady Holland,
                 January 1832, HHP

'He has always affected to admire' *Mrs Arbuthnot's Journal*
'I have been urged by some of my' Duke of Bedford to Lord Grey,
3 March 1832, GP

'You all seem to think that' Duke of Bedford to Lady Holland,
8 April 1832, HHP

'I could not bring myself' Duke of Bedford to Lady Holland,
14 April 1832, HHP

'the whole country' Duke of Bedford to Lady Holland,
13 July 1832, HHP

'My mother's character was' Lord Frederick Hamilton, *The Days
Before Yesterday*

'The gentlemen have had' Ibid
'My father very rarely touched' Ibid
'What's in the wind about Abercorn' Hastings Russell to Lord William
Russell, 1832, WP

'The Duchess went to Woburn with' Ibid
'I am glad that the Duke understands' Duke of Abercorn to Georgina, AP
D/623/A/251/6

'My Scotch Doves are' Georgina to Lord Holland, 13 August
1832, HHP

'I have been a good deal amused' Duke of Bedford to Lady Holland,
October 1832, HHP

'The time approaches my dearest' Duke of Bedford to Lady Louisa
Russell, 1832, AP D/623/A/251/4

'The banks of the Spey' 31 October 1832, *Aberdeen Journal*
'Where all was unique' Ibid
'a pyramid of huge concentric' Ibid
'My hospital report this morning' Duke of Bedford to Lady Holland,
7 January 1833, HHP

'The Duchess of Bedford has' *The Satirist* 1833
'I cannot describe the agony' Georgina to Lord Holland, 22
January 1833, HHP

'You may imagine to what' Duke of Bedford to Lady Holland,
18 January 1833, HHP

'The Duchess is rather better' Lord John Russell to Lady William,
22 February 1833, PRP

'Dearest, Dearest, Dearest Duchess' Lord Holland, poem, HHP
'Now dearest Holly, one word' Georgina to Lord Holland, 26 May
1833, HHP

'Your satire about the Campden' Duke of Bedford to Lord William
Russell, 20 August 1833, WP

'Could you send your fiddle to' Charles Matthews, *The District
Surveyor*

'a warm and irascible temper'   Duke of Bedford to Lady Holland,
22 October 1833, HHP

'in an old home spun shooting'   George D. Leslie, *Riverside Letters*

'Everything here is wild'   Charles Matthews, *The District Surveyor*

'It is without any exception'   Ibid

'Nothing can be more disagreeable'   Ibid

'The Duchess, notwithstanding'   Ibid

'At seven o clock . . . in the midst'   Ibid

'a most agreeable man, a delightful'   Georgina to Lord Holland, 7 October 1833, HHP

'I rejoice that the Bear is so fond'   Georgina to Lord Holland, 17 November 1833, HHP

'If Eugene's son is as captivating'   Georgina to Lord Holland, 16 September 1833, HHP

'more than usually gay, cheerful'   Duke of Bedford to Lady Holland, 1 December 1833, HHP

'No old Nabob after twenty'   Georgina to Lord Holland, 27 December 1833, HHP

'Certainly as far as relates to'   Georgina to Lord Holland, 25 December 1833, HHP

'You can conceive nothing like'   Princess Lieven *Correspondence with Lord Grey*

'I do not think if Charles had tried'   Georgina to Lady Holland, January 1834, HHP

CHAPTER TEN

'Good old Granny with her'   Georgina to Lord William Russell, 9 May 1837, WP

'Think of my having four grandchildren' Georgina to Lord Holland, October 1835, HHP

'What an altered picture, the once lovely' Georgina to Lord William Russell, 9 May 1837, WP

'The great object now seems to'   Lord Tavistock to Lord William Russell, 28 December 1832, WP

'. . . it is curious to see how completely' Ibid

'I cannot describe to you'   Lord Tavistock to Lord William Russell, 1833, WP

'The party at present at Woburn'   *Memoirs of the Duchesse de Dino*

'There is something very unsatisfactory' Lord William Russell's *Diary*, WP

'The Duke of Bedford has written me' Lady William to Lord Holland, 4 May 1834, HHP

'You asked me last night whether'   Duke of Bedford to Lady William, 1834, PRP

'The family believe that it is'   Lady William Russell to Princess Lieven, 1835, PLP

'What splendid luxury, what refinement'   Lord William Russell's *Diary*, WP

'The Duchess spoke to me on'   Ibid

'the Duchess talked to me very'   Ibid

'According to your desire I'   Georgina to Lord William Russell, 11 April 1836, WP

'actual lover is no longer the'   Lady William Russell to Princess Lieven, 23 February 1836, PLP

'I have delayed writing to you from'   Duke of Bedford to Lady Holland, 13 June 1836, HHP

'I cannot conceal from myself'   Georgina to Lord Holland, May 1836, HHP

'The family consists of two'   Allen Thomson to his father, 28 June 1836, TP MS9237 f6

'NB The Dormice above'   Lady Rachel Russell, *Memoirs of a Dormouse and Memoirs of a Doll*

'We jog on here in our usual'   Allen Thomson to his father, 23 October 1836, TP MS9237 f15

'The Duchess is not I suspect'   Ibid

'I said Dear Duchess and twas'   Lord Holland, poem, 24 November 1836, HHP

'When I returned from Glasgow'   Allen Thomson to his mother, 23 November 1836, TP MS9237 f23

'. . . one of the handsomest men'   Allen Thomson to his fiancée Margaret, 5 December 1836, TP MS9237 f25

'Everything here is of course Tory'   Ibid

'there is nothing in the "beautiful" '   Duke of Bedford to Edwin Landseer, December 1836, ELP

'There is nothing remarkable in'   Duke of Bedford to Lady Holland, 7 December 1836, HHP

'In this remote corner we hear'   Duke of Bedford to Lord William, 6 December 1836, WP

'She has an idea that she'   Allen Thomson to his fiancée, 5 December 1836, TP MS9237 f25

'She is very stout, and not'   Allen Thomson to his father, 14 January 1837, TP MS9237 f38

'I thought you knew your informer's'   Georgina to Lord Holland, March 1834, HHP

'we all enjoyed our delicious'   Georgina to Lord Holland, 8 December 1834

'You ought not to be losing'   Count D'Orsay to Edwin Landseer, 1837, ELP

'old shattered frame is so'	Duke of Bedford to Lord William Russell, 23 October 1837, WP
'The Duchess the other day'	Allen Thomson to his mother, 29 January 1837, TP MS9237 f41
'Let me add in the Duke's name'	Georgina to Allen Thomson, 3 June 1837, TP MS9237 f64
'Her great joke against me'	Allen Thomson to his mother, September 1837, TP MS9237 f108
'Paris is indeed a desert'	Duke of Bedford to Lady Holland, December 1837, HHP
'All my anxiety is now about'	Duke of Bedford to Lady Holland, 19 December 1837, HHP
'I did not suffer by my rapid'	Georgina to Lord Holland, 8 January 1838, HHP
'more like advancing towards'	Duke of Bedford to Lady Holland, 18 January 1838, HHP
'I fear the Duke's galanterie'	Georgina to Lady Holland, March 1838, HHP
'I assure you it required all my'	Georgina to Lord Holland, February 1838, HHP
'I perfectly understand his wishing'	Georgina to Lord Holland, April 1838, HHP
'Perhaps after all the trouble'	Allen Thomson to his mother, 4 February 1838, TP MS9237 f107
'The place is delightful and'	Georgina to Lord Holland, February 1838, HHP
'The evenings are somewhat long'	Ibid
'A friend or two would be very'	Ibid
'All came and all heartily partook'	Duke of Bedford to Lady Holland, 16 March 1838, HHP
'You must expect a very dull letter'	Georgina to Lord Holland, 18 March 1838, HHP
'. . . the total absence of judgement'	Georgina to Lord Holland, April 1838
'charming and [she] gains'	Georgina to Lord William Russell, 26 April 1838, WP
'I must confess she looked handsome'	Duke of Bedford to Lady Holland, 30 June 1838, HHP
'Our former friend Brougham is'	Duke of Bedford to Lady Holland, 15 July 1838, HHP
'I sincerely wish he would'	Duke of Bedford to Lord Holland, 18 November 1838, HHP
'It is indeed a severe visitation'	Georgina to Edward Ellice, 6 November 1838, EP MS15051 f3

'When the Duke was well all my'	Georgina to Lady Holland, 10 August 1839, HHP
'In May we arrived at Endsleigh'	Georgina to Lord John Russell, 1841 PRO Kew 30/22/4A
'. . . never was there a more warm-hearted'	Georgina to Lady Holland, 14 August 1839, HHP
'Nothing can go off better than'	Ibid
'I would willingly be there'	Duke of Bedford to Lady Holland, 1839, HHP
'I had not been away more than three'	Edwin Landseer to Frederick Lewis, 15 November 1839, FLP

CHAPTER ELEVEN

'My spirits are so broken'	Georgina to Lord Holland, December 1839, HHP
'My loneliness is dreadful'	Georgina to Lord Holland, 9 December 1839, HHP
'quiet unostentatious'	Duke of Bedford to Lord Tavistock, WP
'Campden Hill and Endsleigh, belonging'	Duke of Bedford to Lord Tavistock, 11 June 1835, WP
'He had not the power or resolution'	Francis, Seventh Duke of Bedford to Lord William Russell, 3 December 1839, WP
'[She] promises if I will send'	Francis, Seventh Duke of Bedford to Lord William Russell, 1841, WP
'Mrs B dwelt so much on your opinion'	Francis, Seventh Duke of Bedford to Lord William Russell, 16 April 1840, WP
'With respect to the Dss. D.'	Francis, Seventh Duke of Bedford to Lord William Russell, WP
'I have enjoyed being with you'	Georgina to Lord John Russell, 1840, WP
'Sister Richmond Me dear'	Georgina to Lord Holland, 29 March 1840, HHP
'My head is considerably addled'	Edwin Landseer to his aunt, 1839, ELP
'You may be quite sure I should'	Edwin Landseer to the Count D'Orsay, 13 July 1840, OP
'I have been very unwell, yesterday'	Georgina to Lady Holland, 1840, HHP
'The accounts of poor Mr Landseer'	Georgina to Lord Holland, 29 March 1840, HHP
'When the body is weakened the mind'	Georgina to Lord John Russell, WP

'Nothing can have been more fortunate' Georgina to Edwin Landseer, 1841, ELP

'Your father and I created it' Georgina to Lord John Russell, 1841, PRO Kew 30/22/4A

'harmless and half simple' Elizabeth Grant, *Journal of a Highland Lady*

'the only person who stirred' Georgina to Lord Holland, 1840, HHP

'Campden Hill would be sad' Georgina to Lord Holland, HHP

'She bears up with great' The Earl of Ilchester, *Chronicles of Holland House 1820–1900*

'To write all I feel would' Georgina to John Allen, 25 October 1840, HHP

'I wish you could cheer' Georgina to Lady Holland May, 1843, HHP

'Every hour I live, I feel' Georgina to Lord John Russell, 1841, PRO Kew PRO/22/4A

'They are very happy and I hope' Georgina to Lady Holland, 7 December 1841, HHP

'Everyone must know how different' Georgina to John Allen, 12 January 1842, HHP

'Not one Russell has written to him' Ibid

'The Duchess I know exists' Francis, Seventh Duke of Bedford to Lord William Russell, July 1842, WP

'As for gratitude or thanks' Francis, Seventh Duke of Bedford to Lord William Russell, 7 March, 1843 WP

'I wish you had mentioned Mr Landseer' Georgina to Lady Holland, 23 August 1842, HHP

'Edwin Landseer, the painter' Mrs Jameson, *Companion to the Most Celebrated Galleries of Art in London*

'I fully enter into the merits' Edwin Landseer to Count D'Orsay, 25 June 1846, OP

'I have just had a second note' Edwin Landseer to Count D'Orsay, OP

'I am <u>obliged</u> to go to Campden Hill' Ibid

'Poor Landseer is very far from well' Georgina to Lord John Russell, 1841, WP

'she evinced during her illness' *The Greville Memoirs 1837–1852*

'She will be regretted by a great' Ibid

'I think no one could find such' *Memoirs of the Duchesse de Dino*

'The churches here are most' Ibid

'The sun, the ever shining sun' Georgina to Lady Holland, 30 January 1844, HHP

'Rachel is quite well and most'	Ibid
'I assure you my affection for you'	Georgina to Lord John Russell, 1841, WP
'John had a very pretty reception'	Spencer Walpole, *The Life of Lord John Russell*
'very intimately acquainted with'	Ibid
'I cannot command the cheerful feelings'	Georgina to Lord John Russell, August 1852, PRO Kew 30/22/10C
'I must pray and hope that the'	Ibid
'Since we met I have been'	Edwin Landseer to Mrs Russell August, 1852, The British Library MSS ADD 57940 f90
'My dear Lanny'	C.R. Leslie to Edwin Landseer, ELP
'The blue waves that roll'	Gaelic, poem, AP D/623/A/251/10

POSTSCRIPT

'I will not dwell upon the painful'	Edward Ellice to Lord Wriothesley Russell, 4 March 1853, EP MS15051 f9
'Poor Rachel is much to be'	Lord Wriothesley Russell to Edward Ellice, 5 March 1853, EP MS15051 f13
'a furious and unreasonable'	Lord Wriothesley Russell to Edward Ellice, EP
'a professional injury to him'	Ibid
'The natural feeling is against'	Edward Ellice to Lord Wriothesley Russell, 14 July 1854, EP MS15064 f150

Bibliography

Adam, William, *A pamphlet printed from the MS in possession of Mr Adam respecting the fifth Duke of Bedford*, 1803

Airlie, Mabell, Countess of, *In Whig Society*, Hodder and Stoughton, London, 1921

Bamford F. and Wellington, Duke of (eds), *Journal of Mrs Arbuthnot*, 2 vols Macmillan and Co., London, 1950

Betham-Edwards, M. (ed), *Autobiography of Arthur Young*, Smith, Elder and Co., London, 1891

Blunt, Reginald (ed), *Mrs E. Montague, Letters and Friendships*, Constable, London, 1923

Blakiston, Georgiana, *Lord William Russell and His Wife*, John Murray, 1972; *Woburn and the Russells*, Constable, 1980

Bedford, John, Duke of, *A Silver Plated Spoon*, Cassell, 1959

Bessborough, Lord *Georgiana, Duchess of Devonshire* John Murray 1955

Brougham, Henry, Lord, *Historical Sketches of Statesmen of the Reign of King George III*, Charles Knight, London, 1843

Bruce, Evangeline, *Napoleon and Josephine, An Improbable Marriage*, Weidenfeld & Nicolson, 1995

Brynn, Edward, *Crown and Castle – British Rule in Ireland 1800–1830*, The O'Brien Press, Dublin, 1978

Clifford, Timothy, *The Three Graces Antonio Canova*, The Trustees of the National Galleries of Scotland, 1995

Cunningham, P. (ed), *The Letters of Horace Walpole*, 9 vols, R. Bentley and Son, 1891

Davis, Frank, *Victorian Patrons of the Arts*, Country Life, 1963

Dickinson, Violet (ed), *Miss Eden's Letters*, Macmillan and Co., London, 1919

Dixon, Sophie, *A Journal of Ten Days Excursion on Western and Northern Borders of Dartmoor*, Plymouth, 1830

Elwin, M. (ed), *The Autobiography and Journals of Benjamin Robert Haydon*, Macdonald, 1950

Fergusson, Alexander, *Henry Erskine and his Kinsfolk*, Blackwood and Sons, 1882

Fitzpatrick, William John, *Lady Morgan – Her Career – Literary and Personal*, London, 1860

Fleming, G.H., *That Ne'er Shall Meet Again*, Michael Joseph, 1971

Forbes, Margaret, *Beattie and his Friends*, Westminster, 1904

Foreman, Amanda, *Georgiana, Duchess of Devonshire*, Harper Collins, 1998

Gordon, Jane, Duchess of, *An Autobiographical Sketch of Jane Maxwell, Duchess of Gordon*, privately printed in Glasgow, 1865

Gordon, Pryse, *Personal Memoirs*, London, 1830

Grant, Elizabeth, *Memoirs of a Highland Lady*, John Murray, 1898

Granville, Castalia, Countess, *Private Correspondence of Lord Granville Leveson Gower 1781–1821*, 2 vols, London, 1899

Graves, A., *Catalogue of the Works of the Late Sir Edwin Landseer*, 1876

Greville, Charles C.F., *The Greville Memoirs 1837–1852*, Longmans and Co., 1888

Grierson, H. J. C. (ed.), *Sir Walter Scott's Letters, Volume 1*, 1932

Hamilton, Lord Frederick, *The Days Before Yesterday*, Hodder and Stoughton, 1920

Haydon, Benjamin R., *Correspondence and Table Talk: with a Memoir by his son Frederic Wordsworth Haydon*, 1876

Healey, Edna, *Emma Darwin, The Inspirational Wife of a Genius*, Headline, 2001

Hibbert, Christopher, *Wellington, A Personal History*, Harper Collins, 1997

Hilliard G.S. (ed), *Life, Letters and Journal of George Ticknor*, 2 vols, Boston, 1909

Holland, Lord, *Memoirs of the Whig Party*, 2 vols, London, 1854

Hunt, J.W., *Reaction and Reform*, Collins, London and Glasgow, 1972

Ilchester, Earl of (ed), *Journal of Elizabeth, Lady Holland*, 2 vols, Longmans and Co., London, 1908; *The Journal of the Hon. Henry Edward Fox 1818–1830*, Thorton Butterworth, London, 1923; *Chronicles of Holland House 1820–1900*, John Murray, 1937; *The Home of the Hollands 1605–1820*, John Murray, 1937; *Elizabeth, Lady Holland to her Son 1821–1845*, John Murray, London, 1946

Jameson, Mrs, *Companion to the Most Celebrated Galleries of Art in London*, 1844

Lennie, Campbell, *Landseer: The Victorian Paragon*, Hamilton, 1976

Bibliography

Lennox, William Pitt, *Reminiscences*, London, 1863

Leslie, George D., *Riverside Letters*, Macmillan and Co., 1896

Leveson Gower, F. (ed), *Countess Harriet Granville Letters, 1810–1845*, 2 vols, Longman, 1894

Lieven, Princess Dorothea, *Correspondence with Lord Grey*, Bentley, 1891

Maltby (ed), *Recollections of the Table Talk of Samuel Rogers*, Appleton and Co., New York, 1856

Manson, James A., *Sir Edwin Landseer RA*, 1902

Martineau, Harriet, *Autobiography*, London, 1877

Massingberd, Hugh and Christopher Simon Sykes, *Great Houses of Ireland*, Laurence King, 1999

Matthews, Charles J., *The District Surveyor*

Maxwell, Sir Herbert, *The Creevey Papers*, John Murray, 1903

McLynn, Frank, *Napoleon: A Biography*, Pimlico, 1998

Mills, A.R., *Two Victorian Ladies*, Frederick Muller, 1969

Monkhouse, W. Cosmo, *The Studies of Sir Edwin Landseer with a History of his Art Life*, London, 1877

Murray, Venetia, *High Society in the Regency Period*, Penguin, 1999

Neale's *Views of Seats*

Ormond, R., *Sir Edwin Landseer*, Philadelphia Museum of Art and Tate Gallery exhibition catalogue, 1981

Ossulston, Lord, *The Chillingham Wild Cattle*, Kingston, 1891

Parissien, Steven, *George IV: The Grand Entertainment*, John Murray, 2001

Pope, William Bissell (ed), *The Diary of Benjamin Robert Haydon*, 5 vols, Harvard University Press, 1963

Preest, J., *Lord John Russell*, Macmillan, 1972

Pugsley, Steven, *Devon Gardens*, Sutton, 1994

Pullitzer, Albert, *The Romance of Prince Eugene*, Edward Arnold, 1895

Radziwill, Princess (ed), *Memoirs of the Duchesse de Dino (1836–40)*, 3 vols, Heinemann, London, 1909–10

Repton, Humphry, *Fragments on the Theory and Practice of Landscape Gardening* London, 1816

Robbins, Alice, *A Book of Duchesses*, Andrew Melrose Ltd, 1913

Robins, Joseph, *Champagne and Silver Buckles – The Viceregal Court at Dublin Castle 1700–1922*, The Lilliput Press, Dublin, 2001

Russell, Constance, *Three Generations of Fascinating Women*, Longmans, 1904

Russell, Lady John, *Letters of Lady John Russell to her Husband 1798–1801* London, 1813

Russell, Lord J. (ed), *Memoirs, Journals and Correspondence of Thomas Moore*, 8 vols, London, 1853–56

Scarlett, Meta Humphrey, *In the Glens Where I was Young*, Siskin, Milton of Moy, 1988

Scott, Sir Walter, *Journal*, Edinburgh, 1972

Shelley, Frances, *Diary of Frances, Lady Shelley*, John Murray, 1912

Smith, Charles Eastlake (ed), *Journals and Correspondence of Lady Eastlake*, John Murray, 1895

Smith, C. Nowell (ed), *Letters of Sydney Smith*, 2 vols, Oxford University Press, 1956

Smout T.C. and R.A. Lambert (eds), *Rothiemurchus Nature and People on a Highland Estate 1500–2000*, Scottish Cultural Press, 1999

Stephens, F.G., *The Early Works of Sir Edwin Landseer RA*, 1869; *Sir Edwin Landseer*, 1881

Stirling, A.M., *Coke of Norfolk and his Friends*, London, 1908

Stockdale, *History of Devon*

Stroud, Dorothy, *Humphry Repton*, 1962

Surr, T.S., *A Winter in London*, 1806

Taylor, Tom (ed), *Charles Robert Leslie RA: Autobiographical Recollections*, London, 1860

Wakefield, Edward, *An Account of Ireland – Statistical and Political*, London, 1812

Walpole, Spencer, *The Life of Lord John Russell*, 2 vols, 1889

Ward, D. R., *Foreign Affairs 1815–1865*, Collins London and Glasgow, 1972

Wheatley, Henry (ed), *Memoirs of Sir N. Wraxall*, 5 vols, Bickers and Son, 1884

Wiffen, *Historical Memoirs of the House of Russell*, London, 1833

Woolley, Benjamin, *The Bride of Science, Romance, Reason and Byron's Daughter*, Pan, 1999

Other Sources

Sir Edwin Landseer by Lady Richmond Ritchie in *Cornhill Magazine*, 1874

A Sympathetic Ear: Napoleon, Elba and the British by Katherine MacDonogh in *History Today*, vol. 44, 1994

Photographic record of Sir Edwin Landseer's work with commentaries, compiled by Caleb Scholefield Mann, Victoria and Albert Museum

Dictionary of National Biography, 1908

Lord Byron, 'Beppo'

Robert Burns, 'Gordon Castle'

J.C. Loudon, *Magazine of Gardening*

The Satirist Magazine, 1833

John Bull, 1820/1821

The Times

Morning Post

Walker's Hibernian Magazine

Dublin Evening Post

Aberdeen Journal, 1832

The Times Literary Supplement, 1982

Country Life, 3 August 1961 and 9 October 1997

Index

Index

Index

Index

Index

Picture Credits

Page 6 – Edwin Landseer by Sir Francis Grant courtesy of the National Portrait Gallery, London.

Page 7 – 'A naughty child' by Landseer (above left) courtesy of the V&A Picture Library, Ladies Louisa and Georgina Russell by A. R. Chalon (above right), and James, first Duke of Abercorn (below left), and Louisa, Duchess of Abercorn (below right) by Landseer by kind permission of the Duke and Duchess of Abercorn/Courtauld Institute of Art.

Page 8 – John, sixth Duke of Bedford, and Georgina, Duchess of Bedford by Landseer by kind permission of the Duke and Duchess of Abercorn/ Courtauld Institute of Art.

Black and white picture section:

Page 1 – Georgina, Duchess of Bedford by kind permission of the Marquess of Tavistock and the Trustees of the Bedford Estates.

Page 2 – Lord Holland by François Xavier Fabre (above) courtesy of the National Portrait Gallery, London and Lady Holland (below) from a Private Collection.

Page 3 – Georgina, Duchess of Bedford by Landseer courtesy of the British Library.

Page 4 – Georgina, Duchess of Bedford by Landseer (above) by kind permission of the Duke and Duchess of Abercorn/Courtauld Institute of Art, and (below) by kind permission of the Marquess of Tavistock and the Trustees of the Bedford Estates.

Page 5 – Georgina, Duchess of Bedford with Lady Rachel Russell by Landseer (above) by kind permission of the Marquess of Tavistock and the Trustees of the Bedford Estates, and Lady Rachel Russell by Landseer (below) by kind permission of the Duke and Duchess of Abercorn/Courtauld Institute of Art.

Page 6 – Sketches by Landseer of Georgina, Duchess of Bedford with Lady Harriet Hamilton (above left), (above right), and (below right) by kind permission of the Duke and Duchess of Abercorn/Courtauld Institute of Art, and with her grandson (below left) by kind permission of the Marquess of Tavistock and the Trustees of the Bedford Estates.

Page 7 – John, sixth Duke of Bedford (above) and the Duke and Duchess of Bedford (below) by Landseer, by kind permission of the Duke and Duchess of Abercorn/Courtauld Institute of Art.

Page 8 – Endsleigh by Landseer (above) by kind permission of the Duke and Duchess of Abercorn/Courtauld Institute of Art and the dining bothie at Glenfeshie by Charles Matthews (below) by kind permission of the Marquess of Tavistock and the Trustees of the Bedford Estates.